Fannie Porter Dickey

Blades O' bluegrass

Choice Selections of Kentucky Poetry, Biographical Sketches and Portraits of

Authors

Fannie Porter Dickey

Blades O' bluegrass

Choice Selections of Kentucky Poetry, Biographical Sketches and Portraits of Authors

ISBN/EAN: 9783337428068

Printed in Europe, USA, Canada, Australia, Japan

Cover: Foto ©Thomas Meinert / pixelio.de

More available books at **www.hansebooks.com**

CHOICE SELECTIONS OF KENTUCKY
POETRY, BIOGRAPHICAL SKETCHES
AND PORTRAITS OF AUTHORS.

COMPILED BY

MRS. FANNIE PORTER DICKEY

LOUISVILLE
JOHN P. MORTON & COMPANY
1892

TO

Colonel R. T. Durrett,

For his love of Literature, his pride in the preservation of
Kentucky History, and the service he has rendered
the State in these things, this Volume is dedi-
cated with the highest respect and
esteem of the Compiler.

PREFACE.

This volume is offered as a miniature representation of Kentucky verse for the one hundred years that it has been a State.

The whole field of poetry has been traversed from the pioneer days to the present time, and an effort made to have every known poet of merit represented.

Besides selections made from published books, there are also many fugitive verses that never went beyond the "Poet's Corner" in a newspaper, while some are here in print for the first time.

That such a book has been made is due to the courtesy and promptness with which the living writers have responded, and to the friends of literature throughout the State who have assisted and encouraged the work, and it is hoped that the collection mirrors a variety of sentiment that will touch a heart in every household and leave a pleasing influence.

Thanks are due The Century Company, Belford's Magazine, The Round-Table, and Detroit Free Press for privilege of poems.

F. P. D.

CONTENTS.

	PAGE
*AINSLIE, HEW,	299
The Ingleside,	281
ALLEN, JAMES LANE, Lexington,	299
Beneath the Veil,	254
In Looking on the Happy Autumn Fields,	276
ALLMOND, MARCUS B., Louisville,	299
A Consolation,	77
A Sabbath in Autumn,	83
ALLGOOD, JOSEPH, Louisville,	300
Uncle Pete's Plea,	169
*ASHTON, EUGENE,	
The Dead Past,	54
Duty,	35
BANGS, S. K., Louisville,	
The Old Church Bell,	74
*BARRICK, J. R.	300
The Beautiful,	268
*BETTS, MARY E.,	301
A Kentuckian Kneels to None but God,	94
BOLTON, SARAH T., Indianapolis, Indiana,	300
Left on the Battle-field,	241
BROTHER, ALLINE, Fort Spring,	300
Castles in the Air,	180
*BROWN, MATTIE N.,	301
Crysanthemums,	273
God's Poem,	225
BROWN, NELLIE LA RUE, Louisville,	
Japanese Wall Paper,	32
BRYAN, STANTON P., Brownsboro,	301
The Wedge,	71
Aspiration,	93
*BUTLER, WILLIAM O.,	301
The Boatman's Horn,	290
*BUTLER, NOBLE,	301
The Bluebird,	293
CARR, ALICE H., Louisville,	
"Sweet Girl Graduate,"	36

*Deceased.

CONTENTS.

CASSEDAY, MISS JENNIE, Louisville, ... 301
    A Night-time Song, ... 258
CAWEIN, MADISON, Louisville, ... 302
    Noëra, ... 167
    Andalia, ... 159
    Chords, ... 151
CHILDRESS, RUFUS J., Louisville, ... 302
    The Moods of You, ... 329
    Ode to A Robin, ... 213
    In the Air, ... 202
CLARK, FLORENCE A., Austin, Texas, ... 303
    A Christmas Pansy, ... 274
COLLINS, MRS. W. LESLIE, Frankfort, ... 303
    A Thought, ... 192
    The Leaf, ... 233
*COSBY, FORTUNATUS, ... 303
    A Song, ... 292
*COSBY, J. V., ... 304
    Song, ... 289
CROCKETT, INGRAM, Henderson, ... 304
    At Yuletide, ... 152
    Late Afternoon in November, ... 175
    We Fade as a Leaf, ... 172
CUNNINGHAM, MRS. J. J., Louisville, ... 303
    Cupid's Arrow, ... 174
    Yon Tiny Stream, ... 157
*CUTTER, GEORGE W., ... 304
    The Song of Steam, ... 284
DAVIE, GEORGE M., Louisville, ... 304
    A Yearn for the Romantic, ... 84
    Night in Venice, ... 78
DAVIS, WILLIAM J., Louisville, ... 304
    Gentleness: A Sonnet, ... 296
DOWNES, MAY SMITH, Somerset, ... 305
    April, ... 126
    The Bird's Song, ... 114
DUKE, BASIL W., Louisville, ... 305
    Song of the Raid, ... 243
    David and Goliath, ... 248
DURRETT, R. T., Louisville, ... 305
    The Old Year and the New in the Coliseum at Rome, . . . 98
    To My Sweetheart, ... 112
DYER, SYDNER, Indianapolis, Indiana, ... 307
    Song of The Sunbeam, ... 68

*Deceased.

CONTENTS.

EVANS, ALEXANDER, Louisville, ... 307
    My Lute So Loved is Now Unstrung, ... 191
    Where the Beautiful River, ... 183
FIELDS, W. H., Louisville, ...
    Yesterday, ... 199
FITZHUGH, NANNIE MAYO, Lexington, ... 307
    Meeting Rivers, ... 256
    Answered, ... 257
FLIPPIN, M. T., Tompkinsville, ... 307
    Rome, ... 43
    The Days of Other Years, ... 51
FORD, THOMAS B., Frankfort, ... 307
    My Violin, ... 67
    The Siren, ... 75
    Dusk, ... 61
FORD, LAURA C., Owenton, ... 308
    The Household Minstrel, ... 81
*FOSDICK, W. W., ... 308
    Light and Night, ... 62
*FOSTER, S. C., ... 308
    My Old Kentucky Home, ... 64
GALLAGHER, W. D., Pewee Valley, ... 308
    The Mothers of The West, ... 76
    May, ... 65
    Woman—Extract, ... 58
    Four Score and One, ... 82
" GERALDINE," . . . .
    What Is It? 39
HAGNER, LAURA S., Buckner, ...
    The Butterfly, ... 15
HAMILTON, ANNA J., Louisville, ... 309
    Death—A Living King, ... 275
    At Set of Sun, ... 215
*HARNEY, JOHN M., ... 309
    Echo and The Lover, ... 129
HARNEY, WILL WALLACE, Pine Castle, Florida, ... 309
    The Stab, ... 95
    In Exile, ... 107
    The Buried Hope, ... 138
    The Bergamot Blossom, ... 110
    South Florida Night, ... 121
    The Twilight of the Heart—Extract, ... 115
HARRIS, ALFRED W., Louisville, ... 309
    Building Castles, ... 277

*Deceased.

CONTENTS.

*HART, JOEL T.,	310
Invocation to the Coliseum at Rome,	23
HAYS, WILL S., Louisville,	310
The Last Hail,	113
The Faithful Engineer,	165
HOPKINS, EDWIN S., Jacksonville,	310
Convolvuli,	63
After Frost,	70
The Old Violin,	57
HOSKINS, JOHN, Louisville,	311
A Lullaby,	97
When Loving Heart's the Goal,	92
Good Morning,	80
JEFFREY, ROSA V., Lexington,	311
A Summer Idyl,	28
Owl in Church,	7
Grecian Poetry Versus Modern Science,	19
JESSEL, KATIE,	
"Earth Has no Sorrow that Heaven Can Not Heal,"	106
JOHNSTON, J. STODDARD, Louisville,	311
A Dream,	116
Parting,	122
To a Marguerite,	108
*KELLEY, A. W. (Parmenas Mix),	313
The Old Scissors' Soliloquy,	227
The Bore,	224
KETCHUM, ANNIE CHAMBERS,	314
A Sea Shell,	223
Amabere Me,	229
KINKEAD, NELLIE TALBOT, Lexington,	
Coquette,	31
Last Night,	27
"KNELM,"	
Solitude	109
*LITTELL, WILLIAM,	
Raptures,	287
LUCAS, OLIVER (Poet of the Asfaltus), Louisville,	314
The Immortal Three,	209
Tobogganing Down the Hill,	221
MCABOY, MARY T.,	314
A Sonnet,	131
MCAFEE, NELLY MARSHALL, Louisville,	314
To-morrow,	155
Hills Look Blue When Far Away,	145
Antithesis,	176

°Deceased.

CONTENTS.

MCBEATH, TOM F., Daleville, Mississippi, ... 315
   Biopsis—Extract, ... 134
MCDOWELL, KATE GOLDSBOROUGH, Louisville, ... 315
   To Whittier, ... 294
MCHENRY, JENNIE T., ... 315
   Evening Thoughts, ... 288
*MCILVAIN, CLARA L., ... 315
   Love, ... 218
   Wedding Bells, ... 206
MCKINNEY, MRS. J. J. (Katydid), Montgomery, Alabama, ... 316
   Twilight in Kentucky, ... 291
   Two Songs, ... 295
   A Bunch of Magnolias, ... 286
   Spring and Summer, ... 239
MERCER, S. C., Hopkinsville, ... 316
   The Strawberry Bowl, ... 261
   The New South, ... 53
   Blonde and Brunette, ... 50
MILLER, HOWARD, ...
   True Greatness, ... 147
   To Poesy, ... 204
MILLER, ELVIRA SYDNOR, Louisville, ... 316
   Edgar Allan Poe, ... 219
   A Dash Through the Lines, ... 279
   A Ballad of Poets, ... 212
*MORRIS, ROBERT, ... 317
   The Level and the Square, ... 203
   Memories of Galilee, ... 255
MORRIS, IDA GOLDSMITH, Glasgow, ... 317
   My Lady Sleeps, ... 149
MORTON, JENNIE C., Frankfort, ...
   Frankfort, ... 141
   The Sweetest Day, ... 158
MUDD, ALICE HAWTHORNE, Louisville, ... 316
   Marble Heart, ... 205
MURPHEY, ELIZABETH LEE, Dallas, Texas, ... 317
   A Letter of To-day, ... 123
   Dixie Land, ... 132
MURRAY, HENRY C., Frankfort, ...
   In Days to Come, ... 34
MURRAY, STUART, Danville, ...
   George Moore, ... 198
NOBLE, VIRGINIA F., Paducah, ... 317
   A May-time Memory, ... 139
   At Dawn of Day. 154

*Deceased.

CONTENTS.

*O'HARA, THEODORE, ... 318
    The Bivouac of the Dead, ... 40
O'MALLEY, CHARLES J., Hitesville, ... 319
    Worthiness, ... 181
    His Birds, ... 188
    A Kentucky Twilight, ... 193
    Enceladus, ... 177
O'MALLEY, SALLIE M., Hitesville, ... 320
    The Child Singer, ... 162
O'SULLIVAN, DANIEL E., Louisville, ... 320
    To Adelina Patti, ... 211
    Margery, ... 179
    Death, ... 160
    To a Pin, ... 186
    A Song, ... 194
PARHAM, EUGENIA, Paducah, ... 320
    Vanished, ... 192
    A Happy Woman, ... 182
PARKER, JO. A., Lagrange, ... 320
    As in the Long Ago, ... 208
    The Kiss I Stole, ... 187
PATTERSON, J. L., Frankfort, ...
    To Silence, ... 30
PIATT, JOHN J., Queenstown, Ireland, ... 320
    Night Thoughts, ... 260
    The Sight of Angels, ... 245
    The Buried Organ, ... 259
PIATT, SARAH M. B., Queenstown, Ireland, ... 321
    A Doubt, ... 13
    Stop the Clock, ... 6
    The Sermon of a Statue, ... 24
POTTS, EUGENIA DUNLAP, Lexington, ... 321
    A Reverie, ... 238
POOL, ARCH., Paducah, ...
    Across the Way, ... 176
*PRENTICE, GEORGE D., ... 321
    Mammoth Cave, ... 9
    To the River in Mammoth Cave—Extract, ... 11
    The Closing Year, ... 21
    The Dream of Life, ... 26
    A Name in the Sand, ... 35
    On Revisiting Brown University—Extract, ... 39
REYNOLDS, T. T., Glasgow, ...
    To L. B.'s Eyes, ... 128

*Deceased.

CONTENTS. xiii

RHEA, FRANK H., Waverly, ... 322
    The Rock, ... 120
    Love's Trinity, ... 148
    November, ... 133
ROBERTSON, HARRISON, Louisville, ... 322
    Aprille, ... 161
    Perspectives, ... 118
    An Idle Poet, ... 150
    The Story of The Gate, ... 130
    Two Triolets, ... 173
    Coquette, ... 140
ROLLSTON, ADELAIDE D., Paducah, ... 322
    In June, ... 164
    If I Had Known, ... 119
    October, ... 127
RUBY, CLINT, Madisonville, ... 323
    The Violet, ... 125
    November, ... 217
SEMPLE, PATTY B., Louisville, ...
    A Madonna, ... 197
SEMPLE, HENRY C., Louisville, ... 324
    Argumentum, ... 47
    Maid of Nazareth—Extract, ... 44
    Faultless, ... 52
*SHREVE, THOMAS H., ... 323
    Midnight Musings, ... 230
SMITH, MATTIE P., Le Sueur, Minnesota, ... 323
    The Prince is Coming, ... 45
SMITH, J. SOULE (Falcon), Lexington, ...
    The Modern Tithonus, ... 196
SPEED, THOMAS, Louisville, ... 323
    Topping the Locusts, ... 216
*SPEED, MAJ. THOMAS, ... 324
    Autumn Leaves, ... 222
SPOTSWOOD, F. M., Lexington, ... 324
    I Love You, ... 96
    Dear Old Southern Home, ... 111
STANTON, HENRY T., Frankfort, ... 324
    The Moneyless Man, ... 33
    Drawing It Fine, ... 1
    The Devil's Hollow, ... 18
    Means to An End, ... 60
    Sweetheart, ... 49
    Double Life, ... 25
    Self Sacrifice—Extract, ... 54

*Deceased.

xiv   CONTENTS.

STAPP, BELLE WILSON, Buckeye, ... 324
   Dreamy September, ... 278
SWING, JEANNETTE, Dayton, ... 325
   The Death of a Soul, ... 38
TEAGER, M. M., Flemingsburg, ... 325
   A Valedictory, ... 270
   The Golden Wedding, ... 282
*THORNTON, SARAH C., ... 325
   Time, ... 174
WALKER, LIZZIE, Hartford, ... 326
   How? 47
   The Old Year, ... 163
   November, ... 269
WALSH, THOMAS, Louisville, ... 326
   The Night Displays the Stars, ... 226
*WARFIELD, CATHERINE A., ... 325
   Spring Thunder, ... 232
*WASHINGTON, WILLIAM A., ... 326
   The Works of Nature, ... 246
WATTERSON, HENRY, Louisville, ... 327
   The Cricket, ... 200
*WELBY, AMELIA, ... 327
   The Rainbow, ... 14
   Musings—Extract, ... 37
*WILSON, LIZZIE, ... 326
   Leoline—Extract, ... 12
WILSON, ROBERT BURNS, Frankfort, ... 327
   A Wild Violet in November, ... 234
   How Spring Comes in the Bluegrass, ... 184
   I Shall Find Rest, ... 195
   The Passing of March, ... 231
*WILSON, FORCEYTHE, ... 327
   To Hersa, ... 16
WOOD, HENRY CLEVELAND, Harrodsburg, ... 328
   Completeness, ... 46
   The Weaver, ... 55
   Beautiful Hair, ... 36
   Gwendolyne, ... 48
   Reproduction, ... 12
WRIGHT, JEAN, Louisville, ... 328
   Ich Liebe Dich, ... 237
   La Glu, ... 240
   5:30 A. M., ... 242

*Deceased.

ILLUSTRATIONS.

WILLIAM D. GALLAGHER.
ROSA VERTNER JEFFREY.
REUBEN T. DURRETT.
HENRY T. STANTON.
GEORGE D. PRENTICE.
SARAH T. BOLTON.
JOHN JAMES PIATT.
SARAH M. B. PIATT.
ROBERT BURNS WILSON.
MADISON CAWEIN.
LIZZIE WALKER.
HENRY CLEVELAND WOOD.
MATTIE P. SMITH.
HENRY COOLIDGE SEMPLE.
JENNIE JONES CUNNINGHAM.
"KATYDID."
INGRAM CROCKETT.
OLIVER LUCAS.
MARCUS B. ALLMOND.
STANTON P. BRYAN.
M. M. TEAGER.
CLINT RUBY.
EUGENIA DUNLAP POTTS.
MRS. FANNIE PORTER DICKEY.
(FRONTISPIECE.)

BLADES O' BLUEGRASS.

DRAWING IT FINE.

IN a shining cloud of meshes,
Where a marge of Summer rushes
  To a noisy water dipt,
Dwelt a prim, maternal spider,
With her grim, brown spouse beside her,
  Like two mummies in a crypt.

And except, perhaps, the shimmer
Of a sunset's silver tremor,
  There was not the slightest breath—
Not the faintest undulation,
In the pendant, hooded station,
  Where they simulated death.

Every tentacle enfolded,
Much as if the parts were molded
  Or were carven so from stone;
There they sat, without emotion,
Staring from a woven ocean,
  From the funnel of their cone.

When the dry, drawn spider's forces
Put its legion pulsate courses
  Thus successfully to rout,
Well, indeed, may silence marvel
How it is this crimson travel
  Of the venous tide goes out.

We have no such tragic actors
As the adept tissue-factors—
　Since they never rant or rave—
And there's not a thing in nature
Wearing such a perfect feature
　Of the unrelenting grave.

True, they *act* this tableau merely,
But they mimic death so nearly,
　Being rigid there and still,
That the blinded insect rushes
Down the silence of their meshes
　To escape some lesser ill.

So, these consorts sat in quiet,
Watching ever for the diet
　To their finished talent due,
Waiting patiently and stilly
For the winged things and silly
　That were intermitting through.

By-and-by, upon her vision
Came a light of clear decision,
　And the sober matron spoke
(She had something like that human,
Active impulse of a woman
　In her tongue—the common joke):

"Having trained our girl and taught her,
As a spider should her daughter,
　All the proper things in life,
It is time she had our blessing—
Though the thought is sore distressing—
　As some decent person's wife.

"I am sure the maid is able
Now to run her line of cable,
　Unassisted, from the spool;
And as weaver and as spinner,
That there's more than common in her,
　I believe, upon my soul!

"Only yesterday I saw her,
For our neighbor, Mistress Drawer,
    Darning places in her net;
Busy there in giving issue
To the finest solar tissue
    I have ever noticed yet.

"She is skilled in all the graces
Of the most exquisite laces—
    Quite invisible to me—
And I think such work would kill me,
With my eyes so very filmy
    I could never, never see.

"There's a wanton mass of bushes
Just above our line of rushes,
    Where to spread the maiden's net;
So, good man, though sad to miss her,
Let us bless the child and kiss her,
    Whilst our lives are steady yet."

And the grim old spider listened,
Till upon his optics glistened
    Something not unlike a tear,
And with quite a man's agreeing
To a woman's way of seeing
    Answered: "As you think, my dear."

Then the mother called her daughter
From a-sporting on the water
    In a little bay below,
And the lady-like young spider
Came and settled down beside her,
    To the sorrow of her beau;

For she ceased at once her skating,
Left the gallant there awaiting,
    Made a courtesy and flew—
Just as every little woman,
When she hears her mother summon,
    Ought undoubtedly to do.

It was charming in the tunnel
Of their silver-sided funnel
　Thus the family to see;
Sitting close to one another
Were the father and the mother
　And the daughter—happy three!

There their plans were all unfolded,
And the maiden's future molded
　In the fancy of the dame;
In the matted brier trellis
She should have her silver palace
　And be given up to Fame.

But alas! like every other
Living thing—that has a mother—
　How these fancies went astray!
All the goodly things we nurture
For the overburdened future
　Pass too fleetingly away.

So it was, this callow weaver,
When her mamma let her leave her,
　Went a little bit too fast;
Though she made a fair beginning
With her cunning kind o' spinning,
　It was not a kind to last.

She was full of life, and agile,
But her shining threads were fragile
　And defective in their length;
For she made her woofing wider
Than her warping justified her,
　And her fabric wanted strength.

We have seen a thousand ladies
On a rapid way to Hades
　By this very common force,
And, exactly like the spinner,
They persist in drawing finer,
　When they ought to draw it coarse.

DRAWING IT FINE.

'T is peculiar to the human—
Where the debutant's a woman—
　To exceed the parent marge;
She rejects the frugal spirit
She should properly inherit,
　And essays to "go it large."

And the rule is just as certain,
When it's time to lift the curtain
　On the drama of her days,
She has found her light ambition
At the margin of perdition
　Through the saddest sort o' ways.

Now, the highest aim that filled her—
And the very thing that killed her—
　Was her foolish love for show;
For our pulsing spider lady
Could n't keep her palace shady
　In the brier-patch below.

But she made her nicest hitches
On some pendulating switches,
　That her glory might be seen;
And she loitered with her lover
All its silver terrace over
　With the leisure of a queen.

And, as might have been expected,
She was readily detected
　By a bandit living near,
For the wily robber sparrow,
Coming downward like an arrow,
　Made a quiet meal of her.

And the prim, maternal spider,
With the grim, brown spouse beside her,
　Sits a silent mummy yet,
And the breaking of each morrow
Brings her such a meed of sorrow
　As she never can forget.

She is full of sad upheavals,
From the crater of her evils,
  For the wrong she did her child,
When she taught her only graces
In the art of making laces,
  By a vanity beguiled.

So the two unhappy tenants
Of the cone are doing penance,
  And their bosoms both are wrung;
He has chronic gout to bother,
And this wicked, wicked mother
  Has paralysis of tongue.
HENRY T. STANTON.

STOP THE CLOCK.

LET this red flower here on the cliffs stay red;
  Let that glad bird sing always in the tree;
Let baby keep this pretty yellow head
  And these two dimples,—do you say to me?

Let these same clouds make this same sky all gold;
  Let these same strawberries last? (You'll tell me how?)
Let's take the world up in our arms and hold
  It where it is, and make forever now?

Let's sit here always in this wind and sun,
  And hear the water dripping from the rock?
Come, then, and tell me how it can be done.
  What, ho, within there! some one stop the clock!
SARAH M. B. PIATT.

OWL IN CHURCH.

In the autumn of 1874 a small gray owl was observed sitting in a niche above the organ of the Episcopal Church, greatly to the amusement of the congregation.

FRONTING us all,
In a niche of the wall,
As if proud of his lofty station,
Like a monk in a cowl
Sat a little gray owl
Looking down on the congregation.

Hymns and chants as they rose
Failed to stir his repose,
A grave mien to the holy place suiting.
Merely looking surprise
With his solemn, round eyes,
He heard them all through without hooting.

His feathers he shook,
And a questioning look
On this wise he cast at the people,
"You are high-church, 't is true,
But I'm higher than you,
For my screeching I do in the steeple.

"If by dropping in here
Once a week ye appear
Thus cleansed from all outward pollution,
How clean I must be,
Living always, ye see,
In the top of this pure institution!"

He glanced through the pews,
As if trying to choose
A few from the many, anointed,
With charity—freed
From ritual creed (?)
I thought that he looked disappointed.

Quoth the wise little owl
In his modest gray cowl,
"What grand dressing!" and then, slyly winking,
"It would be orthodox
To put more in the box
And less in the pews, I am thinking."

Judging men from aloft,
As the righteous do oft,
And women—Oh, owl, have compassion!
For the sees of our church
Would be left in the lurch
If its aisles were forsaken by fashion.

Of our creed justly proud,
We respond very loud,
By holy zeal greatly excited,
And yet look innocent,
As if "us sinners" meant
Not ourselves, but some race more benighted.

Let paid choirs screech,
Let the dear clergy preach,
Don't hoot at them up in the steeple;
It's too high a perch
"To tell tales out of church,"
And might frighten away outside people.

Beware how you chat
To the hawk and the bat;
Church gossip, returned with due culture,
Brings so much to boot
You won't know your own hoot,
And may find yourself changed to a vulture.

It is not orthodox
To peep into our box
And take notes underneath your gray cowl
Of who gives and who don't,
And we hope that you won't,
Or we'll call you a meddlesome owl.

ROSA VERTNER JEFFREY.

MAMMOTH CAVE.

ALL day, as day is reckoned on the earth,
I've wandered in these dim and awful aisles,
Shut from the blue and breezy dome of heaven,
While thoughts, wild, drear, and shadowy, have swept
Across my awe-struck soul, like specters o'er
The wizard's magic glass, or thunder-clouds
O'er the blue waters deep. And now
I'll sit me down upon that broken rock
To muse upon the strange and solemn things
Of this mysterious realm.
     All day my steps
Have been amid the beautiful, the wild,
The gloomy, the terrific. Crystal founts,
Almost invisible in their serene
And pure transparency; high pillared domes,
With stars and flowers all fretted like the halls
Of Oriental monarchs; of rivers dark
And drear and voiceless as Oblivion's stream,
That flows through Death's dim vale of silence; gulfs
All fathomless, down which the loosened rock
Plunges until its far-off echoes come
Fainter and fainter like the dying roll
Of thunders in the distance; Stygian pools
Whose agitated waves give back a sound
Hollow and dismal, like the sullen roar
In the volcano's depths;—these, these have left
Their spell upon me, and their memories
Have passed into my spirit, and are now
Blent with my being till they seem a part
Of my own immortality.
     God's hand,
At the creation, hollowed out this vast
Domain of darkness, where no herb or flower
E'er sprang amid the sands, nor dews, nor rains,
Nor blessed sunbeams fell with refreshing power,
Nor gentle breeze its Eden message told

Amid the awful gloom. Six thousand years
Swept o'er the earth ere human footprints marked
This subterranean desert. Centuries
Like shadows came and passed, and not a sound
Was in this realm, save when at intervals,
In the long lapse of ages, some huge mass
Of overhanging rock came thundering down,
Its echoes sounding through these corridors
A moment, and then dying in a hush
Of silence, such as brooded o'er the earth
When earth was chaos. The great mastodon,
The dreaded monster of the elder world,
Passed o'er this mighty cavern, and his tread
Bent the old forest oaks like fragile reeds
And made earth tremble. Armies in their pride
Perchance have met above it in the shock
Of war, with shout and groan and clarion blast,
And the hoarse echoes of the thunder-gun;
The storm, the whirlwind, and the hurricane
Have roared above it, and the bursting cloud
Sent down its red and crashing thunder-bolt;
Earthquakes have trampled o'er it in their wrath,
Rocking earth's surface as the storm-wind rocks
The old Atlantic;—yet no sound of these
E'er came down to the everlasting depths
Of these dark solitudes.
                    How oft we gaze
With awe or admiration on the new
And unfamiliar, but pass coldly by
The lovelier and the mightier! Wonderful
Is this lone world of darkness and of gloom,
But far more wonderful yon outer world
Lit by the glorious sun. These arches swell
Sublime in lone and dim magnificence,
But how sublimer God's blue canopy,
Beleagured with his burning cherubim
Keeping their watch eternal! Beautiful
Are all the thousand snow-white gems that lie
In these mysterious chambers, gleaming out

Amid the melancholy gloom and wild,
These rocky hills and cliffs and gulfs, but far
More beautiful and wild the things that greet
The wanderer in our world of light; the stars
Floating on high like islands of the blest;
The autumn sunsets glowing like the gate
Of far-off Paradise; the gorgeous clouds
On which the glories of the earth and sky
Meet and commingle; earth's unnumbered flowers
All turning up their gentle eyes to heaven;
The birds with bright wings glancing in the sun,
Filling the air with rainbow miniatures;
The green old forests surging in the gale;
The everlasting mountains, on whose peaks
The setting sun burns like an altar-flame;
And ocean, like a pure heart rendering back
Heaven's perfect image, or in his wild wrath
Heaving and tossing like the stormy breast
Of a chained giant in his agony.
                              GEORGE D. PRENTICE.

——— O, SOMBER stream,
Whence comest thou, and whither goest? Far
Above, upon the surface of old Earth,
A hundred rivers o'er thee pass and sweep,
In music and in sunshine, to the sea;
Thou art not born of them. Whence comest thou,
And whither goest? None of earth can know.
No mortal e'er has gazed upon thy source—
No mortal seen where thy dark waters blend
With the abyss of Ocean. None may guess
The mysteries of thy course. Perchance thou hast
A hundred mighty cataracts thundering down
Toward Earth's eternal center; but their sound
Is not for ear of man. All we can know
Is that thy tide rolls out, a specter stream,
From yon stupendous, frowning wall of rock,

And, moving on a little way, sinks down
Beneath another mass of rock as dark
And frowning, even as life—our little life—
Born of one fathomless eternity,
Steals on a moment and then disappears
In an eternity as fathomless.

"*The River in the Mammoth Cave.*" GEORGE D. PRENTICE.

'TWAS night, and all the burning stars were set
Like flaming gems in Nature's coronet—
There was a wild wail in the wind's low sigh
Like the last tone of human agony.
Odors from myriad flowers were borne along,
And wild and sweet arose the night bird's song.
'T was midnight, when the awestruck spirit feels
That nature her most awful power reveals.

"*Leoline.*" LIZZIE WILSON.

REPRODUCTION.

Two on a sunset gazed in rapturous hush,
  One was a poet, one a child of art;
A canvas glowed beneath a master's brush,
  A song divine gushed from the poet's heart.

HENRY CLEVELAND WOOD.

A DOUBT.

It is subtle, and weary, and wide;
It measures the world at my side;
  It touches the stars and the sun;
It creeps with the dew to my feet;
  It broods on the blossoms, and none,
Because of its brooding, are sweet;
It slides as a snake in the grass,
Whenever, wherever I pass.

It is blown to the South with the bird;
At the North, through the snow, it is heard;
  With the moon from the chasms of night
It rises, forlorn and afraid;
  If I turn to the left or the right
I can not forget or evade;
When it shakes at my sleep as a dream,
If I shudder, it stifles my scream.

It smiles from the cradle; it lies
On the dust of the grave, and it cries
  In the winds and the waters; it slips
In the flush of the leaf to the ground;
  It troubles the kiss at my lips;
It lends to my laughter a sound;
It makes of the picture but paint;
It unhallows the brain of the saint.

The ermine and crown of the king,
The sword of the soldier, the ring
  Of the bride, and the robe of the priest,
The gods in their prisons of stone,
  The angels that sang in the East—
Yea, the Cross of my Lord, it has known;
And wings there are none that can fly
From its shadow with me, till I die.

Sarah M. B. Piatt.

THE RAINBOW.

I SOMETIMES have thoughts, in my loneliest hours,
That lie on my heart like the dew on the flowers,
Of a ramble I took one bright afternoon,
When my heart was as light as a blossom in June;
The green earth was moist with the late fallen showers,
The breeze fluttered down and blew open the flowers,
While a single white cloud to its haven of rest,
On the white wing of peace, floated off in the west.

As I threw back my tresses to catch the cool breeze,
That scattered the raindrops and dimpled the seas,
Far up the blue sky a fair rainbow unrolled
Its soft tinted pinions of purple and gold.
'T was born in a moment, yet, quick as its birth,
It had stretched to the uttermost ends of the earth,
And, fair as an angel, it floated as free,
With a wing on the earth and a wing on the sea.

How calm was the ocean! how gentle its swell!
Like a woman's soft bosom it rose and it fell;
While its light sparkling waves, stealing laughingly o'er,
When they saw the fair rainbow, knelt down on the shore.
No sweet hymn ascended, no murmur of prayer,
Yet I felt that the spirit of worship was there,
And bent my young head, in devotion and love,
'Neath the form of an angel that floated above.

How wide was the sweep of its beautiful wings!
How boundless its circle! how radiant its rings!
If I looked on the sky, it was suspended in air;
If I looked on the ocean, the rainbow was there;
Thus forming a girdle, as brilliant and whole
As the thoughts of the rainbow that circled my soul.
Like the wing of the Deity, calmly unfurled,
It bent from the cloud and encircled the world.

There are moments, I think, when the spirit receives
Whole volumes of thought on its unwritten leaves,
When the folds of the heart in a moment unclose
Like the innermost leaves from the heart of a rose.
And thus, when the rainbow had passed from the sky,
The thoughts it awoke were too deep to pass by;
It left my full soul, like the wing of a dove,
All fluttering with pleasure and fluttering with love.

I know that each moment of rapture or pain
But shortens the links in life's mystical chain;
I know that my form, like the bow from the wave,
Must pass from the earth and lie cold in the grave;
Yet O! when death's shadows my bosom encloud,
When I shrink at the thought of the coffin and shroud,
May Hope, like the rainbow, my spirit enfold
In her beautiful pinions of purple and gold.

AMELIA B. WELBY.

THE BUTTERFLY.

SAILING so airily over the clover,
  Bending so lovingly over the rose,
Who would envy thee, beautiful rover?
  What dost thou know of our life and its woes?

Thou hast forgotten thy former existence—
  Wingless and sad 'mid thy mates of the clod—
So shall our earthly life fade in the distance,
  When we arise in the likeness of God!

LAURA S. HAGNER.

TO HERSA.

Maiden, there is something more
Than raiment to adore:
Thou must have more than a dress,
   More than any mode or mould,
More than mortal loveliness,
   To captivate the cold.

Bow the knightly when they bow,
To a star behind the brow:
Not to marble, not to dust;
   But to that which warms them:
Not to contour nor to bust;
   But to that which forms them:
Not to languid lid nor lash,
Satin fold nor purple sash;
But unto the living flash
So mysteriously hid
Under lash and under lid.

But—vanity of vanities—
If the red rose in a young cheek lies,
   Fatal disguise!
For the most terrible lances
Of the true, true Knight,
   Are his bold eyebeams;
And every time that he opens his eyes
The falsehood that he looks on dies.

If the heavenly light be latent,
It can need no earthly patent.
Unbeholden unto art,
     Fashion or lore,
     Scrip or store,
     Earth or ore
     Be thy heart,
Which was music from the start,
Music, music to the core.
Music, which, though voiceless,

WILLIAM D GALLAGHER.

TO HERSA.

    Can create
Both form and fate,
As Petrarch could a sonnet.
That, taking flesh upon it,
    Spirit noiseless,
Doth the same inform and fill
With a Music sweeter still,—
Lives, and breathes, and palpitates,
Moves, and moulds, and animates,
And sleeps not from its duty
Till the maid in whom 't is pent,
From a mortal rudiment,
    From the earth-cell
    And the love-cell
    By the birth-spell,
    And the love-spell,
    Come to beauty.

Beauty is music mute,
Music's flower and fruit,
    Music's lute:
Music's lute be thou,
Maiden of the starry brow,
(Keep thy heart true to know how!)
A Lute which he alone,
As all in good time shall be shown,
Shall prove and thereby make his own,
Who is god enough to play upon it.

Happy, happy maid is she
Who is wedded unto Truth!
Thou shalt know him, when he comes,
    (Welcome youth!)
Not by any din of drums,
Nor the vantage of his airs;
    Neither by his crown,
    Nor his gown,
Nor by any thing he wears.
He shall only well known be
By the holy Harmony
That his coming makes in thee!

                    FORCEYTHE WILSON.

THE DEVIL'S HOLLOW.*

On Devil's Hill the Day-king still
  His amber robe is trailing;
Floats up to sight the Queen of night,
  Her white, sweet face unveiling.
In silver cars the courtier stars
  With leal allegiance follow,
As kling-go-ling, the cow-bells ring,
  Adown the Devil's hollow.

How smooth and hard the boulevard
  This Autumn eve for walking;
Beneath the cliffs, in misty skiffs,
  I hear the fishers talking;
Above the bridge 'round Devil's Ridge
  Still flits the tardy swallow,
And kling-go-ling, the cow-bells ring
  Adown the Devil's Hollow.

O perfect scene! The still ravine,
  The bridge, the elm, the river;
For love and rhyme the twilight time
  Should linger here forever.
No meeter field was e'er revealed
  For Daphne and Apollo,
As kling-go-ling, the cow-bells ring
  Adown the Devil's Hollow.

Though nights to be come fair to me,
  Beyond my fancies' bringing,
Where light shall steer some gondolier
  With maids to gitterns singing,
From distance long shall float the song
  Above their tra-la-la-la,
The klang-go-lang the cow-bells rang
  Adown the Devil's Hollow.

HENRY T. STANTON.

*A picturesque ravine near Frankfort, Ky.

GRECIAN POETRY VERSUS MODERN SCIENCE.

The startling information is given by a modern chemist of the possibility of preparing alcohol from quartz and flints.—*Harper's Scientific Record* (*old number*).

THERE dwelt a youth in ancient Thrace,
  Where voice and lyre entrancing
Bewitched with song the human race,
  And set creation dancing.
The gods and goddesses above
  Heard him in silent wonder;
Juno forgot to lecture Jove,
  And Jove forgot to thunder;
The sea-snakes heard and wagged their tails,
  The porpoise burst with pleasure;
The fishes weighed it on their scales,
  And found a perfect measure;
The mermaids gathered round in flocks,
  And strewed his path with corals;
The sirens heard, and from the rocks
  Cast down their watery laurels;
The trees picked up their trunks and swayed
  About in measures mazy;
The rocks rolled 'round and danced and played
  In waltzes wild and crazy.
There comes a thrill down listening years
  Throughout creation ringing,
Perchance the "music of the spheres"
  Still echoes his sweet singing.
Now, Orpheus loved a maid who died
  The day they were united;
He wished below to seek his bride,
  And Pluto's realm delighted
By striking soft his "golden shell."
  I never have forgiven
This seeking for his love in hell
  Before he searched through heaven.

'T was like a man to go there first,
    And scarcely worth remarking—
But Tantalus forgot his thirst
    And Cerberus ceased barking.
Things without motion swayed about
    While Ixion's wheel stopped turning;
And fire was stirred, but not put out,
    And Orpheus left it burning.
The vulture even forgot to prey
    While listening to that lyre:
Some creatures of the present day
    Might show a like desire.
But truth must triumph. Lo! a glance
    Our modern science merits,
She says no wonder rocks can dance
    When they're possessed by spirits.
A savant gives mysterious hints
    That modern quartz are leaking,
And that the fiery hearts of flints
    With vinous streams are reeking.

* * * * * * * *

Let modern humbug still increase:
    I fling with fierce defiance
The gauntlet of Poetic Greece
    At prosy modern science.
I swear the strains of Orpheus' lyre
    Did cause the stones to frolic,
And left them all with hearts of fire
    And nature's alcoholic!
O shade of Bacchus! see with scorn
    Thy purple glories flicker,
When mortals, drunk on rye and corn,
    Press rocks for stronger liquor.

                        ROSA VERTNER JEFFREY.

THE CLOSING YEAR.

'T IS midnight's holy hour—and silence now
Is brooding, like a gentle spirit, o'er
The still and pulseless world. Hark! on the winds
The bell's deep tones are swelling. 'T is the knell
Of the departed Year.
      No funeral train
Is sweeping past; yet on the stream and wood,
With melancholy light, the moonbeams rest,
Like a pale, spotless shroud; the air is stirred
As by a mourner's sigh; and on yon cloud,
That floats so still and placidly through heaven,
The spirits of the seasons seem to stand—
Young Spring, bright Summer, Autumn's solemn form,
And Winter with his aged locks—and breathe
In mournful cadences, that come abroad
Like the far wind-harp's wild and touching wail,
A melancholy dirge o'er the dead Year,
Gone from the earth forever.
      'T is a time
For memory and for tears. Within the deep,
Still chambers of the heart, a specter dim,
Whose tones are like the wizard voice of Time
Heard from the tomb of ages, points its cold
And solemn finger to the beautiful
And holy visions that have passed away
And left no shadow of their loveliness
On the dead waste of life. That specter lifts
The coffin-lid of hope, and joy, and love,
And, bending mournfully above the pale
Sweet forms that slumber there, scatters dead flowers
O'er what has passed to nothingness.
      The Year
Has gone, and with it many a glorious throng
Of happy dreams. Its mark is on each brow,
Its shadow in each heart. In its swift course
It waved its scepter o'er the beautiful,

And they are not. It laid its pallid hand
Upon the strong man, and the haughty form
Is fallen, and the flashing eye is dim.
It trod the hall of revelry, where thronged
The bright and joyous, and the tearful wail
Of stricken ones is heard, where erst the song
And reckless shout resounded. It passed o'er
The battle-plain, where sword and spear and shield
Flashed in the light of midday—and the strength
Of serried hosts is shivered, and the grass,
Green from the soil of carnage, waves above
The crushed and mouldering skeleton. It came,
And fadeth like a wreath of mist at eve;
Yet, ere it melted in the viewless air,
It heralded its millions to their home
In the dim land of dreams.
       Remorseless Time!
Fierce spirit of the glass and scythe!—what power
Can stay him in his silent course, or melt
His iron heart to pity? On, still on
He presses, and forever. The proud bird,
The condor of the Andes, that can soar
Through heaven's unfathomable depths, or brave
The fury of the northern hurricane
And bathe his plumage in the thunder's home,
Furls his broad wings at nightfall, and sinks down
To rest upon his mountain-crag.—But Time
Knows not the weight of sleep or weariness,
And night's deep darkness has no chain to bind
His rushing pinion. Revolutions sweep
O'er earth, like troubled visions o'er the breast
Of dreaming sorrow; cities rise and sink,
Like bubbles on the water; fiery isles
Spring, blazing, from the ocean, and go back
To their mysterious caverns; mountains rear
To heaven their bald and blackened cliffs, and bow
Their tall heads to the plain; new empires rise,
Gathering the strength of hoary centuries,
And rush down like the Alpine avalanche,

Startling the nations; and the very stars,
Yon bright and burning blazonry of God,
Glitter awhile in their eternal depths,
And, like the Pleiad, loveliest of their train,
Shoot from their glorious spheres, and pass away
To darkle in the trackless void: yet Time,
Time the tomb-builder, holds his fierce career,
Dark, stern, all-pitiless, and pauses not
Amid the mighty wrecks that strew his path,
To sit and muse, like other conquerors,
Upon the fearful ruin he has wrought.

GEORGE D. PRENTICE.

INVOCATION TO THE COLISEUM AT ROME.

A THOUSAND years ago, and thou
  Wert then a thousand old;
The mightiest wreck of splendor now
  Time lingers to behold,
And, like thy victims, torn and pale,
And falling thou wouldst tell thy tale.

Thy subject realms from zone to zone,
  Their trophies sent each sea,
The suppliant from the shrine, the throne,
  Their tributes borne to thee,
While Parian throngs in forms divine
And gods were ministers of thine.
*   *   *   *   *
And Time hath writ upon thy brow
  Pride and ambition's fall;
Wealth, pageant, glory, empire, thou
  Hast reared and buried all;
In stern decay, sublime and lone,
Art now a moralist in stone.

JOEL T. HART.

THE SERMON OF A STATUE.

(IN WESTMINSTER ABBEY.)

SUDDENLY, in the melancholy place
   With sculptured king and priest and knight assembled,
The music called us. Then, with kindly grace,
   On a gold head was laid a hand that trembled:
"You little stranger, come," the verger cried,
"And hear the sermon." "No," the child replied.

A moment standing on his new-world will,
   There in the corner of the poets, holding
His cap with pretty reverence, as still
   As any of that company, he said, folding
His arms: "But let that canon wait." And then:
"I want to stay here with these marble men.

"If they could preach, I'd listen!" Ah, they can,
   Another thought. It pleased the boy to linger
In the pale presence of the peerless man
   Who pointed to his text with moveless finger.
Laughing with blue-eyed wonder, he said: "Look,
This one (but do you know him?) has a book!"

. . . I know him. Ay, and all the world knows him—
   Among the many poets the only one!
On that high head the stainèd gloom was dim;
   In those fixed eyes the look of gods was lonely.
Kings at his feet, to whom his hands gave fame,
Lay, dust and ashes, shining through his name.

I heard him. With the still voice of the dead
   From that stone page, right careless of derision,
Sad jesters of a faithless age! he read
   How the great globe would vanish like a vision,
With all that it inhabit. . . . And hath he
Then writ but one word, and that—Vanity?

S. M. B. PIATT.

DOUBLE LIFE.

OVER pools of purest water,
  Lying silent, there will come,
Soon, or late, the green enamel
  Of a quickened herbage-scum,
Taking color from the vesture
  That the margin grasses wear,
Till it hides the lambent sparkle
  Of the liquid crystal there.

So the poet-nature shadows
  All its glory with a cloud,
That the soul-light may not dazzle
  In the ordinary crowd;
So they hide their real beings,
  So they live and act a part,
Making nature but an adjunct
  To the perfectness of art.

Oh! I hate this outward seeming,
  This unreal, double life,
Where the face is full of quiet,
  While the heart is full of strife;
For our latent inner-currents
  Would to other currents run,
Though the waters of the spirit
  May be hidden from the sun.

We may live upon the surface,
  We may wear the mantle green,
And among the outer beings
  Be as outer beings seen;
But the spheres of souls magnetic
  Are beyond the common thrall,
And the true life of the poet
  Pulseth under, after all.

HENRY T. STANTON.

THE DREAM OF LIFE.

'T was but a bubble—yet 't was bright,
And gaily danced along the stream
Of life's wild torrents in its light
Of sunbeams sparkling, like a dream
Of heaven's own bliss for loveliness—
For fleetness like a passing thought;
And ever of such dreams as thee
The tissue of my line is wrought.
For I have dreamed of pleasures when
The sun of young existence smiled
Upon my wayward path, and then
Her promised sweets my heart beguiled;
But when I came those sweets to sip
They turned to gall upon my lip.

And I have dreamed of friendship, too;
For friendship's thought was made
To be man's solace in the shade
And glad him in the light, and so
I fondly thought to find a friend
Whose mind with mine would sweetly blend,
And as two placid streams unite,
And roll their waters in one bright
And tranquil current to the sea,
So might our happy spirits be
Borne onward to eternity.
But he betrayed me, and with pain
I woke—to sleep and dream again.

And then I dreamed of love, and all
The clustered visions of the past
Seemed airy nothings to that last
Bright dream. It threw a magical
Enchantment o'er existence—cast
A glory on my path so bright
I seemed to feel and breathe its light;
But now that blissful dream is o'er,
And I have waked to dream no more.

Beyond the farthest glimmering star
That twinkles in the arch above,
There is a world of truth and love
Which earth's vile passions never mar.
O, could I snatch the eagle's plumes
And soar to that bright world above,
Which God's own holy light illumes
With glories of eternal day!
How gladly every lingering tie
That binds me down to earth I'd sever,
And leave for that blest home on high
This hollow-hearted world forever.

GEORGE D. PRENTICE.

LAST NIGHT.

WHAT was it then? The trick of some wild thought,
Unguarded, swift, like sudden lightning's flight,
Whose ruthless blade doth stab the slumb'rous night
And rouse to fierce awaking, passion-fraught,
The silent earth? What strange delirium brought
Us two, soul-starved—beyond the years of blight,
Beyond the weary conflict for the right,
And all the hard-earned lesson duty taught—
To look once more into each other's eyes,
As they who love, yet dare not love too well,
To feel again the old, glad, sweet surprise,
And maddening pain the heart half feared to tell?
Did I, or you, dear, lose the long control
That left us thus, one moment, soul to soul?

NELLIE T. KINKEAD.

A SUMMER IDYL.

PICTURES of sunset, yester eve,
  The still lake underlying,
So charmed us we forgot to grieve
  For the sweet summer dying.
O sunny noons! O warm suns set
  Where crystal waters quiver!
Days without shadow, save regret
  That they are gone forever!
O lambent skies, so pure and bright,
  While realms beyond draw nearer;
Our rapt souls wonder, steeped in light,
  If Heaven itself is fairer!
O long sweet drives through leafy ways
  Of forests dim and olden,
Where softly steal the subtle rays,
  Turning their green shades golden!
Through dewy lanes, where summer came
  To blazon her sweet story
In cardinal tufts of scarlet flame,
  And mark a path of glory;
Down long, bright miles of golden-rod,
  Born of the Day-god's shadow,
From sunbeams sown along the sod,
  A nimbus round the meadow;
Where flash pale marguerites, starry-eyed,
  Beside their sister daisies,
With violet colors, streaked and pied,
  Clust'red in purple mazes;
Down where the sweet wild roses thrill
  Faint fragrance to the rushes,
And regal lilies, paler still,
  In contrast with their blushes;
Unmarked, the hours, like golden darts,
  Through summer vistas flying,
Till green leaves turn their bleeding hearts
  To tell us they are dying.

A SUMMER IDYL.

The summer smites through sunny clouds
    Her treasures green and tender,
To fit them for their crimson shrouds
    And autumn's funeral splendor.
O matchless eves! your glories sweep
    So low where twilight closes
Her purple gates, yon crystal deep
    Looks heaped with cloud-land roses.
And, while I gaze, night's Rembrandt shade
    Falls where the red is waving,
Till sun-flushed views, dissolving, fade
    To moonlight's soft engraving.
O summer friends of vanished days,
    So calm, so blest, so fleeting,
When all have gone their separate ways,
    Where next will be our meeting?
Perchance before another year
    Shall bring us summer's blessing,
In chains of friendship woven here
    Some dear link may be missing.
Fresh childhood, youth, maturer age,
    Swept off by Death's dark tidal,
Might leave, alas! one clouded page
    In this, our summer idyl.
Old Time will bind with icy chain
    The blue lake's dulcet murmur,
And cold storms chant a wild refrain
    Where sang the sweet-voiced summer.
But memory sails through sparkling waves,
    And drifts on waters glowing,
With sunset fires our path she paves
    Out to the westward rowing.
O dreamy scenes of joy and love,
    My soul in beauty steeping,
Your pictures live as treasure trove
    In Memory's holy keeping.
The songs we sang still steal to me
    From out a mystic gloaming;
Ferns wave their plumes, wild-flowers I see
    Through tender vistas blooming.

Friends of one fleeting summer-time,
  'Mid falling leaves we sever;
But in my heart, as in this rhyme,
  I hold you fast forever.
                    ROSA VERTNER JEFFREY.

TO SILENCE.

FALL on my senses
  Soft as the drop of drifting snow,
And soothe my restlessness, sweet Silence.

Here in this glade, just still
  From vanished song-bird's varying air,
Thy presence doth fulfill
  His melody—though sweet to hear,
    Far sweeter in the memory.

The very stream rests in her run,
  Or, if she resteth not, thy full embrace
Keeps her to dance so lightly on
  As not to stir the daisies in her dress,
    The lilies on her bosom.

Here would I lie o' lazy hours,
  Where noiseless nooks make thy retreat,
Where butterflies tiptoe upon the flowers
  And naught disturbs thee save the sweet,
    Sad treble of the trees.

Fall on my senses
Soft as the drop of drifting snow;
Enfold me in thy peace, sweet Silence.
                    J. L. PATTERSON.

COQUETTE.

'MID hot-house blooms and rarest plants,
   She stood apart a moment's space,
A dainty maiden, clad in white,
   And waved her fan with careless grace.

(The merry dancers passed her by
   To strains of sweetest minstrelsy.)

"For once you deign to speak to me.
   At last," he said, "I find you here.
Ah, well! perhaps you can forget,
   But I—I have so loved you, dear."

One moment in his manly clasp
   He held her little, shapely hand,
One moment felt with sudden thrall
   The mystic spell of Circe's wand.

And then he spoke with bitter jest
   Of woman's faith and woman's love,
And strove, with cool indifference,
   Her utter heartlessness to prove.

(The dancers passed with rhythmic tread;
   A softened light shone overhead.)

But when the time for parting came,
   With broken voice, "I make you free.
O love," he said, "just for this once,
   Why need you turn away from me?"

The small brown head was lower bent,
   A softened light shone overhead,
An upward glance was swiftly lent,
   "Because I love you, John," she said.

(The dancers passed unheeded by
   The strains of sweetest minstrelsy.)

                  NELLIE TALBOT KINKEAD.

JAPANESE WALL-PAPER.

WAIFS from carvings arabesque,
Framed in arcs and squares grotesque;
Esthetes call this droll burlesque,
Quaint, novel, dainty, picturesque.

Roses red with hearts ecru,
Ragged robins, gold in hue,
Hyacinths, I never knew
Earth to give birth to such as you.

Lilies dark that love the light;
Pansies in a sad, sad plight;
Poppies, with their breath of night,
Keep guard o'er sleep in gilding bright.

Daisies sporting mammoth crowns;
Feathery ferns in russet gowns,
Flora can't suppress her frowns
At seeing that you dress in browns.

Bells of blue in whorls of red,
Freaks of art, Dame Nature's dread;
Fancy born and fancy bred,
You never grew in garden bed.

Grasses tall, but not of green,
Glints of garnet here are seen;
Also grays of softer sheen,
Lines meant for vines run just between.

Flowers found on chamber wall,
Placed in vases far too small;
Printed paper, else you'd fall;
Bee, bird, and lea disclaim you all.

NELLY LA RUE BROWN.

ROSA VERTNER JEFFREY.

THE MONEYLESS MAN.

Is there no secret place on the face of the earth,
Where charity dwelleth, where virtue has birth?
Whose bosoms in mercy and kindness will heave
When the poor and the wretched shall ask and receive?
Is there no place at all where a knock from the poor
Will bring a kind angel to open the door?
Ah, search the wide world wherever you can,
There is no open door for a Moneyless Man!

Go, look in yon hall where the chandelier's light
Drives off with its splendor the darkness of night,
Where the rich-hanging velvet in shadowy fold
Sweeps gracefully down with its trimmings of gold,
And the mirrors of silver take up, and renew,
In long, lighted vistas, the 'wildering view:
Go there! at the banquet, and find if you can,
A welcoming smile for a Moneyless Man!

Go, look in yon church of the cloud-reaching spire,
Which gives to the sun his same look of red fire,
Where the arches and columns are gorgeous within,
And the walls seem as pure as a soul without sin;
Walk down the long aisles, see the rich and the great
In the pomp and the pride of their worldly estate;
Walk down in your patches and find, if you can,
Who opens a pew to a Moneyless Man!

Go, look in the Banks, where Mammon has told
His hundreds and thousands of silver and gold;
Where, safe from the hands of the starving and poor,
Lie piles upon piles of the glittering ore!
Walk up to their counters—ah, there you may stay
Till your limbs grow old, till your hairs grow gray,
And you'll find at the Banks not one of the clan
With money to lend to a Moneyless Man!

Go, look to yon Judge, in his dark-flowing gown,
With the scales wherein law weigheth equity down;
Where he frowns on the weak and smiles on the strong,
And punishes right while he justifies wrong;
Where juries their lips to the Bible have laid,
To render a verdict—they've already made:
Go there, in the court-room, and find, if you can,
Any law for the cause of a Moneyless Man!

Then go to your hovel—no raven has fed
The wife who has suffered too long for her bread;
Kneel down by her pallet, and kiss the death-frost
From the lips of the angel your poverty lost:
Then turn in your agony upward to God,
And bless, while it smites you, the chastening rod,
And you'll find, at the end of your life's little span,
There's a welcome above for a Moneyless Man!

HENRY T. STANTON.

IN DAYS TO COME.

IN days to come,
What thoughts may live, what dreams may rise,
To move thy heart, to melt thine eyes?
It may be he thou scornest to-day
Will hold in undisputed sway
    Thy soul, thy life—
    In days to come.

In days to come
It may be that thy breast of snow
Love's unrequited pang shall know;
Alone within thy heart may be
A sigh for him who plead with thee
    And craved thy love—
    In days to come.

HENRY CHURCHILL MURRAY.

A NAME IN THE SAND.

ALONE I walked the ocean strand,
A pearly shell was in my hand,
I stooped and wrote upon the sand
  My name, the year and day.
As onward from the spot I passed,
One lingering look behind I cast,
A wave came rolling high and fast,
  And washed my lines away.

And so, methought, 'twill quickly be
With every mark on earth of me;
A wave of dark oblivion's sea
  Will sweep across the place
Where I have trod the sandy shore
Of time, and been to me no more—
Of me, my day, the name I bore,
  To leave no track or trace.

And yet, with Him who counts the sands,
And holds the waters in his hands,
I know a lasting record stands
  Inscribed against my name,
Of all this mortal part has wrought,
Of all this waking soul has thought,
And from these fleeting moments caught,
  For glory or for shame.
                         GEORGE D. PRENTICE.

DUTY.

NEVER did artist execute work
  That looked in his own eyes perfected;
Never a day drew to its close
  But it saw some duty neglected.
                         EUGENE ASHTON.

"SWEET GIRL GRADUATE."

DRINKING sunshine, dew receiving,
Gathering fruits of Life's good-giving;
Trophy-laden, laurel-crowned,
Into larger life out-bound—
 "Sweet girl graduate!"

Life that wakes, and lifts, perfecting;
Life, the light received, reflecting;
Broadening, deepening into giving,
Reaching out to real living—
 "Sweet girl graduate!"

Turn again your gleaming face,
Scan the scene with loving gaze;
Know your feet will never more
Touch on youthland's care-free shore—
 "Sweet girl graduate!"

ALICE H. CARR.

BEAUTIFUL HAIR.

THERE is no glimmer
 Nor shimmer,
Nor golden gleams,
Like molten streams
 Of sunlight,
To dazzle the sight
In the beautiful hair,
Not golden nor fair,
 That I prize.

I leave caresses
 For tresses,
Floating so light,
Darker than night,
 To others,

Who have no mothers
With silvery hair,
Turned thus with the care
    Of long years.

But I will render
    And tender
Love for the care
That turned her hair
    So snow-white,
    From golden bright.
Ah! beautiful hair,
Not golden, nor fair,
    That I prize.

I love to linger,
    And finger
O'er the dear bands
Of silvery strands;
    My treasures,
    That bring more pleasures
Than would jewels rare.
Oh, silvery hair,
    So precious!
                HENRY CLEVELAND WOOD.

THE twilight hours, like birds, flew by
    As lightly and as free;
Ten thousand stars were in the sky,
    Ten thousand on the sea;
For every wave with dimpled face
    That leaped upon the air
Had caught a star in its embrace
    And held it trembling there.
                            AMELIA WELBY.
"*Musings.*"

THE DEATH OF A SOUL.

"THE soul that sinneth"—the words came slow
From the lips of a woman bending low
O'er a couch where death was drawing nigh,
" The soul that sinneth, it shall die."

With a dull, bitter feeling she looked away
From the drawn, pinched face of the man who lay
So silent there, with slow-drawn breath;
She listened to hear the coming of death.

His soul! Had it sinned? Did the Bible mean
That a *soul could die?* Then never again
In all the years of an infinite sphere
Would she meet him, the love of her lifetime here?

She *knew* he had sinned, aye, well she knew
That his life had been wicked. Her own had been, too.
His life course was passing; his body was mortal.
His soul? Would it not meet her own at some portal

Of heaven or hell? She did not much care,
If only he waited and watched for her there.
And now he was dying! Did she have to stay
In existence, when his soul was quite passed away?

Even so! Death had come with a touch light and quick
As a candle will flicker and wrap round its wick,
He was dead—*soul and spirit.* For who could deny
The words of the Bible—"*it surely shall die.*"

JEANNETTE SWING.

WHAT IS IT?

'T is in the running brooklet as it bubbles on its way;
'T is in the purple violet, that blooms with modest ray;
'T is in the quiet moonbeam, when it sleeps upon the wave;
'T is in the daisy pure and fair, which decks the lonely grave.
'T is in the golden sunset, and in silvery twilight, too;
'T is in the gorgeous sunrise, and in the sparkling dew
That adorns the earliest, fairest flowers that open to our view.

'T is in th' awe-inspiring thunder as it sounds thro' earth and sky,
Followed by the vivid lightning's blaze flashing from on high;
'T is in the music of the dense old woods, the rustling of the leaves,
Around us a tender melancholy a hallowed influence weaves.
There is language in all nature! Did we not ungrateful prove,
Did we let her faithful teaching our hearts but rightly move,
We 'd learn from e'en the tiniest flower this sacred truth,
"God is love."

GERALDINE.

THE PAST! the silent Past! pale Memory kneels
Beside her shadowy urn, and with a deep
And voiceless sorrow weeps above the grave
Of beautiful affections. Her lone harp
Lies broken at her feet, and, as the wind
Goes o'er its mouldering chords, a dirge-like sound
Rises upon the air, and all again
Is an unbreathing silence.

GEORGE D. PRENTICE.
"*On Revisiting Brown University.*"

THE BIVOUAC OF THE DEAD.

THE muffled drum's sad roll has beat
    The soldier's last tattoo;
No more on life's parade shall meet
    That brave and fallen few.
On Fame's eternal camping-ground
    Their silent tents are spread,
But Glory guards, with solemn round,
    The bivouac of the dead.

No rumor of the foe's advance
    Now swells upon the wind;
No troubled thought at midnight haunts
    Of loved ones left behind;
No vision of the morrow's strife
    The warrior's dream alarms;
No braying horn nor screaming fife
    At dawn shall call to arms.

Their shivered swords are red with rust,
    Their pluméd heads are bowed;
Their haughty banner, trailed in dust,
    Is now their martial shroud.
And plenteous funeral tears have washed
    The red stains from each brow,
And the proud forms, by battle gashed,
    Are free from anguish now.

The neighing troop, the flashing blade,
    The bugle's stirring blast,
The charge, the dreadful cannonade,
    The din and shout are past;
Nor war's wild note, nor glory's peal,
    Shall thrill with fierce delight
Those breasts that never more may feel
    The rapture of the fight.

Like the fierce northern hurricane
That sweeps his great plateau,
Flushed with the triumph yet to gain,
Came down the serried foe.
Who heard the thunder of the fray
Break o'er the field beneath,
Knew well the watchword of that day
Was "Victory or death."

Long has the doubtful conflict raged
O'er all that stricken plain,
For never fiercer fight had waged
The vengeful blood of Spain;
And still the storm of battle blew,
Still swelled the gory tide;
Not long our stout old chieftain knew
Such odds his strength could bide.

'T was in that hour his stern command
Called to a martyr's grave
The flower of his beloved land,
The nation's flag to save.
By rivers of their fathers' gore
His first-born laurels grew,
And well he deemed the sons would pour
Their lives for glory too.

Full many a norther's breath has swept
O'er Angostura's plain—
And long the pitying sky has wept
Above the moldering slain.
The raven's scream, or eagle's flight,
Or shepherd's pensive lay,
Alone awakes each sullen height
That frowned o'er that dread fray.

Sons of the Dark and Bloody Ground,
Ye must not slumber there,
Where stranger steps and tongues resound
Along the heedless air.

Your own proud land's heroic soil
  Shall be your fitter grave;
She claims from War his richest spoil—
  The ashes of her brave.

Thus 'neath their parent turf they rest,
  Far from the gory field,
Borne to a Spartan mother's breast
  On many a bloody shield;
The sunshine of their native sky
  Smiles sadly on them here,
And kindred eyes and hearts watch by
  The heroes' sepulcher.

Rest on, embalmed and sainted dead,
  Dear as the blood ye gave,
No impious footstep here shall tread
  The herbage of your grave;
Nor shall your glory be forgot
  While Fame her record keeps,
Or Honor points the hallowed spot
  Where Valor proudly sleeps.

Yon marble minstrel's voiceless stone
  In deathless song shall tell,
When many a vanquished age hath flown,
  The story how ye fell;
Nor wreck, nor change, nor winter's blight,
  Nor Time's remorseless doom,
Shall dim one ray of glory's light
  That gilds your deathless tomb.

THEODORE O'HARA.

ROME.

BESIDE the Tiber's sluggish stream
  Behold the seven giant hills
  Gleam dark above the murm'ring rills,
Like mountains in some troubled dream!

I see the sullen spider creep
  Through ruins of two thousand years;
  I feel the bitterness of tears
That Kings and Consuls used to weep.

I see the timid sunbeams steal
  Down through a time-worn ruined arch,
  Where slave and master used to march
To martial trumpet's ringing peal.

Again I look! and deep-blue skies
  Bend o'er the smiling, joyous earth;
  I hear the shout, the song, the mirth
Of Plebeians and Triumvirs rise.

I see the shade of many a sage,
  I hear the voice of Cicero,
  And Virgil's witch-notes soft and low,
As in the distant Golden Age.

I see the hues of black and green,
  I see a deeper, darker shade
  Than painter ever dared or made,
Steal o'er the weird and haunted scene.

I feel the awful spirit-spell
  Of ages past creep o'er my soul,
  I hear the volleying thunders roll,
The victor shout, the fun'ral knell.

A warlike spirit, fierce as death,
  Broods o'er these grim, majestic plains;
  And yet another spirit reigns
As gentle as an infant's breath.

I gaze again! the pageant wild,
Of legions, banners, bugles, marches,
Has died amid the broken arches,
Where captives wept and victors smiled.

But now the flashing flags are furled,
And crumbled now the splendid dome;
This is th' Eternal City—Rome,
The ancient Mistress of the World.

MANLIUS T. FLIPPIN.

CANTO II.

THE massive pile of Nazareth stood
Deep-capped in midnight's sable hood.
A chilly dampness gathered 'round,
And all was silence save when sound
Of sudden gust the tree-top shakes,
Or hooting owl the quiet breaks.
And now and then a dash of rain
Bursts wildly down, and in its train
The lightning's flame and thunder's roar
Flung open wide the Storm-king's door.
In truth it was a fearful night
To those who love and do the right;
More fearful still and terribly
It threatened foul iniquity.
No moon nor stars lent kindly light
To set the lonely traveler right;
But gloom and chill and tempest's crash
Were varied by the Fire-god's flash.

"*Maid of Nazareth.*"   HENRY COOLIDGE SEMPLE.

THE PRINCE IS COMING.

I.

THE PRINCE is coming, coming!
O robin, do you hear?
The Prince is coming, coming
With sword and shining spear.
O all ye blooming grasses,
You'll know him when he passes,
The sun will shine so clear.

II.

The Prince is coming, coming!
O fields, put on your green!
He has a wondrous palace,
And I shall be his queen.
You'll know him, wild bee rover,
For when he smiles the clover
Will blush with rosy sheen.

III.

The Prince is coming, coming!
Away with toil and care,
I'll bind the red, red roses
All in my bonny hair.
O birdies, sing your loudest,
O roses, blaze your proudest,
And make me passing fair.

IV.

The Prince is coming, coming!
Across the bright blue sea;
O robin in the tree-top,
Do you his great ship see?
His sails will be the whitest,
His pennons stream the brightest
The day he comes for me.

V.

The Prince is coming, coming!
  O daisies, would you see?
Crowd closely all the roadside,
  And find how grand we 'll be
With breeze-tossed plumes a-dancing,
And milk-white palfreys prancing
  To kirk across the lea.

VI.

Then we 'll go sailing, sailing!
  O bright will be the day,
With all the waves a-glancing,
  And all the winds at play;
O breezes blowing after,
Crowd all your sails with laughter
  As we go down the bay.

MARTHA PEARSON SMITH.

"*Appha*," *an unpublished poem.*

COMPLETENESS.

"WHY use these dull and dingy hues?" I said;
The weaver paused, and smiled, and shook his head,
And answered, " 'T is a background for the brighter thread;
  When all is finished, you will see
  How bright the pattern be."

I pondered o'er the weaver's words and ways;
Might it not be that Fate sent darker days
That we might trace thereon in shining deeds of praise?
  So that Life finished, one might see
  How bright the pattern be.

HENRY CLEVELAND WOOD.

ARGUMENTUM.

When Cupid e'er the human heart
    To daring deeds doth urge,
How well one plays deceptive part,
And dabbles deep in shamming art,
    What chains of cunning forge.

No bolts or bars resist the power
    Of truly loving souls;
No altitude of lofty tower,
No rugged walls or steel-bound door
    Their course of love controls.

The vigilance of watchful eyes
    Is but precaution vain;
The dauntless swain all care defies,
And, bearing off the cherished prize,
    E'en mocks decorum's bane.

When man once loves, his reason flies,
    All cowardice doth flee;
Nor dreams of future woe arise,
Nor sorrow caused by severing ties
    Of sweetest sanctity.

"*Maid of Nazareth.*"

HOW?

Pray, how could I help it—
With the gate just between,
All covered with sweet-smelling vines for a screen?
And her red lips—Ah, dear me,
So temptingly near me!
Pray, how could I help it—
With the gate just between?

                    Lizzie Walker.

GWENDOLYNE.

'NEATH the dusky cottage eaves
Is a window framed in leaves,
Through them golden sunshine cleaves,
And strange patterns ever weaves,
Yellow as the harvest sheaves;
   And sweet Gwendolyne
Spins each day her flax with care,
Dimpled shoulders, white and bare,
And, the rounded arms so fair,
Seen through braids of golden hair.
Hath she not a pretty air,
   The peasant Gwendolyne?

From the dewy forest glade,
Where the deer in freedom strayed,
Through the long arcades of shade,
Came a princely cavalcade,
And they saw the peasant maid,
   The pretty Gwendolyne.
On they came with stately tread,
Each with plume above his head,
Some of white, and some of red.
"By my faith!" the leader said,
"Methinks you is the one to wed,"
   And points to Gwendolyne.

The brave knight wooed without delay,
The maiden set her wheel away,
And with the cavalcade so gay,
Just at the closing of the day,
They reached the castle, old and gray,
   The Knights and Gwendolyne.
And no more did the hands so fair
Know aught of toilsome work or care;
But gleaming in her golden hair,
And on her breast were jewels rare,
Rich-broidered silks had she to wear,
   The Lady Gwendolyne.

                HENRY CLEVELAND WOOD.

R T. DURRETT.

SWEETHEART.

SWEETHEART—I call you sweetheart still,
  As in your window's laced recess,
When both our eyes were wont to fill,
  One year ago, with tenderness.
I call you sweetheart by the law
  Which gives me higher right to feel,
Though I be here in Malaga,
  And you in far Mobile.

I mind me when, along the bay
  The moonbeams slanted all the night;
When on my breast your dark locks lay,
  And in my hand, your hand so white;
This scene the summer night-time saw,
  And my soul took its warm anneal
And bore it here to Malaga
  From beautiful Mobile.

The still and white magnolia grove
  Brought wingéd odors to your cheek,
Where my lips seared the burning love
  They could not frame the words to speak;
Sweetheart, you were not ice to thaw,
  Your bosom neither stone nor steel;
I count to-night, at Malaga,
  Its throbbings at Mobile.

What matter if you bid me now
  To go my way for others' sake?
Was not my love-seal on your brow
  For death, and not for days to break?
Sweetheart, our trothing holds no flaw;
  There was no crime and no conceal,
I clasp you here in Malaga,
  As erst in sweet Mobile.

I see the bay-road, white with shells,
  I hear the beach make low refrain,
The stars lie flecked like asphodels
  Upon the green, wide water-plain—
These silent things as magnets draw,
  They bear me hence with rushing keel,
A thousand miles from Malaga,
  To matchless, fair Mobile.

Sweetheart, there is no sea so wide,
  No time in life, nor tide to flow,
Can rob my breast of that one bride
  It held so close a year ago.
I see again the bay we saw;
  I hear again your sigh's reveal,
I keep the faith at Malaga
  I plighted at Mobile.
                              HENRY T. STANTON.

BLONDE AND BRUNETTE.

Two clouds, gold and purple, at sunrise contending,
Two chords of rare music contrasting and blending,
Through the Carnival flying, like sunshine and shadow
Pursuing each other o'er mountain and meadow,
Swept our Blonde and Brunette, all radiant with joy—
Cleopatra of Egypt and Helen of Troy.

The Blonde is a dew-spangled morning in June,
When birds, breeze, and bee with the sun are in tune;
Her lips and the rose scent the crystalline air,
And the sunshine is lost in the gold of her hair.
The Brunette is a ray of the mystical light
Which falls from the moon on a Midsummer night,
And visions celestial of Dream-land arise
From the luminous depths of her violet eyes.
                              S. C. MERCER.

THE DAYS OF OTHER YEARS.

'T is true I may not seem to weep,
   Or grieve at gath'ring cares;
But jealous guard doth memory keep
   O'er days of other years.

These days may ope their golden store,
   And yield the wealth that's theirs;
But oh! they never can restore
   The days of other years.

Less golden now the evening shadow,
   Or morning's blush appears;
More bright the sheen of field and meadow
   In days of other years.

The moonlight on the glassy mere,
   Fond memory endears;
How bright the birds and blossoms were
   In days of other years!

Sometimes no joy comes to repress
   The flood of falling tears;
And then in memory I bless
   The days of other years.

In vain I wander in my dreams
   From these discordant years,
And gaze back at the light that gleams
   In days of other years.

Dear mem'ry sometimes comes to me,
   And takes my hand in hers,
And down her vista lets me see
   The days of other years.

Far back in glorious setting cast,
   The brightest hour appears;
And I must seek my joys at last
   In days of other years.

                              MANLIUS T. FLIPPIN.

FAULTLESS.

MANUS PULCHERRIMA QUAM UNQUAM VIDI.

Like a mould of flawless marble,
  With the hue of fallen snow,
Perfect in each curve and dimple,
  Is the fairest hand I know.
It is soft and smooth as satin,
  And each vein is like a thread,
Faintly colored with the azure
  Of the Summer sky o'erhead.

And each finger is a pattern,
  Far beyond the sculptor's tool,
Graceful as the drooping willow,
  Bending near some silent pool;
Tipped with color of the moss-rose,
  Lovely as the fleur-de-lys—
Ever will my admiration
  For that fairy hand increase.

E'en its touch is light and tender,
  Gentle as the zephyr's breath;
Just the hand to press the forehead
  Paling 'neath the blight of death.
Feeble words can ne'er the beauty
  Of that angel hand portray;
O forgive me if this measure
  Taketh from its charms away.

Henry Coolidge Semple.

THE NEW SOUTH.

Sweet were my dreams along thy streams,
  Old South, in bygone days,
Till war's red cloud, 'mid thunders loud,
  Consumed them in its blaze:
Suwanee's old plantation scenes,
  Where wild bees filled the comb;
The banjo and the moonlight dance
  Of old Kentucky Home.

The New South wakes! the New South shakes
  The dew-drops from her mane,
For idle grief brings no relief;
  The past comes not again.
To manly hearts and patient souls
  Heaven sanctifies each loss;
Two angels, Toil and Patience, bear
  To heaven the Southern Cross.

New South! New South! unseal thy mouth,
  Thy golden age is come,
Invention's soaring harmony
  And labor's busy hum.
The Old South dies; with beaming eyes
  The New South hastens in—
So boyhood's toys are cast aside
  When manhood's deeds begin.
                              S. C. Mercer.

THE DEAD PAST.

The dead past will not bury its dead;
The corpses of lost hopes will rise
From their half-covered graves, and fill
The present with their ghostly cries:

"That still shall be which once has been!"
Till the present is a death levee,
Where the past in warning tones
Shows the future what it will be.

We can not rise to goodly deeds,
But an attendant ghostly train
Bids us mistrust our very strength,
And in our joy prepare for pain.

The faithless ones we trusted rise,
And will not dwell amid the past,
But make us fear that each new friend
May prove a faithless one at last.

EUGENE ASHTON.

——"ONLY such as keep in storage
Goodly bins, from Summer forage,
 May the barren days defy;
For the dreamy thing that lingers
With the blossom in its fingers,
 When the Winter comes, may die."

"*Self Sacrifice.*" HENRY T. STANTON.

THE WEAVER.

MORNING.

THE sun climbed up the eastern hills,
  And through the dewy land
Shot gleams that fell athwart the rills,
  That sang on every hand.

Upon the wood and in the air
  There hung a mystic spell,
And on the greensward everywhere
  Soft shadows lightly fell;

And in a cottage where the bloom
  Of roses on the wall
Filled all the air, there was a loom
  Well built of oak, and tall.

All through the fragrant Summer day
  A maiden, blithe and fair,
Sat at the loom, and worked away,
  And hummed a simple air:

SONG.

"Oh! idle not, ye leafy trees,
  Weave nets of yellow sun,
And kiss me oft, O balmy breeze!
  My task is but begun."

NOON.

Still higher in the hazy sky
  The sun climbed, on and on,
Then Autumn winds came rushing by,
  For Summer flowers were gone.

Now sat a mother at the loom,
  The shuttle flew along
With whirr that filled the little room
  Together with her song:

SONG.

"O shuttle! faster, faster fly,
    For know ye not the sun
Is climbing high across the sky,
    And yet my work's not done?"

TWILIGHT.

The sun shot gleams of amber light
    Along the barren ground,
And shadows of the coming night
    Fell softly all around.

And in the little cottage room,
    From early dawn till night,
The weaver sat before the loom,
    Her hair was snowy white.

The hands were palsied now that threw
    The shuttle to and fro,
And as the fabric longer grew,
    She sang both sweet and low:

SONG.

"Half hidden in the rosy west,
    I see the golden sun,
And I shall soon begin my rest,
    My task is almost done!"

The Spring again brought joy and bloom,
    And kissed each vale and hill,
But in the little cottage room
    The oaken beam was still.

The swaying boughs with rays of gold
    Wove nets of yellow sun,
And cast them where a headstone told
    The weaver's task was done.

                    HENRY CLEVELAND WOOD.

THE OLD VIOLIN.

"Then shall the virgin rejoice in the dance, both young men and old together." Jer. xxxi, 13.

WHEN the old man taps with his foot on the floor,
    As the bow trips over the strings,
And the violin sighs to its quivering core,
    Like love when the bluebird sings,
There's a jubilant ring to the schottische and waltz,
    And the jigs and the reels he plays,
That flushes the cheeks while it quickens the pulse
    For a whirl in the redolent maze.

When the tense bow rocks to the equinox
    Of a wild melodious rain,
And the violin screams like a girl in dreams
    At the kiss of an amorous swain,
Then the old man sighs with a mist in his eyes
    As he hugs it up to his chin,
And he holds it near that his soul may hear
    The ravishing strains within.

When the room resounds with the jocund sounds
    Of the tunes that are always new,
And the waltzers go like sparks that glow
    When the backlog burns in two,
Then his joy runs o'er like a dripping oar
    'Mid waves of widening rings,
Till its ripples pour on the far-off shore
    Where Memory's galleon swings.

And he dreams he plays of departed days
    With Love in the heart of June,
And the lips he kissed laugh out of the mist
    Of the haze of the honeymoon,
And his fingers twitch as they catch the pitch
    Of the measures she loved to tread,
Till the sweet old air is a voicing rare
    Of the dream of a waltzer dead.

                    EDWIN S. HOPKINS.

WOMAN.

In acknowledgment of a copy of "Lucile" presented by a friend.

IN the highways of Life, here and there, now and then,
Amid muslin call'd ladies, and buckram call'd men,
One meets, though the race is now hardly styled human,
A man that's a man, and a woman that's woman;
Such scorn not to drink of the waters of truth,
That flow, pure and cool, from the fountains of youth;
Nor reject, for roast beef and plum-pudding, the meal
Fitly seasoned and served by the hand of Lucile.

Lucile! oh thou sweetest of self-immolators
That e'er walk'd the walks of the world in French gaiters;
Thou purest of Sisters, and bravest of Nuns,
Thou shouldst have borne daughters — thou shouldst have left sons;
But failing of these—perhaps Life's lesser part—
Thou still hast left offspring that sprang from thy heart,
Having just enough falsehood truth's force to reveal,
And just enough art art's device to conceal.

It is true — is it not? that the beings we know
As the beings of mind, are the beings that flow
From nearer the sources of trial and truth,
From nearer the fountains of freshness and youth,
Than the beings of muslin and buckram we meet
In the gilded saloon, or the church, or the street;
The alembic of Genius from which they proceed,
From the sickness and sin of humanity freed,
From the gloss of its crime, and the grime of its error,
From its frenzy, its fume, its despair, and its terror,
Gives existence to purer and loftier lives
Than are borne to most husbands by most of their wives.
  *   *   *   *   *   *   *   *   *   *
Ah, Lucile—Alfred Vargrave—Eugene de Luvois—
If well "put on the stage," what "large houses" you'd draw!

But as given to the page of Life's prophet, the Poet,
You draw better still, and the "trade sales" all show it.
From which I conclude,—as I'm certain I may,—
That the world has still some men and women who pay
Willing tribute to all that ennobles the race,
And due homage to woman whene'er she displays
The uplifting emotions, the purposes high,
The unchanging resolve or to do or to die
For the truth of the tongue, and the faith of the heart,
Which we feel were Lucile's—which Lucile could impart.
* * * * * * * * * *
Woman's strength is her virtue—her will—her desire—
That exalt her, sustain her, forbid her to tire;
The priestess of Nature, interpreting God,
She is like much that Nature spreads grandly abroad;
Yet she's not the strong river that flows to the sea,
Nor the wild waste of waves that engulf it is she,
But the vine that clings close to the husbanding wall,
Having faith it will not be permitted to fall—
Neither it nor its fruit. She's the angel that brings
Down the jewels of heaven to the crowns of earth's kings;
Though unheeded so oft, she's the voice that to man
Speaks as not e'en the voice of an archangel can.

Woman's strength is her virtue—her will—her desire
For a love that is purer—a life that is higher—
A truth that is surer—a faith that is stronger—
A hope that is brighter—a charity longer,
And broader, and deeper, and oh! much benigner;
With an impulse that ever incites her to twine her
White arms and sweet purposes round what is pure,
And serene, and unselfish, and sinless and sure.
What the rose to the garden, the leaf to the tree,
And the grass to the plains, to man's mansion is she;
Like the sun to the earth—like the stars to the skies—
She's the warmth of his love, and the light of his eyes;
But she's more than all this: she's companion, friend, wife,
Without whom man might live—but, would living be Life?

W. D. GALLAGHER.

MEANS TO AN END.

WOULD you compass this world in your limit of time,
No desert to cross and no mountain to climb,
With passage by rivers in meadows so sweet
That everywhere flowers fall fresh at your feet?
Would you subjugate soul, and for life's recompense
Take only such grail as will gratify sense?
There's a way—and it's clear as the light to your eye—
For Pleasure's a thing that your money can buy.

Do you wish to sit high in the councils of men,
In places attained by the one of the ten,
In seats for the good, and the great, and the grand,
Who utter the laws and are lords of the land?
Do you wish to be ruler and guide of your kind,
With never a right from the patent of mind?
There's a way—and it's short—you may sit very high—
Position's a thing that your money can buy.

Do you care to be famous for wisdom or wit,
By reason of words that another has writ,
By reason of logic in eloquent speech,
Or figures or fancies far out of your reach?
Do you wish for renown from the tongue and the pen,
When, to measure your brain, you must go to the wren?
If you do, it is yours—though your life is a lie—
For Fame is a thing that your money can buy.

Do you seek to be coupled with beauty and grace,
Perfection of manner, of form, and of face,
With her who approaches an angel so near
That earth is evanished and heaven is here?
Do you seek to be wed and be drowned in the bliss
Of the arms and the lips of a creature like this?
There's a way—but, alas! be it said with a sigh—
A Wife is a thing that your money can buy.

Thus Pleasure, Position, and Fame, and a Wife
You may find on the earth in your limit of life;
You may live as a bee in the heart of a rose,
With never a care for your soul to the close,
With only life's nectar exhausted from bloom,
And open before you the gate of the tomb;
But life after death with the angels on high
Is one of the things that your money can't buy.

HENRY T. STANTON.

DUSK.

OUT from the phantom forests of the West
  The black-winged bats of the night are flying,
The whippoorwill drowsily chants of rest,
And the brown owl, crooning within its nest,
  Moans o'er the couch of the daylight dying.

And the swallows circle above the trees
  In the purple haze, yet slightly golden,
While, softly, the fluttering, whispering breeze
Low murmurs in tremulous melodies
  Of by-gone hours and of legends olden.

And the clime of the Sun-set far away,
  Known only in dreams or magic story,
Is seen through a mist, as the dying day
A moment lingers, with parting ray,
  Then disappears in a cloud of glory.

THOMAS B. FORD.

LIGHT AND NIGHT.

Out through the loom of light,
When comes the morning white,
Beams, like the shuttle's flight,
　　Other beams follow,
Up the dawn's rays so slant,
Forth from his roof and haunt,
　　Darts the swift swallow.

Back like the shuttle's flight
Sink the gold beams at night,
Threads in the loom of light
　　Grow dark in the woof,
All the bright beams that burn
Sink into sunset's urn—
Swallows at night return
　　Home to their roof.

Thus we but tarry here
A moment, a day, a year—
Appearing, to disappear—
　　Grosser things spurning,
Departing to whence we came,
Leaving behind no name—
Like a wild meteor flame
　　Never returning.

Back to the home of God
　　Soul after soul departs,
　　And the enfranchised hearts
Burst through the sod;
Death does but loose thé girth
Buckling them on to earth,
　　Promethean rack!
Then from the heavy sod
Swift to the home of God
The Soul, like the Shuttle and Swallow, flies back.

The Swallow, Shuttle, Soul and Light,
All things that move or have a breath,
Return again to thee at night—
To thy dark roof, O ancient Death!

WILLIAM W. FOSDICK.

CONVOLVULI.

BLOW open, bugles of bloom,
O beautiful bugles of bloom!
Wake to life at the kiss of the dew,
Untwist in the odorous gloom;
Wake to die at the death of the dew,
O beautiful bugles of bloom!

Blossom in purple and white,
In crimson and scarlet and white,
Tempt the kiss of the amorous sun,
Bloom of the midsummer night;
Lift your lips to the amorous sun
In crimson, scarlet, and white.

Blush into roseate red,
From pink into roseate red,
Tremble and droop at his hot caress,
Till faded and withered and dead;—
Dead for the love of his hot caress,
Mingle your purple and red.

EDWIN S. HOPKINS.

MY OLD KENTUCKY HOME.

THE sun shines bright in our old Kentucky home;
'T is summer, the darkies are gay;
The corn top's ripe and the meadow's in the bloom,
While the birds make music all the day;
The young folks roll on the little cabin floor,
All merry, all happy, all bright;
By 'm-by hard times comes a-knockin' at the door,—
Then, my old Kentucky home, good night!

CHORUS.

Weep no more, my lady; O weep no more to-day!
We'll sing one song for the old Kentucky home,
For our old Kentucky home far away.

They hunt no more for the 'possum and the coon,
On the meadow, the hill, and the shore;
They sing no more by the glimmer of the moon,
On the bench by the old cabin door;
The day goes by, like a shadow o'er the heart,
With sorrow where all was delight;
The time has come when the darkies have to part,
Then, my old Kentucky home, good night!

The head must bow, and the back will have to bend,
Wherever the darkey may go;
A few more days and the troubles all will end
In the field where the sugar canes grow;
A few more days to tote the weary load—
No matter, it will never be light;
A few more days till we totter on the road;
Then, my old Kentucky home, good night!

STEPHEN COLLINS FOSTER.

HENRY T. STANTON.

MAY.

WOULD that thou couldst last for aye,
Merry, ever merry May!
Made of sun-gleams, shade and showers,
Bursting buds and breathing flowers!
Dripping-lock'd and rosy-vested,
Violet-slipper'd, rainbow-crested;
Girdled with the eglantine,
Festoon'd with the dewy vine:
Merry, ever merry May,
Would that thou couldst last for aye!

Out beneath thy morning sky!
Dian's bow still hangs on high!
And in the blue depths afar
Glimmers, here and there, a solitary star.
Diamonds robe the bending grass,
  Glist'ning early flowers among—
Monad's world, and fairy's glass,
Bathing fount for wandering sprite—
  By mysterious fingers hung
In the lone and quiet night.
Now the freshening breezes pass—
Gathering, as they steal along,
Rich perfume, and matin song—
And quickly to destruction hurl'd
Is fairy's diamond glass, and monad's dewdrop world.
Lo! yon cloud, which hung but now
Black upon the mountain's brow,
Threatening the green earth with storm—
See! it heaves its giant form,
And, ever changing shape and hue,
But still presenting something new,
Moves slowly up, and spreading rolls away
Toward the rich purple streaks that usher in the day;
Bright'ning, as it onward goes,

Until its very center glows
With the warm, cheering light the coming sun bestows:
As the passing Christian's soul,
Nearer the celestial goal,
Bright and brighter grows, till God illumes the whole.

Out beneath thy noontide sky,
On a shady slope I lie,
  Giving fancy ample play;
And there's not more blest than I,
  One of Adam's race to-day.
Out beneath thy noontide sky;
Earth, how beautiful!—how clear
Of cloud or mist the atmosphere!
What a glory greets the eye!
What a calm, or quiet stir,
Steals o'er Nature's worshiper—
Silent, yet so eloquent,
That we feel 't is heaven-sent—
Waking thoughts that long have slumber'd
Passion-dimm'd and earth-encumber'd—
Bearing soul and sense away,
To revel in the Perfect Day
That 'waits us, when we shall for aye
Discard this darksome dust—this prison-house of clay!

Out beneath thy evening sky!
Not a breeze that wanders by
But hath swept the green earth's bosom—
Rifling the rich grape-vine blossom,
Dallying with the simplest flower
In mossy nook and rosy bower—
To the perfum'd green-house straying,
And with rich exotics playing—
Then, unsated, sweeping over
Banks of thyme, and fields of clover!
Out beneath thy evening sky!
Groups of children caper by,
Crown'd with flowers, and rush along
With joyous laugh, and shout, and song.

Flashing eye, and radiant cheek,
Spirits all unsunn'd bespeak.
They are in Life's May-month hours—
And those wild bursts of joy, what are they but Life's
    flowers?

Would that thou couldst last for aye,
Merry, ever merry May!
Made of sun-gleams, shade and showers,
Bursting buds, and breathing flowers;
Dripping-lock'd, and rosy-vested,
Violet-slipper'd, rainbow-crested;
Girdled with the eglantine,
Festoon'd with the dewy vine;
Merry, ever merry May,
Would that thou couldst last for aye!

W. D. GALLAGHER.

MY VIOLIN.

ACROSS the trembling, thrilling strings,
  Entranced I draw the magic bow,
And all the quivering twilight rings,
  With echoes of the long ago.

With sweet, sad strains of by-gone years,
  Once waked by her who died so young,
The mingled notes of smiles and tears,
  In love's exquisite accents sung.

The tender, wailing air ascends,
  Till drifting down through golden bars,
An Angel's anthem with it blends,
  That floats from far beyond the stars.

THOMAS B. FORD.

SONG OF THE SUNBEAM.

I'M the bright sunbeam;
I flit as I dream,
Which gently comes down from the skies,
When sleep with delight
Holds infancy bright,
To close up its soft silken eyes.

O'er lake and o'er sea,
As tripping with glee,
Reflected my beauties I trace;
So rapt is the wave,
As lightly I lave,
It trembles as still we embrace.

I lie in the rose,
When freshly unclose
Its leaves to the sun and the breeze;
I skip o'er the plain
And ripe waving grain,
Or glide o'er the leaves on a tree.

I shun not the cot,
Where poverty's lot
Holds often the wise and the good;
Through hatch and through pane
I leap in again,
A gift all unsullied from God.

I shrink from the halls
And thick curtained walls,
Where wealth lies in sorrow all day;
But in at the door
Where dwelleth the poor
A daily warm visit I pay.

I never will shrink
From the cataract's brink,
But paint on its moisture my bow;
And down on the stream
With radiance gleam,
As stars flashing up from below.

On Death's pallid cheek
I often will-seek
To glow with the beauty of even;
But, finding has fled
The soul of the dead,
Will mount with it gladly to Heaven!

The night for a while
May shadow my smile,
Then Nature in sorrow will reek;
I'll come o'er the lawn
At first peep of dawn
And wipe each sad trace from its cheek.

In each opened grave
I'll pour in my wave
To show there is light in the tomb;
And smiling will say,
Come, this is the way
To where I eternally bloom!

SYDNER DYER.

AFTER FROST.

When the leaves are off the bushes and the quails begin to
  pipe,
An' the hickory nuts are fallin' an' the pawpaws good and
  ripe,
An' the twigs you step so careful on are sure to snap an'
  crack,
An' you whistle to the setter, an' the squirrel jaws you
  back—
Oh, them's the kind o' days fer me to meet the risin' sun,
With huntin' boots an' trousers an' a double-barreled gun;
When the woods are full of happy sounds of every sort an'
  type,
An' the leaves are off the bushes an' the quails begin to
  pipe.

There's a kind o' free-like feelin' broken loose inside o' you,
An' you want to holler awful, but you know you dassen't to;
Fer the frosty woods is allus full o' skeery-hearted things,
From the fussy little partridge, with its whizzin', whirrin'
  wings,
To the leapin', long-eared cotton-tail, 'at goes a-skippin'
  hence,
An' the frisky little chipmunk on the top rail o' the fence,
Where he giggles till he doubles up as if he had the gripe,
When the leaves are off the bushes and the quails begin to
  pipe.

There's a sort o' dreamy sadness too, a feller often feels,
With his game-bag full o' pheasants an' the setter at his
  heels,
As he plods across the medders at the settin o' the sun,
An' thinks about their whirrin' wings an' bangin' of his gun;
An' things 'll come to him about the souls of birds an' men,
An' happy huntin' grounds 'at's in the everlastin' when,
'At makes his heart as tender as a piece o' pickled tripe,
When the leaves are off the bushes an' the quails begin to
  pipe.   Edwin S. Hopkins.

THE WEDGE.

ONCE I wandered down a hill-side,
  Reckless where the pathway led,
Gathering wild flowers sweet and lovely
  To adorn a fair one's head,
Till I reached a little river,
  Rippling in its pebbly bed.

Sat I on its verdant border
  Where a clump of violets grew;
Some were white, and some were yellow,
  Some were amethystine blue;
So I gathered of each color
  Just a few—the choicest few.

Long I sat and watched the river,
  Listening to its cheerful song;
For it sang in gentle murmurs
  As it slowly flowed along,—
Glanced sweet notes from the smooth pebbles
  Which the waters flowed among.

Gently leaping, slowly creeping,
  Down a hollow in the hill,
O'er the pebbles, through the grasses,
  Wound a tiny, tinkling rill,
Till it leaped into the river,
  Whose broad bed it strove to fill.

Where the rivulet and river
  Sweetly mingled into one,
Scores of little fragile bubbles
  Danced and glistened in the sun;—
Dancing, jostled one another
  Like wee children in their fun.

Lying just below the junction,
　With its apex toward the shore,
Pointing very slightly upward,
　Large, and smoothly polished o'er,
Was a long, broad, wedge-like pebble—
　Edgewise on the sandy floor.

And it reached above the waters,
　For they were not very deep;
Scarce a single wavelet, playful,
　Ventured o'er the wedge to leap;
But they slowly wended 'round it,
　Lulling the cold wedge to sleep.

And the bubbles, gaily floating,
　All attracted by the wedge,
Rushed with bold precipitation
　'Gainst its smoothly polished edge;
Some swept past its upper border,
　Some along its lower ledge.

Those that gained the upper current
　Soon were far out in the stream,
Riding buoyantly and proudly,
　Glistening in the golden gleam,
Dazzling with their iris colors,
　Like a youthful poet's dream.

Those that with the lower current
　Swept along the wedge's side,
In a little whirling eddy
　For a moment paused to ride;
Then, escaping from the whirlpool,
　Floated down the river's side.

And they slowly, slowly floated,
　Clinging to the weedy shore,
Half concealed amid the shadows
　Of the broad leaves drooping o'er,
Till they *perished* in the shadows
　Of the rank weeds on the shore.

THE WEDGE.

Two I saw of equal merit,—
Or at least I viewed them so,—
Fondly clinging to each other,
To the heartless pebble go;
One just gained the upper border,
And the other passed below.

One I saw in vacillation
Clinging to the smooth, sharp edge;
Once I thought it past redemption
Borne along its lower ledge,
When a fitful breeze a-puffing
Lifted it above the wedge.

Then I asked myself the question—
"Is it just, O, is it fair,
That a single line of difference,
Interposing as it were,
Should divide the proud and buoyant
From those drooping in despair?"

Thus it is with other bubbles—
Human bubbles they, alas!
Thus a single line divideth
'Twixt the *poet* and the *ass;*
And th' opinion of the critic
Is the stony wedge they pass,
While the fitful breeze a-puffing
Is the plaudit of the mass.

S. P. BRYAN.

THE OLD CHURCH BELL.

From an unpretentious steeple
It is calling to the people,
In a sweet, strong voice, "Come along,
Come ye high and come ye lowly
To the Temple of the Holy,
And swell our hallelujah with your song."

"Come along, come along, come along,"
Is the clear interpretation of its song,
And the child that stops to listen can very plainly tell,
When its iron voice is saying,
"I'm ashamed of your delaying,
It's enough to try the patience of the Old Church Bell."

Years to us it thus has spoken,
Tho' in accents somewhat broken,
And no sound is more familiar and none we love so well,
When a rosy, cheerful dawning
Ushers in a Sunday morning
With the urgent invitation of the Old Church Bell.

Ah, how merrily it swings
When the marriage call it rings,
And the fair young bride is coming, with no secret now to tell,
·The belfry's tongue may ring it
On the waves of sound that bring it
From the palpitating bosom of the Old Church Bell.

But its glad notes seem to alter,
And its iron tongue to falter,
When it's called upon to utter the slowly measured knell,
Then its spirits seem to languish
And to share in human anguish
With all the tender sweetness of the Old Church Bell.

Tho' apart from it we go
On a tide that wills it so,
We shall hear it when our thoughts on old times dwell;
We'll then recall again
All the pleasure and the pain
Blent with the intonations of the Old Church Bell.

S. K. BANGS.

THE SIREN.

THERE is a cruel Siren always singing unto me,
Of a bright and happy future and of things that are to be;
And her songs they are enchanting, as beneath a crescent moon,
She chants of bounteous harvests and a golden-freighted June.

And she has sung those songs to me through all the weary years,
And I have watched and waited long in hopes and doubts and tears;
A watching, and a waiting for the happy things to be,
That this cruel, cruel Siren sings so constantly to me.

But still the night grows longer, and the stars begin to wane;
As o'er my rough and rugged way still falls that mocking strain;
And still I struggle onward, toward a silent, unknown sea,
While this deceitful Siren sings of things that are to be.

THOMAS B. FORD.

THE MOTHERS OF THE WEST.

THE mothers of our Forest-Land!
　Stout-hearted dames were they;
With nerve to wield the battle-brand,
　And join the border fray.
Our rough land had no braver
　In its days of blood and strife—
Aye, ready for severest toil,
　Aye, free to peril life.

The mothers of our Forest-Land!
　On old Kentucky's soil,
How shared they, with each dauntless band,
　War's tempest and life's toil!
They shrank not from the foeman,
　They quail'd not in the fight,
But cheer'd their husbands through the day,
　And sooth'd them through the night.

The mothers of our Forest-Land!
　Their bosoms pillow'd Men;
And proud were they by such to stand
　In hammock, fort, or glen;
To load the sure old rifle—
　To run the leaden ball—
To watch a battling husband's place,
　And fill it should he fall.

The mothers of our Forest-Land!
　Such were their daily deeds;
Their monument—where does it stand?
　Their epitaph—who reads?
No braver dames had Sparta—
　No nobler matrons Rome—
Yet who or lauds or honors them,
　Ev'n in their own green home?

The mothers of our Forest-Land!
  They sleep in unknown graves;
And had they borne and nursed a band
  Of ingrates, or of slaves,
They had not been neglected more.
  But their graves shall yet be found,
And their monuments dot here and there
  "The Dark and Bloody Ground!"

W. D. GALLAGHER.

A CONSOLATION.

IF the bird but sing its sweetest
  While it poises on the wing,
If the bud is the completest
  In the rosy wreath of Spring,

If the dew-drop's pearly beauty
  Gives new joy unto the leaf,
This is life, for this is duty;
  This is life, though it be brief.

In a thousand thousand morrows,
  Read it through your blinding tears,
Twenty winters with their sorrows
  Are a weary length of years;

Twenty summers with their flowers,
  With their birds and bees and braes,
Are but one of all the hours
  In the shortest of the days.

MARCUS BLAKEY ALLMOND.

NIGHT IN VENICE.

(AFTER ALFRED DE MUSSET.)

In Venice, the sea's daughter,
No boat awakes the water;
No fisher rows benighted,
No torch moves, to and fro.

On his column, grim and dark,
The Lion of Saint Mark
Crouches, with foot uplifted
On the horizon.

Around him, moored in groups,
Ships, barges and sloops
Sleep on the smoking water,
Like herons, in circles.

Bare as from winter blasts,
Rise a forest of masts;
In the fitful breaths of midnight
Interlacing their pennons.

As a maiden from her lovers,
The Night her moon-face covers
With veil-like clouds; bejeweled
Diamond-like, with stars;

Or, like a Nun, benighted
In the lonely skies, affrighted,
Draws her black-rolled hood of clouds
Down on her surplice.

The ancient towers, the arches,
The halls, the pillared porches,
The stately marble stairways
Of the merchant kings;

NIGHT IN VENICE.

The statues, white as moons,
The bridges, the lagunes
Whereon the breezes sprinkle
The broken star-beams;

All are silent: save the guards
Trailing their hallebardes
As they tramp the battlements
Of the grim arsenals.

How many eyes now glisten,
How many ears now listen,
To catch a form or footstep
As the lover comes.

How many, half arrayed
For the midnight masquerade,
O'er their beauty, at their mirrors,
Draw the black mask down.

On her perfumed couch, enshrined,
La Vanina now, reclined,
Still presses to her bosom
Her lover as she sleeps.

Gay Narcissa, wild with folly,
Hither, thither, heedless wholly,
In her gondola unguided,
Gives the night to revel.

Who, save we, are melancholy
In this land of love and folly?
Who, save we, give not to rapture
Such hours as these?

Let us look no more,—my Fair,—
On the moonlight-mellowed air;
On the sea, the sleeping city
Of loveliness and loves:

Let yon antique horologe
On the palace of the Doge
Count its long *ennuis* of hours,
Through the silent night:

Let us leave to it, its duty;
Let us only count, my Beauty,
On thy haughty lips the kisses
Given, and forgiven;—

Count thy heart's throbs, and hushes,
And the flushing, fading blushes;
And the tears of tender languor
In thy violet eyes.

And, in Venice, the sea's daughter,
When morn awakes the water,
Let us, like the sea-born city,
Dream anew the past!
GEORGE M. DAVIE.

"GOOD MORNING."

"GOOD MORNING!" saith the rosy God
  Of new-born day. "Good morning,"
As from the eastern skies he sweeps
The clouds away, and, blushing, peeps
Upon the waking earth, that leaps
  From sleep, fresh robes adorning.
Bedeck'd with drops of pearly dew
  Is ev'ry leaf and spray,
And flowers peep out, of every hue,
  To greet the God of day.
May thy good mornings cloudless be,
  Thy heart be of good cheer;
Thy bright star yet beams bright for thee,
  My star-eyed sister, dear.
JOHN HOSKINS.

GEORGE D. PRENTICE.

THE HOUSEHOLD MINSTREL.

An enchanter, I ween,
Is the singer unseen
Whose note—when the sky becomes starred—
Riseth up from the screen
Which lieth between
Ourselves and the queer little bard.

There are symphonies grand
In the wondrous bird-land;
Chords seeming of magical birth;
But in all the broad scope
No minstrel can cope
With the cricket that chirps in the hearth!

Not one of them flies
To the heart and there lies
So warm in our mirth or our grief—
None charms from the eyes
The tears as they rise
Like that home-song, sweet, tender, and brief!

So while everywhere
There's a plenteous share
Of music to gladden the earth,
There is none can compare
To the minstrel so rare—
The cricket that chirps in the hearth!

LAURA C. FORD.

"FOUR SCORE AND ONE."

We wait for the gates to open,
   Wait together, Faith and I,
And the twilight of Life comes sweetly,
   As the years glide gently by.
From the past loved voices call us,
   That call from the future too;
And we know, by the tokens left us
   Of a life serene and true,
That soon, on some bright to-morrow,
   When the wings of this flesh are furl'd,
We shall join them again, and forever,
   In that brighter and better world.

We know not, we ask not, we think not—
   For we do not care to learn—
If the gates to that world are of jasper,
   Or on golden hinges turn;
Nor whether, when once within them,
   On diamonded streets we tread,
So that there, in the light and the glory
   Of God, we shall meet with the dead—
With the dead, who have gone before us,
   And the wings of the spirit unfurl'd
To the beauty and brightness and glory
   Of that other and better world.

Still the old familiar faces
   From old coverts sweetly look,
And we hear glad voices singing
   With the breeze and with the brook;
Yet we know that they are but echoes
   And reflections from above;
So, from earth we turn to heaven
   For the beings of our love.
And we wait for the gates to open,
   Wait together, Faith and I,
While the Night* comes down with its shadows,
   And the Day† is drawing nigh.
                       W. D. Gallagher.

*Death.   †The Resurrection.

A SABBATH IN AUTUMN.

DULL, stately day of stark repose,
    All nature steeped in listless awe:
The sky with gray clouds hooded o'er
    Locked in inexorable law;

Sere leaves from drooping boughs flit down
    And deck the earth in sombre dress,
While woodland birds their notes prolong
    Piped in a voice of sore distress.

The rose has left its parent stem,
    The honey-suckle lost its sweet,
Gray grasses bow their flayed brown heads
    Down at the meadow-oak's broad feet.

The rich man cheers his gloomy thought
    With wine and song and change of scene;
The poor man longs for Labor's stroke
    To make this arid desert green.

The callow youth whom Summer lured
    To dreams Utopian in their build,
Grow restless, cheerless, and now find
    The voices of their love-notes chilled.

A fitting scene—a cortége moves
    Along the drenched streets to the tomb;
The dead-march fills and thrills and stills
    The crushed heart of this day of gloom.

                    MARCUS BLAKEY ALLMOND.

A YEARN FOR THE ROMANTIC.*

"Knighthood's dauntless deed,
And Beauty's matchless eye."

[In view of the lamentable tendency of late toward the modern inanities of Æsthetics, the following has been prepared, by one of the Old Romantic School, with the endeavor to restore a healthy taste for the Mediæval and the Strong, to induce a return to the chivalric pages of Scott, of Bulwer, and of G. P. R. James, and to lead to a revival of feeling for the stalwart old days of Knighthood and of the Troubadour.]

I.

THE DAYS OF OLD.

WHEN a-weary of this living, with its gaining and its giving,
And its toiling and its traffic, and its tame pursuit of gold—
I recall at what a high rate lived the Poet, Knight and Pirate,
As they fought, and sung, and swaggered, in heroic days of old!

II.

THE KNIGHT ERRANT.

With a chivalry romantic, and with love and honor frantic,
With a cross upon his armor, and a spur upon his heel,
He would bind him in indentures to impossible adventures,
And to rid the world of evil—or to never take a meal!

Then, to slay the dark deceiver, or the wicked unbeliever,
He would swim the deepest river, and would sleep upon the sward;
To subdue a horrid schism, he would risk the rheumatism—
All, to prove his high devotion to his Lady, and his Lord.

*This poem, which has been pronounced the finest joco-serious in the language, was written by George M. Davie, an eminent lawyer of Louisville, Ky., and in its first form, shorter than now, published in the "Bric-à-brac" of the *Century* for April, 1882. The exquisite Section IV ("The Ladye-Love") has been added since.—ED.

Then it was not looked absurd on, if he wore a lady's guerdon
  Whom he loved to desperation—but he didn't know by sight—
Or would ride a distant journey, to indulge in joust or tourney,
  To maintain her matchless beauty over any caitiff Knight.

Then, their statutory vapor, upon parliamentary paper,
  Couldn't dwarf his noble nature with debilitating "laws";
For he stopped not to construe 'em, with their horrid "meum," "tuum,"
  But survival of the fittest proved the justice of his cause!

He would glare and shake his lances, for belligerent advances,
  While his armor clanked and rattled from his head unto his toe;
From his helmet of pot-metal, like the steam from out a kettle,
  He would blow his fierce defiance at his mediæval foe:

Then, confiding in his science, and the Saint of his reliance,
  With his battle-axe and bludgeon he would cut, and thrust, and guard,
Till their shields would clang together, like the bells in foggy weather,
  And the blows upon their armor clattered like a boiler-yard!

Then, to slay a brazen Dragon wasn't thought a thing to brag on;
  As to massacre a Giant was an every-day affair;
And 'twas nothing but a wassail to assail an Ogre's castle
  And deliver noble damsels, who were hanging by the hair.

He would swear on sword and altar that he'd never halt or falter
  Till he'd help the True Religion sack the Saracenic hive;

Then, the unbelieving village was the prey of pious pillage,
That the Turk could be converted—if he happened to survive.

That his valor, so resplendent, might be wholly indepen-
dent,
He was bothered not with baggage, and the other minor ills;
From Jerusalem to Gaza there was scarce a comb or razor,
And an almost utter absence of all washerwoman's bills.

When the long Crusade was over, then he'd rest awhile in clover;
And around the kingly table he would royster and regale;
Jolly monks would utter benison o'er the haunch of royal venison,
And the beards would wag with wisdom as they quaffed the yellow ale.

Thus, a-battling and a-bouting, and a-rioting and routing,
From Palestine to Paris, on the land and on the sea,
Though perhaps a little gory, yet he led the life of Glory—
Ah! how brave, and true, and noble was the Knight of Chivalry!

III.

THE TROUBADOUR.

With a jaunty cloak and swagger, and a jewel-handled dagger,
And a lute across his shoulder by a ribbon—blue, at that!
And his breeches never bigger than would show his shapely figure,
And a fascinating feather in his funny little hat;

Not fat and roly-poly—like that parody Brignoli
Singing sentiment affected to a mercenary tune—
But a Poet, young and slender, he would charm the tender gender,
As he sighed his soul in music at the maiden, or the moon.

A YEARN FOR THE ROMANTIC.

He would rove the land and ocean, on the slightest whim or notion;
He would sing the tender rondeau; he would tell the merry tale;
He would thrill the fierce Crusader; he would turn a serenader;
He would banquet in the castle; he would billet in the jail.

And the Queens and noble maidens doted on his serenadings,
And they dropped him down a ribbon, or a glove, or lock of hair;
Or, in lieu of rope or stringlets, loosed their long and silken ringlets,
And the minstrel, bold and loving, climbed up—as you might a stair!

Thus, he poached on others' manors, and he fought for others' banners,
And he dined at others' tables, and he droned in others' hives;
And he livened others' journeys, and he rhymed of others' tourneys,
And he emptied others' flagons, and he flirted others' wives.

So, he wandered forth a-warring, and a-rhyming and guitaring,
And, in attitudes artistic, tinkled lum-te-tum-ty airs;
And the ladies all adored him, and the gallants aped and bored him,
And his tunes were legal-tender for his lodging, everywheres.

Thus, a-humming and a-strumming, and a-wooing and a-cooing,
Dealing ditties by the dozen, making sonnets by the score—
Where the glamour of the amour hid the stammer of the grammar—
Ah! so gay, and free, and happy was the merry Troubadour!

IV.

THE LADYE-LOVE.

She was hardened not with knowledge of the boarding-
school or college;
She was sung at oft in language that she did not under-
stand;
But was learned in all romancing, and in dancing, and in
glancing—
Stately, fair, and tender-hearted was the Ladye of the
Land.

Though she dressed in shocking fashion, she inspired the
deepest passion,
And a tune upon her lutelet was a very dangerous thing;
For her smile, were all imploring, and her sigh set all
adoring,
And she strung the hearts around her like the beads
upon a string.

Now, at tourneys, gaily quartered, she would see her beaux
be slaughtered,
Till the solitary relic crawled to crown her "Beauty's
Queen";
Then, from tops of balustradings, she would sigh to sere-
nadings,
Or, with hawk or hound, and suitors, she would gallop
o'er the green.

Any summer morn, awaking, full of sentiment and quaking
At the ditties and the clatter of her lovers keeping
guard,
She'd behold, with charming satisfaction—peeping through
her lattice—
Scores of guitars and of gallants shattered all about her
yard!

Any day she'd feel neglected, if not forcibly selected
As the booty of some Baron, who would make her will
his law;
Any night she'd slumber, hoping to be wakened by eloping
On the pommel of the saddle of a Knight she never saw.

A YEARN FOR THE ROMANTIC. 89

Then, how charmingly exciting! setting twenty Knights to
    fighting,
And to have to wed the victor, who would come to claim
    her glove!—
Or to have to sit for hours in the tallest kind of towers,
On the thinnest sort of diet, till her heart would learn
    to love!

They would call her cold and cruel: yet they'd fight the
    daily duel,
And lay vows of love eternal and despairing at her
    shrine;
When at last some one would win her, they would oft
    neglect their dinner,
And would talk for days of dying, or of far-off Palestine.

When her Liege would go crusading, or his neighbors' lands
    invading,
Then from highest turret windows would she wave her
    lily hands;
Or perchance, ere seeking Vandals, he would lock her safe
    from scandals,
And she'd pine, from quiet convents, for her lord in
    Paynim lands.

Thus, a-smiling and a-sighing, and a-laughing and a-crying,
With her eyes as stars or diamonds, and her hair as silk
    or gold—
Never maid so sentimental, never matron half so gentle,
Never love so true and tender, as the Ladye-Love of old!

V.

THE PIRATE.

With his raven beard, and visage that would terrify in
    this age,
And with eyes as fierce as eagles' when they swoop from
    mountain crag,
With his jack-boots of raw leather, and a Spanish cloak
    and feather,
And a fragment torn from Midnight for his horrifying
    flag—

With the winds and waves he'd wrestle, in a somber sort
   of vessel,
   And in search of strange adventures, he would ravage
      every shore;
Now to rob the Lapland lubbers of their walrus teeth and
   blubbers,
   Now to depredate the natives on the coast of Labradore!

On the track of Turkish zaccas, or of Portuguese polaccas,
   Or of argosies of Venice, heavy laden with their gain,
Or of Amsterdam's fat traders, or of homeward-bound Arma-
   das,
   He would scour the Northern Ocean, or would sweep the
      Spanish Main.

Now, on summer isles Pacific, he would hold his haunt
   terrific,
   With his dreadful bark at anchor in some tropical lagoon;
There to rest a while and revel, and to traffic with the
   Devil,
   And to bury tons of Treasure in the darkness of the
      moon.

Thence, he'd strike for fame and plunder, midst the hurri-
   cane and thunder,
   While the jagged flash of lightning hissed behind him
      from the clouds;
And, with curses of bravado, dare the tempest and tornado,
   While the winds, as ghosts of victims, were a-shrieking
      through the shrouds!

When the foe would strike their colors, with their doubloons
   and their dollars,
   He would give the night to riot, and to jolly jest and
      cheer;
And would, free from weak emotion, walk the captives in
   the ocean—
   Ah! so bold, and free, and bloody was the roving Bucca-
      neer!

VI.
THIS DEGENERATE AGE.

Ah! those days have gone forever, with their splendid fire
and fever,
And their lofty scorn of living, and undying thirst for
fame!
When Faith and Beauty filled them, and when Love and
Glory thrilled them,
And the sacred light of Honor led them like a flitting
flame!

And the Minstrels, tender-hearted—now are silent and departed,
With their amatory melodies, so delicate and sweet;
Now, we never sigh to hear them, but we fly them and we
fear them—
Grinding melancholy organs on the corners of the street.

Gone, the Pirate and the Sea-King, and the Buccaneer and
Viking:
Furled, the banner of the Rover, hushed his cannon's
heavy roar,
And the only reminiscence of his nautical existence
Is the banging of the big drum in the play of "Pinafore."

Gone's the glamour and the glory of the Knights of song
and story,
With their love and high endeavor, and their noble deeds
and aims;
Of heroic days behind us, now there's nothing to remind us
But the "Solitary Horseman" in the narrative of James!

For, the Knights so celebrated, in these days degenerated
Would be madmen or marauders—we should ridicule their
cause;
And the Pirate of the shipping would be hanged, or get a
whipping;
And the Troubadours be prisoned, under local vagrant
laws!

Now, the soul that scorns to grovel, has no solace but the
    novel
Of Sir Scott, or James, or Bulwer, on the Times of Long
    Ago!
When were Brian de Bourbeon, and the mighty Cœur de
    Lion,
And Sir Launcelot, and Arthur, and immortal Ivanhoe.

For, the prosy and pedantic have extinguished the romantic,
    And the pomp and pride of Chivalry are driven from the
        stage;
All is now so faint and tender that the world has lost its
        gender,
    And the enervate Æsthetic is the model of the age!

GEORGE M. DAVIE.

WHEN LOVING HEART'S THE GOAL.

How oft he's praised those eyes of mine,
And in them says, "Heav'n's light doth shine,
    Reflecting Heav'n's own blue."
But does he know that in his own
The depths of soul e'er in them shone,
    Evincing love most true?
That all he sees in mine to praise
Reflects the love in those that gaze
    So tenderly in mine?
How all my inmost soul goes out,
In perfect trust—without a doubt,
    In those dark orbs that shine!
I feel and know he loves me true—
Love beams from dark eyes as from blue—
    They mirror forth the soul.
They speak—tho' no words tell the tale;
More potent are—for love's avail,
    When loving heart's the goal.

JOHN HOSKINS.

ASPIRATION.

WHO would not be a boy again
With all the impulse of his youth,
With life wild-throbbing in each vein,
And in his soul the soul of truth;

With hopes as fresh as matin dew—
As roseate as the sunset glare;
With aspirations high and true,
And future prospects, O how fair!

Ah! who e'er lived to be a man
And realized his boyhood dreams?
Wealth, honor, fame, are spectres wan,
Untinted by hope's magic beams.

The mountain which we looked upon,
And thought so high in childhood days,
Seems, when its highest height is won,
A little hill to manhood's gaze.

And just beyond another hill
Still lures us with its mellow haze;
When it is reached another still
Gleams faintly on our ravished gaze.

Thus on and on, forever on,
Our path of duty upward lies;
Nor will its utmost height be won
Till we shall scale yon starry skies.

S. P. BRYAN.

A KENTUCKIAN KNEELS TO NONE BUT GOD.

[Colonel Crittenden, nephew of John J. Crittenden, United States Senator for Kentucky, commanded the filibuster forces taken prisoners at sea, near Havana, August 15, 1851. Doomed to death by the Cuban authorities, and ordered to be shot on the 16th, they were all commanded to kneel. Colonel Crittenden spurned the command with these words, "*A Kentuckian kneels to none but God.*"]

AH! tyrant, forge thy chains at will—
  Nay, gall this flesh of mine;
Yet thought is free, unfettered still,
  And will not yield to thine.
Take, take the life that Heaven gave,
  And let my heart's-blood stain thy sod;
But know ye not Kentucky's brave
  Will kneel to none but God?

You've quenched fair Freedom's sunny light,
  Her music tones have stilled,
And with a deep and darken'd blight
  The trusting heart have fill'd!
Then do you think that I will kneel
  Where such as ye have trod?
Nay, point your cold and threat'ning steel;
  I'll kneel to none but God.

As summer breezes lightly rest
  Upon a quiet river,
And gently on its sleeping breast
  The moonbeams softly quiver—
Sweet thoughts of home lit up my brow,
  When goaded with the rod;
Yet these can not unman me now—
  I'll kneel to none but God.

And though a sad and mournful tone
  Is coldly sweeping by,
And dreams of bliss forever flown
  Have dimm'd with tears mine eye—

Yet mine's a heart unyielding still—
Heap on my breast the clod;
My soaring spirit scorns thy will;
I'll kneel to none but God.

MARY E. WILSON-BETTS.

THE STAB.

"Of sudden stabs in groves forlorn."—*Hood's Eugene Aram.*

[John James Piatt says of this: "Nothing could be better; it is a tragic little night-piece which Heine could not have surpassed in its simple graphic narration and vivid suggestiveness."]

ON the road, the lonely road,
Under the cold, white moon,
Under the ragged trees, he strode;
He whistled, and shifted his heavy load—
Whistled a foolish tune.

There was a step, timed with his own,
A figure that stooped and bowed;
A cold white blade that gleamed and shone,
Like a splinter of daylight downward thrown—
And the moon went behind a cloud.

But the moon came out so broad and good
The barn cock woke and crowed,
Then roughed his feathers in drowsy mood,
And the brown owl called to his mate in the wood
That a dead man lay on the road.

WILL WALLACE HARNEY.

I LOVE YOU.

I LOVE you! I love you!
In vain have I tried
To banish your image, 't is now at my side:
I see your bright smile, I hear your sweet voice,
I wish, Oh I wish, that I were your choice!
You know not the anguish that burdens my heart,
And the keen sense of shame that your scorn can impart;
I fain would forget it, would hide it away,
But haunting me ever, a voice seems to say,
    "I love you! I love you!"

I love you! I love you!
But without avail;
Love unrequited is such a sad tale;
Slighted and jilted, I longingly sigh,
For one little smile, as you pass by.
You look with indifference upon my despair,
You do not, you would not, my least sorrow share;
I've vowed to forget you, so frequent, so oft,
But then comes the voice, so sweet and so soft,
    "I love you! I love you!"

I love you! I love you!
I can not control
This great load of love, it burdens my soul:
I pine and I languish alone in my grief,
You, and you only, can bring me relief.
But think not I chide you, indeed I do not—
If you would request it, 't would all be forgot;
My heart wants for nothing when you are nigh,
But when you are absent, ah, then comes the sigh,
    "I love you! I love you!"

I love you! I love you!
Yes, love is my theme;
Through the long hours of night, 't is of love that I dream

When the spring time returns, when winter has fled,
Will you think of me only as of one that is dead?
When the soft summer breeze sings the flowers to rest,
When hearts are so happy, so free from distress,
Oh, will you remember, when in the gay throng,
That there is one singing, that this is his song?
 "I love you! I love you!"
FREDERICK M. SPOTSWOOD.

A LULLABY.

Oh! baby fair,
With dark brown hair,
 And eyes of heaven's own blue;
Where, seems to me,
I think I see
 An Angel peeping through.

Oh! sacred joy!
My darling boy,
 I feel that thou art giv'n
Unto my care,
And over there
 An Angel less in heav'n.

Oh! sacred trust!
As God is just,
 I'll lavish all my care
On thee, my love,
Till heav'n above
 Shall call my Angel there.
JOHN HOSKINS.

THE OLD YEAR AND THE NEW IN THE COLISEUM AT ROME.

Now chaste Diana, like a Dorian maid,
Across the star-sown fields of light pursues
The God of Day. Companions of the chase,
The steady planets and the twinkling stars,
With noiseless glide, press onward in their course
Upon the burning trail of Helios.
In wild pursuit full half Italia's sky
Is passed, and now the Huntress-Goddess stands
Upon the zenith with her bended bow.
There, pausing, peerless in her silver robes,
She views the shoreless sea of ether spread
Around, above, beneath, and cheers her train.
Meanwhile swift Sol, with half the sky 'twixt him
And those that follow in his glowing path,
Has forced his coursers o'er the midland sea
And whirls his chariot toward Aurora's gate.
'T was thus that race began when sun and moon
And stars were fashioned out of nothingness;
And thus it must continued be till all
The hosts of earth and sea and sky return
Again to Chaos wild.
      But oh! fair moon,
How kind thy mellow beams do soften down
Uncomeliness and beautify these ruins!
The Coliseum in its splendors new
Had ne'er more solemn loveliness than now,
With its majestic wrecks so softly draped
In thy pure snowy light. These crevices
Through which uncounted twinkling stars do peep,
As if the sky looked down with Argus eyes
Upon the rents of ruthless time; these walls
Which rough destruction has deprived of all
Their polished marbles, chiseled erst in forms
That seemed to speak, and o'er them drawn instead
The furrows deep of desolation's plow;

This vast elliptic sweep of walls around
The Gladiator's circus, compassing
The famed arena, like to giant hills
Around the placid lake, embosomed deep
Within the circuit of their lofty peaks;
These myriad plants and varied flowers, that grow
Among the rents and o'er the mouldering rocks,
Decay has scathed with her dissolving breath;
This matchless relic of the mighty dead,
Though coming down to us, wrapped in the charm
And potent spell which hoar antiquity
E'er throws around the hallowéd works of art,
Seems yet more lovely now with all its wrecks,
While yonder pitying Moon doth fold it round
With her pure winding sheet. Nor less dost thou,
Fair Queen of Night, the soft enchantment of
Thy mellow beams impart to skeletons
Of other structures, which Eternal Rome,
In times since numbered with the distant past,
Erected round this spot.
　　　　　　　　Lo! from these walls'
Proud height the classic eye doth search and rest,
At intervals, upon the seven hills—
The little mounts immortalized in song—
Now dwindled down, by Time's effacing hand,
Beneath their lofty height on glory's page.
The modern Romans, when they lost the high
Thoughts of empire held by ancient Romans,
Quitted the seven hill-tops and builded
Where the Campus Martius compassed lowlands.
And even the hills themselves, so high in Rome
Of old, have sunken downward to the plane
Of these degenerate sons of noble sires.
The Quirinal and Capitol show life,
But not the life of ancient Rome.
　　　　　　　　　　　The eye
Turned southward rests upon the mighty ruins
Of Caracalla's Baths, a giant pile,
Attesting in its fall the pomp and power

Of him who o'er the world did tyrannize,
And bathe his fratricidal hand in blood
That warmed the gentle Gaeta's heart. Whilome
The gifted Shelley, musing o'er these walls,
Amid the flowers that fed upon their ruins
And filled the willing air with wild perfumes,
Did catch the inspiration shadowed forth
In his Prometheus; and from such wrecks,
Arising like enchanted images,
There came some of the sweetest thoughts that e'er
Exalted Byron's muse.
      Now turns the eye
Unto the west, where, like a spotless sheet
Of Alpine snow, the moonbeams do enrobe
The Cæsar's palace, wonder of the world.
See shattered arch, and column crushed, and walls
To dust and fragments crumbled. Trees have grown
To giant strength upon the mighty waste,
And twined and fixed their deeply planted roots
In halls that once resounded with the harp
And held the sovereignty of mighty Rome.
Now poisonous weeds and hoary ivy, grown
Until its tendrils seem the trunks of trees
Upon whose growth long centuries were spent,
Usurp saloons and halls and royal rooms
Once graced by Roman Emperors and filled
With all the noblest works of ancient art.
Envenomed reptiles creep o'er frescoed roofs
And o'er mosaic floors that erst did feel
The haughty presence of Imperial dames.
That royal palace now remains a heap
Of wrecks o'er which confusion reigns supreme.
From out the solemn pile the wailing wind
Is heard, as o'er Campagna's plain it floats;
All else is hushed and silent like the tomb.
But further on the yellow Tiber bears
His mountain flood and murmurs in his course
The storied origin of Rome, and tells
The weird legends which immortal bards

Did sing upon his classic shores, when Rome
Was mistress of the world.
                            Lo! northward now
The Forum opens to the eye, and calls
To mind the proud assemblies of the State,
While all around majestic temples stood,
And statues of the Gods, and busts of men,
And Tully thundered from the rostra words
That honied eloquence ne'er spoke before.
Above the Forum see the Capitol,
Still lifting high into the air its tower
With solemn antique grace! Beneath its walls,
Imbedded in the Capitolian mount,
The prisons frown which Ancus Marcius built
When Rome was but an infant colony.
Imprisoned here, in these unholy cells,
In which Jugurtha starved and Catiline's
Accomplices did share the traitor's death,
Our Lord's Apostle Peter once was chained
By stern decree of Nero's bloody code.
At his command a limpid spring
Gushed forth from out the dungeon's rock, as pure
And cool and pearly as Egeria's fount;
And still it bubbles there to quench the thirst
Of pilgrims to the consecrated spot.
Lo! further in the distance rises, like
A globous cloud suspended in the air,
The noblest dome that man throughout all time
E'er lifted to his God—an emblem fit
And model worthy of the concave sky
Which forms the dome of nature's temple proud.
'T is worthy there to hang and to adorn
St. Peter's, fairest church that man e'er built
And consecrated to the living God;
Yes, prouder far than all the temples old
Which superstition reared unto the Gods
Whom Pagans have adored.
                         The noon of night
Has come, and thoughts more wild than this wild scene

Crowd on the mind. The Old Year and the New
As Gladiators seem in mortal strife
Within the Coliseum's fated walls.
A conflict more almighty was not when
The arch fiend, with his hosts of ruined angels,
In heaven's broad purlieu met the sons of light,
Led on to battle by Omnipotence;
Nor when the storied giants Ossa piled
On Pelion to dethrone the Thunderer.
The glad spectators of this scene are not
The eighty thousand sons of Rome who filled
These seats while Titus sat as arbiter,
And with his festivals an hundred days
Did dedicate to feats of strength and shows
Of wickedness this wondrous theater.
Now goblins, ghosts, and spirits, forms divine,
And shapes satanic fill the air and crowd
These seats as numerous as the sands that bleach
Old ocean's storm-lashed shore. Here Life and Death,
Youth and Age, Disease and Health, War and Peace,
Famine, Pestilence, and Mortality,
The Past, the Present, and the Future dark,
With other forms as numerous as the stars,
Together now have congregated all,
From every quarter of the universe,
To see the noble Gladiator die;
While old Eternity, enthroned above
In Fate's dread chair, sits arbiter sublime
And views the awful strife.
                          The noon of night
Impends. One moment more must pass, and then
The Year that wears the diadem will fall,
Forever fall, into the changeless past.
How pregnant is this moment with rapt thoughts!
This moment! It doth to the future bind
The past and make of them one boundless, vast,
Sublime Eternity. It is that link,
Without which in duration's endless chain
All past, all future and the present time

Were disconnected parts confounded worse
Than dire confusion's self. In its brief span
Swift memory waves her life's restoring wand
And calls up from the past immortal things,
Whose genesis was far beyond the date
Of the Cloaca Maxima and tomb
Of Scipio. Events which filled long times
And great discoveries in the realm of art
And science, which the dragging centuries
Had scarce made known, now flash like vivid dreams
Across the mind. The changeless stars which saw
Arcadian shepherds watch their nightly flocks
Upon yon Palatine, ere Romulus
Had founded there the Citadel of Rome,
Shine o'er us now. And yon same moon, that threw
Her mellow beams upon the Pantheon,
The shrine of all Rome's Gods and Goddesses,
Two thousand years ago, rolls on unchanged
Upon the silver chariot of the night.
Yon deep blue sky, the pride of tropic climes,
Looks on us with the same bright starry eyes
That watched the City of the Seven Hills
As from the work of Romulus it rose
To majesty and grandeur ne'er surpassed.
Yon Tiber winds his wonted course along
The shores which once were clad with glory's pomp,
And bears his waters from the Appenines
Into the midland sea just as he did
When, centuries ago, Æneas came
With all the Gods had spared of fallen Troy
And landed on his banks. All else how changed!
The Eternal City wears ephemeral hues,
The Cæsar's palace, once the pride of Rome,
Remains a heap of ruins wild. The hills,
Upon whose crests the famous City stood,
Have crumbled down and scarcely seem to rise
Above the rubbish which two thousand years
Have piled around their base. The Forum lies
Deep buried 'neath the waste of centuries.

War, Famine, Pestilence and flood and flame
Have swept o'er ancient Rome, and naught remains
To tell where glory dwelt, save mighty wrecks
Which greet the eye like to immortal deaths.
The Gods who erst were worshiped here are gone,
And crumbled into dust their gorgeous shrines,
And borne away their comely busts of bronze
And marble statues to adorn the halls
Of those their sculptors deemed barbarians.
Unto the memory of the Christian dead,
Whom wild beasts tore and fire consumed to make
A holiday for Roman elegance,
This vast arena has been set apart
And consecrated by his Holiness,
And prayers ascend now to the Triune God,
Where Jove was throned and warrior Gods displayed
In men the showman's arts.
      That moment brief,
So full of thought, is gone. The olden year
Beneath his adversary lies. The Past
Has claimed him as his spoil and bears him off,
While Time proclaims Eternity's decree,
And gives the empire of the universe
Unto the glad New Year, the victor proud.
No shout goes up to rend the air, as did
Of old when victory was here proclaimed,
And countless Latin and Barbaric tongues
Made the welkin ring with joy. The olden
Year his given span of life has measured;
The cold has chilled the current of his soul;
The winds have sung his solemn requiem,
And Time with one hand pointing forward to
The future's dark and mystic canopy,
The golden chronoscope which measures out
The moments and the hours that multiply
Themselves in days and years and centuries,
And with the other reaching backward to
The frowning past, the tablet and the style
With which he makes the record of all things,

Has noted all the Old Year's deeds or good
Or bad upon Eternity's vast scroll
That changes never more.
            All hail New Year!
Welcome upon the vacant seat of Time!
During thy reign may flourish all the arts
And sciences that do make their progress
In Beauty's realm or in the wide domain
Of usefulness. Thou mayest promote good
Learning until mortal men and women
Do write and send abroad immortal books,
Whose words of wisdom and philosophy
May give forth thoughts on whose eternity
The fate of governments and peoples rest.
In thy allotted reign may be accomplished
More for human welfare than centuries
Of old could yield to slower footed life.
Thy progress o'er the world by mortal woes
Must needs be marked and loved ones oft be sent
Into the spirit land. But who can blame
Thee for such deeds? Their three-score years and ten
Have been assigned to mortals all; but crimes
And wrongs and wasteful modes of living life
Have made their years contract, and, worse than that,
Entailed upon their offspring yet unborn
The elements of dire and fixed disease
And death. Were mortals what they should be now,
And had their days been all well spent, their death
Had come with worn-out life and proved a kind
And gentle breeze to waft their souls away,
And wing them off to amaranthine climes.
Yes, of all the agencies with which thy
Deeds are wrought, New Year, that one whose emblem
Is the glass and scythe must bring to mortals
The saddest sorrows. Yet this should not be.
When dire disease shall come upon the good
And, ghastly and emaciate, their forms
Shall scarce sustain the waning vital spark
That lights its fragile tenements, and fierce

And racking tortures make all life a curse,
Oh! then thou mayest unto them bring sweet death,
The hush of groans, the calm of sorrow's sea,
The grand emancipation of the soul
From all its earthy trammelings of flesh,
That it may soar among the stars and drink
New life from fountains of perennial bliss.

ROME, January 1, 1856.   R. T. DURRETT.

"EARTH HAS NO SORROW THAT HEAVEN CAN NOT HEAL."

THE poet hath said, that whate'er be our grief—
  No matter what sorrow the heart may feel—
We must look to Heaven to find relief,
  For "Earth has no sorrow that Heaven can not heal."

So the poet hath said, and surely we know
  That such blessed relief from our sorrow is given;
But how many turn, when all look below,
  To seek for one ray of the sunshine of Heaven.

When the heart with some mighty sorrow is torn,
  And we bend like a reed 'neath affliction's strong might,
O, who can believe, when so sad and forlorn,
  That day will succeed such a dark dreary night?
And who, in his anguish, can look up and feel
That "Earth has no sorrow that Heaven can not heal?"

O, all ye who struggle and toil upon earth,
  Whose hearts are made heavy by misery and grief,
Look upward! The power that gave sorrow birth
  Will send to a poor soul some heavenly relief,
And God will His infinite mercies reveal,
For "Earth has no sorrow that Heaven can not heal."

                                        KATIE JESSEL.

IN EXILE.

An exile to the pine and palm,
  I see the far-winged summer brood,
Through azure depths of endless calm,
  Above a nursling solitude.

On ample breadths of bloom unfurled,
  As sweet as that voluptuous South,
When Antony gave the Roman World
  For Egypt's Cleopatra mouth.

All things of sight and sound appear
  To breathe of nothing but content,
As if, unheeded through the year,
  The vagrant season came and went.

Yet often, when I hear the rain,
  In fleecy vapor, whisper low,
Like ghosts about the window pane,
  My heart would leap to see the snow.

To see, beyond the frozen meres,
  In chalk and crayon's black and white,
The river hills, through atmospheres,
  Wind-blown in dazzling points of light.

In smooth white level lies the croft,
  A mound of snow the boxwood shines;
Still sweep the trowels white and soft,
  In sloping curves, and sweeping lines.

Soft flurries, as a shadow blurs
  The page in passing, light and fleet,
Of soft warm faces wrapped in furs,
  Of faces passing on the street.

I see them through the falling rain,
  Through all the years that flow between,
Like ghosts about my window pane,
  Among the musk and evergreen.

Old boyish friends, the fair young wife,
　Who watched with me so long ago;
As if across another life,
　In all the softly falling snow.

While yearning in the pine and palm,
　The winds do chide uncounted hours,
Whose unspent summers dull the calm,
　In soft still utterances of flowers.

WILL WALLACE HARNEY.

TO A MARGUERITE.

SOME love the rose in blushing pride,
　And some the lily sweet,
But let them both in envy hide,
　I love the Marguerite.

The air is filled with sweet perfume
　Of flowers at my feet,
The prairie glistens with their bloom,
　And chiefest, Marguerite.

I love the fair and modest flower
　Where'er its smile I meet,
It lends a charm to every hour,
　The cheerful Marguerite.

O, spirit pure embalmed in bloom,
　O, soul and form complete,
O, eyes that can dispel all gloom,
　Ye dwell in Marguerite.

J. STODDARD JOHNSTON.

SOLITUDE.

OFT have I strolled alone where it did seem
   The foot of man before had ne'er intruded,
By cliff or cave, or by some lonely stream,
   Or forest dense where night through day still brooded;
And 'round, above, beneath me—everywhere,
Nature and nature's works alone were there.

By glimm'ring light of star I've walked alone
   Some old churchyard, wand'ring among the dead;
There paused to rest on some sepulchral stone,
   And muse upon the scene about me spread,
While gray bats flitted 'twixt me and the sky,
And ghostly winds passed like a human sigh.

And I have been where man had come and gone,
   Had built and lived and left all to decay;
And weed and grass before the door had grown
   Where human feet had wont to make their way;
But reptiles now made it their habitation,
And all desertion was, and desolation!

And yet 'mong all of these so solemn places,
   Where deepest loneliness would seem to brood,
Found I less solitude than 'mong the faces
   That doth the streets of some great city flood;
Gliding me past till they as ceaseless seem
As autumn leaves borne on a forest stream.

There where the grass is hid 'neath paving stone,
   The sky shut out by roof, or blurred by smoke,
And the loud tumult ceaselessly upborne,
   More solemn grows than silence never broke;
Where man mingles with man, and yet, at heart,
Doth stand as dumbly as the stars apart!

Where from communion or with God or nature
  We are shut out, till lost is sympathy
Or with the Creator or with the creature,
  And life grows madness, or vacuity!
Ah, this is loneliness, is solitude,
  In which the soul most blightedly doth brood!

KNELM.

THE BERGAMOT BLOSSOM.

WE had no other gifts to give,
  But just one withering flower;
We had no other lives to live,
  But just that sweet half hour,
So small, so sweet, its freight of musk
Makes fragrant all Life's after dusk.

For this the summer toiled and spun,
  With fairy fingers silken shot,
Till moonlight's milky threads were run,
  In the scented, creamy bergamot,
That gives one dear remembered hour
The fragrance of the orange flower.

Through Love and Parting this remains;
  A memory, like a faint perfume,
More dear than all Life's loss and gains,
  About a withering orange bloom,
Whose fading leaves in dusky green
Keep sweet the thought of what has been.

WILL WALLACE HARNEY.

DEAR OLD SOUTHERN HOME.

IN de summer time at night, when de stars am shinin'
	bright,
An' when I heah de sighin' ob de breeze,
I always takes a turn, an' oh, dis heart does yearn,
	As I watch de moon a-peepin' frough de trees:
It takes me to my home whar long fo' I was grown
	I passed so many happy hours away;
De tall palmettos wave above my brudder's grave,
	Wid whom I used to frolic all de day.

It 'pears as if sometimes I heah de same sad chimes
	Dat rung when little Missy come to die;
Sumpin' whispahs in my eah 'bout my mudder deah,
	An' it says dat I shall jine her by an' by.
When de Lo'd shall gib comman', den I shall rise an' stan'
	'Fo' my brudder an' my little missy deah;
An' my mudder's face I'll see, an' ergin she'll sing ter me,
	An' den I'll laugh at all dis foolish feah.

Dar's a spot dat's mighty deah to dis ole darky heah,
	Way down whar de sweet magnolias bloom;
Oh, de 'membrance ob de pas' shall be wid me to de las',
	An' dribe away dese thoughts ob care an' gloom.
But now I'll soon be free, an' I 'low dat I shall see
	De faces ob de ones dat's dead an' gone:
De Heb'nly bells will ring, and once ergin I'll sing
	Wid de lubbed ones on de resurrection morn.

FRED. M. SPOTSWOOD.

TO MY SWEETHEART.

I PRAY for you when rising
   Aurora spreads her wings,
And o'er retiring planets
   Her golden mantle flings;
I pray for you when evening,
   Enrobed in twilight hues,
On zephyrs gently wafted,
   Dispenses pearly dews.

I see you in the blushing
   Of flora-plumaged vales,
Where nectared waters flowing
   Rehearse enchanted tales;
I see you with bright Iris,
   While arching glory's sky,
For all things which have beauty
   Present you to mine eye.

I hear you in sweet music
   As on the breeze it floats,
In vernal songs of warblers
   That carol dulcet notes;
I hear you in the whisper
   Of gentle gales that bring
The sweet perfume of flowers
   To glad angelic Spring.

And when the day is folded
   In night's endarkling cloud,
And all the world as pulseless
   As Silence in her shroud,
The sleep which comes upon me
   Is oft a vision bright
Of you beside me sitting,
   The Angel of the night.

CINCINNATI, July 1, 1850.   R. T. DURRETT.

THE LAST HAIL.

"MATE, get ready down on deck,
    I'm heading for the shore,
I'll ring the bell, for I must land
    This boat forevermore.

"Say, pilot, do you see that light—
    I do—where angels stand?
Well, hold her jack-staff hard on that,
    For there I'm going to land.

"That looks like Death that's hailing me,
    So ghastly grim and pale;
I'll toll the bell—I must go in—
    I never passed a hail.

"Stop her! Let her come in slow—
    There! That will do—no more;
The lines are fast, and angels await
    To welcome me ashore.

"Say, pilot, I am going with them,
    Up yonder, through that gate,
I'll not come back; you ring the bell,
    And back her out—don't wait.

"For I have made my trip of life,
    I've found my landing-place,
I'll take my soul and anchor that
    Fast to the Throne of Grace."
                  WILL S. HAYS.

THE BIRD'S SONG.

(T-WIT, T-WEE.)

T-WIT, t-wee,
    Come sit by me
Up here in this old cedar tree.
    Everywhere
      Far and near,
    All is bare,
      Cold and drear.
    There is now
      To be seen,
    Save this bough,
      Nothing green;
Nothing growing—winds a-blowing,
Must be time that we were going.

T-wit, t-wo,
    Not long ago
I wooed you dear, I loved you so.
    We made a nest,
      A tiny thing,
    To snugly rest
      And lightly swing
    With every breeze
      That chanced to sway
    The leafy trees
      All through the day.
Winds a-blowing, flowers growing,
Hidden nest—what else? No knowing.

T-wit, t-way,
    One summer day
Our cherished nestlings flew away;
    And there was left
      To idly swing
    A home bereft
      Of everything

That made it dear
    To you and me—
    Save what is here—
    Save memory.
Winds a-blowing, plainly showing
It is time we, too, were going.

T-wit, t-woo,
    Well then, adieu
To all that in those days we knew.
    To all I say,
        Excepting you,
    This cheerless day,
        Adieu! Adieu!
    From you, sweet life—
        Sweet soul—sweetheart—
    My precious wife,
        I shall not part.
Winds are blowing, old we're growing,
Yes, my dear, we're going—going.

MAY SMITH DOWNES.

——I SEEM to see the smiling eyes,
    That loved me long ago,
Look down the pale and tranquil skies
    In all the after-glow;
The still delight, the smiles and tears
Come back through all the silent years
    In which we are apart,
    As if they wished to say,
        Now comes the twilight of the Heart,
    More beautiful than Day!

WILL WALLACE HARNEY.

"*The Twilight of the Heart.*"—*The Century.*

A DREAM.

I DREAMED a sweet and beauteous dream. Methought
I walked 'mid flowers abloom, whose fragrant breath
Was wafted in the moon's pure light to where
I stroll'd along the graded terrace front.
I dreamed that by my side a graceful form,
Embodiment of beauty's self, kept pace,
Her arm within mine own so gently laid
That scarce I felt her presence—save only
By the hallowing sense which fills the soul
When forms supernal are revealed to man.
And ever and anon, as threading shady walks
With fleckered moonlight streaming in our path,
Her silvery voice was whispered in the night
Like sweetest music from the crimson shell.
Soft words of love were spoken, and the heart
Whose pulses warmed the bosom of my love
Beat quickly, and I felt Elysian bliss—
An ecstacy more sweet than all of earth
Can give. And as I gazed into her face,
'Round which a halo circling seemed to dwell,
I scanned its features with a lover's eye,
And then the beauties which were centered there:
Eyes which the wild gazelle in freedom born
Might vainly strive to rival, while their flash
Was softened by the darkest silken lash
Which ever curtained Peri's lids. Her lips
Like Grecian bow at rest were sweetly drawn,
As if a golden arrow deftly aimed
Had erstwhile sped on Cupid's mission bound.
Between the ruby portals of that mouth
Two rows of pearls, such as adorn the bride
Or lend a lustre to a Queenly crown
When decked in regal glory and the State
Listens to know Her Majesty's commands.
Smiled on my gaze and spoke in accents plain
Of rosy breath and purity and health

A DREAM.

An oval face such as Medici claimed
Immortalized in fair Carrara's stone,
Radiant with life and joy and all in one
Blending the lily in unsullied white
With sunset tints that paint the rose's leaf.
Confined about the brow, with simple grace
Her nut-brown tresses on her shoulders fell
Snowy as Alpine summits bathed in light.
Methought that as this vision filled my view
Sure Heaven itself had sent its brightest star
To cheer my gloom and shed its light
Upon a heart all blasted with despair.
Still as I gazed in endless wonder fixed,
And as we paused in silence to survey
The passing beauty of the night's bright cheer
And nature's rich profusion spread afar,
She reached her hand toward a neighboring shrub
And with her graceful fingers plucked a flower.
Great was my joy when to my wistful glance
I saw the fragile token proffered to myself,
And eagerly I reached to seize the prize
When slumber ceased, and with it fled
The vision sweet, which so had thrilled my soul.
And I awoke to find that, save in dreams
And in the realms of Angels, only dwell
Such fair creations as my dream disclosed.

Long years I nursed the memory of that dream,
And ever bright as to my quickened sense
Had come this fair creation of a night.
I roamed the world and felt the battle's shock
'Mid bloody years of war and carnage wild,
And in my waking hours and dreams I saw
Through all these years the same bright form and face,
Whilst 'mong the living things I sought to find
Its counterpart on earth. But vain the task
Till lately on a summer's eve I strolled
Where roses bloomed beneath a Southern sky.
Magnolias with their snowy cups were there,

And plants exotic to more Northern climes
Secure from frosts their fragrant tribute paid.
As moodily I mused in silent thought
Suddenly I chanced upon a form
Graceful in outline, and every mien
Suggesting thoughts of her whose witching face
Revealed in slumber long had filled my soul.
She plucked a rose, and as I came near by
Turned to my wandering gaze a face so fair,
So like in feature to my long lost love,
That as our glances met each seemed to feel
The recognition of long parted friends.
And ever since that blessed eve whereon
My dream came true, and to my loving heart
There came the real presence of my love,
I've worshipped only at her throne, and life
Has been but one long day of happiness.

J. STODDARD JOHNSTON.

PERSPECTIVES.

I.

LIVING, he threads the maze below,
And looking beyond, he saith,
"Ah, me! to penetrate and know
The greatest of mysteries, Death!"

II.

Dead, he wanders the phantom-land,
And viewing behind, the strife
Of the world, he cries, "Ah, to understand
The greatest of mysteries, Life!"

Harper's Monthly. HARRISON ROBERTSON.

IF I HAD KNOWN.

She lay with lilies on her pulseless breast,
 Dim woodland lilies wet with silver dew,
"Dear heart," he said, "in life she loved them best,
 For her sweet sake the fragrant buds were blown';
 For her in April-haunted nooks they grew—
  O love, if I had known!

"If I had known when yesterday we walked,
 Her hand in mine, along the hedges fair,
That even then, the while we careless talked,
 The shadow of a coming loss was there,
And death's cold hand was leading us apart!—
If I had known the bud she would not wear
Nor touch, lest she should mar its perfect grace,
To-day would press its dewy, golden heart
  Against her poor, dead face!

"Last year, when April woods were all a-glow,
 She said, 'If it be death to fall asleep,'
And, bending, kissed the lilies sweet and wet,
 'A dreamless sleep from which none wake to weep—
When I lie down to that long slumber, dear,
 And life for you has dark and empty grown,
Come to me then, and tho' I shall not hear,
 Lay your sad lips to mine, and whisper low:
'If I had known! O love, if I had known
  That you would not forget!'"

ADELAIDE D. ROLLSTON.

THE ROCK.

I KNOW a great, gray-lichened rock,
   Its rugged face impassive, stern,
   Rough-bearded with sere-frouded fern,
And brow defiant, upreared to mock
The fiercest storm's fire-bolted shock.

With hoary majesty it stands,
   Bold, sturdy, fixed, and dauntless forth,
   With mien and visage which the North
In ruder days with mail-clad hands
Stamped on his wild barbaric bands.

And Time's memorial fingers trace
   On granite tablets gravures deep,
   Which lore of storied aeons keep;
While Death's blade, broken at its base,
Lies garland-twined with bloomy grace.

Here world a-weary and alone
   I lean my heart upon its breast,
   With list'ning, longing ear close-pressed
Against the Sphinx-like lips of stone,
For counsel of the Ages Gone,

Lean long to catch the faintest sound
   Which, wave-like, beats the Shores of Sense,
   And sigh that each soft ripple hence,
From keels white-winged and "outward bound,"
Is *by my own heart's tumult drowned!*

Lost, lost each echo hither blown,
   Charged with a soul's electric fire!
   The frail connecting spirit wire
Which speeds the thoughts from Lands Unknown,
By hands of flesh is broken down!

So from the wounds that never cure,
  These voiceless lips of lasting stone,
  I con the only counsel known
To wisest sage or witless boor:
  Be strong, mute, patient, and endure!

                              DR. FRANK H. RHEA.

SOUTH FLORIDA NIGHT.

THE rain floats off: a crescent moon
  Holds in its cup a round of dusk,
Like palm buds in the month of June,
  Half breaking through its vernal husk,
While breathes a low sweet undertone,
  Like brooks that grieve through beds of fern,
As if by curve and pebble stone
  The moon had spilled her silver urn.

Night-blooming agaves part the sheaf
  To catch the light distilled in showers,
Till, overflowing cup and leaf,
  Its cluster breaks in midnight flowers;
Like merchants breaking beds of nard,
  And jars of olives, desert born,
Pine-apples lift a prickly shard
  And show the seeds of fragrant corn.

Like Hebrew maids the citrons hold
  Their pitchers to the vapor spring,
And fill the hollow rinds of gold
  With midnight's musky offering;
So once, I think, Earth knew her Lord
  In lands like these, of palm and vine,
When midnight gave the sweet accord
  That turned the water into wine.

Atlantic Monthly.   WILL WALLACE HARNEY.

PARTING.

Another's arms will fold the form
  Which mine have lately pres't;
Another's lips will kiss the cheek
  Once pillow'd on this breast.

Another's hand will twine the hair
  Which thrill'd me in its stroke;
Another's heart will swell to thine,
  While mine, alas! is broke.

Another's soul will know the joy
  Of love's requited bliss,
While there remains alone to me
  The mem'ry of a kiss.

Another's voice will wake the fires
  Which slumber in thy blood;
Another's hand will pluck the rose
  While I have nursed the bud.

We part. I go. Perhaps no more
  To me shall be the boon
To feel the joys I once have known—
  Ended, alas! too soon.

But, should I never know the joy
  Awakened in this heart,
I crave one promise ere I go—
  One pledge before we part:

When duty shall enforce the claim
  Denied to love and me,
Oh! heave one swelling sigh for him,
  Who, dying, thinks of thee.

J. Stoddard Johnston.

A LETTER OF TO-DAY.

DEAR EDITH: Our ball is just over;
    As the French say, 't was quite *recherche*—
Such music, such lights, and such dancing!
    My breath was quite taken away.
Of course not a soul was invited
    Save the choice "four hundred" in town;
They came too, and ma was delighted,
    As she stood in her new velvet gown,
So grand, so serene, and so smiling,
    By papa, who pays all our bills.
Not a soul in the room dreamt they'd ever
    Made *"Moonshine" in Cumberland Hills.*

You know we are just home from Europe,
    And our house is the finest in town;
Then we live right next door to the Astors,
    And Brown's not so bad when spelled *Browne.*
So when all of these things are considered,
    You can see in a moment, my dear,
That as far as getting into society
    We had nothing whatever to fear—
To be sure, papa's somewhat old-fashioned,
    But then he pays all of our bills,
And looks too genteel to have ever
    Made *"Moonshine" in Cumberland Hills.*

You should see my new dresses from Paris;
    The one that I wore at our ball
Had a train that was perfectly startling,
    But no waist, to speak of, at all.
I laugh in my sleeves sometimes, Edith,
    At the many things money can do,
And ofttimes I peep in my mirror,
    And I say to myself, Is this you,
The girl who once lived in the mountains,
    Went barefooted, worked at the "stills"
Helping pa and the men make "moonshine"
    'Way back in the Cumberland Hills?

And I moralize thus, as I stand there:
"Who cares what you were in the past?
The present is yours and the future—
So long as your money shall last."
But I find that each day there is creeping
A scornful contempt in my heart
For the people who "toady" around us.
Were we and our money to part,
Then all of our past would be opened;
Could papa no longer pay bills,
Then all of our friends would be sure to find out
We'd made Moonshine in Cumberland Hills.

But to come back to news—oh, such scandals!
When one's wealthy, 'tis quite *apropos;*
Things grow so dreadfully stupid,
And times are so awfully slow
That a genteel and well-got-up scandal
Is considered rather swell in a way,
And lends such an interest to people
Whom we meet in our set every day.
Now old-fashioned, sensible papa,
Who does little but pay off our bills,
Says a scandal is even much lower
Than *moonshining* in Cumberland Hills.

And sometimes I think so myself, dear,
And I long for the old, happy life,
When I roamed o'er the piney wood mountains,
Knowing nothing of discord or strife.
Ah, Edith, those days—they were blissful!
Do you remember my old lover, Joe?
Mamma says that I never must name him,
That it's quite too dreadfully low—
To bury the dead past as she has;
And I have tried with a might and a will,
But my heart must be buried if the past is
In a grave in the Cumberland Hills.

But good-bye to such foolish fancies,
　That now in my life hold no part;
I am worldly, and scheming, and soulless,
　Yet know, dear, that down in my heart
Is a spot warm and true and untainted
　For you, the sweet friend of my youth,
Kept green with the tears of remembrance
　Girt round with a strong wall of truth,
That I brought with me over the mountains,
　That I cherish and keep with me still,
As the only memento that's left me
　Of my life in the Cumberland Hills.

ELIZABETH LEE MURPHEY.

THE VIOLET.*

I FOUND my first violet to-day,
　A silent messenger of Spring,
Alone in the deep wood-way,
　A poor little frightened thing.

The gaunt limbed oaks towered high
　While it shyly knelt at their feet,
And the pilfering breeze, strolling by,
　Caught its fragrance, rare and sweet.

Alone in the deep wildwood,
　An exile pale and fair,
The tiny darling stood
　Until I wandered there.

I found it in its helmet blue,
　A pale and shivering thing;
I culled it, and brought it to you,
　A dainty off'ring of Spring.

CLINT RUBY.

*Written at the age of twelve years.

APRIL.

EARLY birds singing,
Heather-bells swinging,
And crocuses breaking in long slender blades;
Lilacs are budding,
Creeks are all flooding,
And wind-swept and misty the upperland glades.

Gray limbs are bending,
Outward they're sending
The tenderest shoots of the daintiest green;
Winds are a-blowing,
Grass spears are showing,
With delicate snow-drops blooming between.

Daffodils brighten,
Spring-beauties whiten
The meadow's broad bosom e'en down to the pond;
Long lily blades shiver
Within their brown quiver,
And wake-robins bloom in the woodlands beyond.

Liverwort nestles
On moss-covered trestles,
Where trickles the water down—down to the pool;
Anemones, cresses,
And lady-fern tresses,
Are dropping and hiding where shadows fall cool.

The clouds are all weeping
For Life gone a-sleeping
And tucked 'neath the cover of old Autumn leaves;
A softer breath blowing
Will hasten the growing
And stir a new hope in the bosom that grieves.

Are you glad—are you cheerful?
Are you sad—are you tearful?
Let sorrow fly free—see, the sun's shining now.

The world is broad smiling
Each sad thought beguiling;
Let frowns disappear from the shadowed brow.

Ah, gusty and rainy is April,
But promising pleasanter weather;
And lovelier meadows and flowers
Will follow the blossoming heather.

MAY SMITH DOWNES.

OCTOBER.

THROUGH glimmering mists the warm light drifts
　Sleepily over the dun, wet fields,
Where the sumac burns, and the wild rose lifts
Its pale, sweet face 'mid the odorous gifts
　That the golden harvest yields.

There's a moan from the heart of the waving pine,
　Wind-tossed by the creek's dim shore,
And a hint of death on the purpling vine,
Though still in the shadowy dingles shine
　The violets that April bore!

In the cool, gray light of the dayspring fair,
　Ere the skies take on their blue,
A strange, wild beauty the woodlands wear,
And the sedges sway in the scented air,
　A-glitter with silver dew.

Till the day, with its slumb'rous, purple glow,
　A wonderful splendor weaves
On the hazy fields where the soft winds blow,
And the fading rose with its heart of snow
　For the vanishing summer grieves.

ADELAIDE D. ROLLSTON.

TO L. B.'S EYES.

Dedicated to a young lady who possesses the rare charm of having one brown and one blue eye.

O TELL me if, when waking,
   Thy spirits stray,
And through thine eyes come taking
   My cares away?
For ever in my dreaming
   Come visions bright,
Oft in my slumbers teeming
   Sweet stars of night.

Deep in the beaming portals
   Of thy brown eye,
Gems and silicious opals,
   Rare pebbles, lie.
To tell thy blue eye's praises,
   A hundred hues
Sparkle, as on the daisies
   The morning dews.

Mild looking, not vindictive,
   Each eye contrives,
And happily seems instinctive
   With separate lives.
The spirit dies—no, never—
   But O it sighs
That ever life should sever
   From thy sweet eyes.

                   T. T. REYNOLDS.

SARAH M. B. PIATT.

ECHO AND THE LOVER.

LOVER. Echo! mysterious nymph, declare
　　　　Of what you're made and what you are—
ECHO. 　　　　　　　　　　　　"Air!"

LOVER. 'Mid airy cliffs and places high,
　　　　Sweet Echo! listening, love, you lie——
ECHO. 　　　　　　　　　　　"You lie!"

LOVER. You but resuscitate dead sounds—
　　　　Hark! how my voice revives, resounds!
ECHO. 　　　　　　　　　　　"Zounds!"

LOVER. I'll question you before I go—
　　　　Come answer me more apropos!
ECHO. 　　　　　　　　　　"Poh! poh!"

LOVER. Tell me, fair nymph, if e'er you saw
　　　　So sweet a girl as Phœbe Shaw?
ECHO. 　　　　　　　　　　　"Pshaw!"

LOVER. Say, what will win that frisky coney
　　　　Into the toils of matrimony?
ECHO. 　　　　　　　　　　"Money!"

LOVER. Has Phœbe not a heavenly brow;
　　　　Is it not white as pearl—as snow?
ECHO. 　　　　　　　　　　"Ass, no!"

LOVER. Her eyes! was ever such a pair!
　　　　Are the stars brighter than they are?
ECHO. 　　　　　　　　　　"They are!"

LOVER. Echo, you lie, but can't deceive me;
　　　　Her eyes eclipse the stars—believe me.
ECHO. 　　　　　　　　　　"Leave me!"

LOVER. But come, you saucy, pert romancer,
　　　　Who is as fair as Phœbe? answer.
ECHO. 　　　　　　　　　　"Ann, sir!"

　　　　　　　　　　　JOHN M. HARNEY.

THE STORY OF THE GATE.

Across the pathway, myrtle-fringed,
Under the maple, it was hinged—
　　The little wooden gate.
'T was there, within the quiet gloam,
When I had strolled with Nellie home,
　　I used to pause and wait

Before I said to her good-night,
Yet loath to leave the winsome sprite
　　Within the garden's pale;
And there, the gate between us two,
We'd linger, as all lovers do,
　　And lean upon the rail.

And face to face, eyes close to eyes,
Hands meeting hands in feigned surprise
　　After a stealthy quest—
So close I'd bend, ere she'd retreat,
That I'd grow drunken from the sweet
　　Carnations on her breast.

We'd talk—in fitful style, I ween—
With many a meaning glance between
　　The tender words and low;
We'd whisper some dear trite conceit,
Some idle gossip we'd repeat;
　　And then I'd move to go.

"Good-night," I'd say; "Good-night—good-bye!"
"Good-night!"—from her, with half a sigh—
　　"Good-night!" "*Good*-night!" And then—
And then I do *not* go, but stand,
Again lean on the railing, and—
　　Begin it all again.

Ah! that was many a day ago—
That pleasant summer-time—although
　　The gate is standing yet;
　　A little cranky it may be,
　　A little weather-worn—like me—
　　　Who never can forget

The happy—"End?" My cynic friend,
Pray save your sneers—there was no "end."
　　Watch yonder chubby thing!—
　　That is our youngest—hers and mine;
　　See how he climbs, his legs to twine
　　　About the gate and swing.
　　　　　　　　　HARRISON ROBERTSON.

SONNET.

THE thistle-down soared up to meet the sun—
　　The way-side nursling of the summer shower—
　　A matchless purple tint its only dower,
That blanched to whiteness ere the day was done.
Though carelessly her web the spider spun
　　To hide the splendors of the day-god's power,
　　Yet vainly still the veiled and fettered flower,
The thistle-down, soared up to meet the sun.
The wind's wild playmate through the summer days
　　Soared to the sun it worshiped from afar;
The whiteness caught the glint of golden rays
　　In triumph passed beyond a rainbow bar;
The wondering world looked on with words of praise
　　And lips inspired named *the flower* A STAR.
　　　　　　　　　MARY THORNTON MCABOY.

DIXIE LAND.

An old Italian came into our yard last night,
   And humbly begged permission that his wandering band
Might play for us some old, forgotten airs.
   I bowed assent, and straightway "Dixie Land"
Fell on my ears. Forgotten? No, my pulses throbbed and
     thrilled—
   And was it weakness that mine eyes were filled with tears?
Ah, well, perhaps it was; but that old song
   Is but a grave-stone o'er the buried hopes of other years.

And as the notes swelled out, now high, now low,
   I saw between the chords, in letters bright and red,
The birth, the life, the age of that Lost Cause
   That ne'er will be forgotten, e'en though dead.
The stricken South, with unstrung bow in hand,
   I saw again, amid her mournful scenes,
Her arrow sped too high, and lying lost
   Among a myriad host of sweet, dead dreams.

Could you, my friend, stand by the grave of one you loved
   And think on any faults that he in life possessed—
Would you not rather dwell on nobler traits
   That put to shame and darkness all the rest?
So, dreaming o'er that past brought back to me,
   No errors saw I, but before my sight
A vision only came of noble, loyal men
   Fighting, yea, dying, for a cause to them both just and right.

As listening to the music die away, one scene arose
   Whose pathos ne'er on canvas can be given,
A troop of ragged soldiers weeping o'er a flag *
   All riddled, battle-stained, but dear as hopes of heaven.
And one, the gentlest memory of our world,
   Stood in their midst, his figure sadly grand,
Saying good-bye to them and to the day
   When life no longer could be given for Dixie Land.

* Lee's surrender.

And that old song our fathers loved so well,
  Whose words were oft times breathed with their last breath,
Should be to every one of Southern birth as dear
As loved "remembered kisses after death."
A fitting "In Memoriam," so it seems to me—
Grief softens anger, and from it a ray
Makes warm our hearts for those who wore the blue,
  While strengthening love and pride for those who wore the gray.

ELIZABETH LEE MURPHEY.

NOVEMBER.

THE gloaming of an Autumn eventide,
  Sullen and red, deep in the waning west,
  Like iron-throated furnace in whose breast
Some smith Titanic wrought where yet abide
The smouldering fires, the Day reluctant died.
  A clump of oaks its dismal branches pressed
  Sheer of the sombre glow, and from the crest
Of hither hills I caught the scene and sighed,
  Because the Autumn of my heart was here!
And on th' horizon of its sky, where gleamed
  The ling'ring light of Hope departed, were
The dim, sweet silhouettes of fancies deemed
  By Youth and Love immortal! Thus Despair
Oft comes as Autumn to bright Summers dreamed
  In ardent Spring, and like the leafless oak
Whose naked limbs do piteously invoke
  Of Winter the chill charity of snow,
She adjures Death to shroud her wintry woe.

DR. FRANK H. RHEA.

BIOPSIS.

It can not be that this sweet life of ours,
So grand, so glorious and so beautiful,
So full of mighty promises, is but
The clash of blind and senseless atoms, and
At last dissolves in empty nothingness!
It can not be that its bright, crystal stream
Runs darkling to the deeps of endless death,
When every wave that wooes the winding banks
Sings of the summer skies from whence it came!
What is this in this tenement of clay
That like a caged wild bird beats its wings
Against its prison bars, unless it be
A captive spirit fretting 'neath the chains
Of conscious slavery, struggling to be free?
This ceaseless longing after better things
Than earth hath ever promised, or can give,
Whence comes it, if the yearning, homesick soul
Hath not had visions of some happier sphere
To our dim eyes invisible, or else
There lingers still, like some half-waking dream,
Sweet memories of a former glory lost?

O grand, invisible, and potent essence, Life!
In vain the student seeks with chemic test
To fathom thy deep mystery! All in vain
With fierce and fiery questions would he wring—
Poor tortured Nature writhing on the rack—
Confession from her suffering silent lips
Of THAT MYSTERIOUS, SUBTLE POWER that moves,
Controls, and regulates her wondrous works.
He sees it laughing in the budding flower;
He hears it trilling in the sky-lark's song;
He feels it throbbing in the fiery flood
That leaps like liquid lightning 'long his veins,
And, maddened at the mockery of his powers,
Calls bold, unblushing Science to his aid.

BIOPSIS. 135

Who, armed with scalpel and retort, pursues
With patient search the protean phantom down
Through system, organ, member, molecule,
And atom, but to find for all her pains
There's THAT within the lowliest thing that lives
That will not yield to his analysis.

In nature is no death, unless that death
Be called, which is but change to newer forms
Of ever upward reaching life. In all
This ceaseless change beginning finds she none,
Nor prophecy of end. NO FURTHER SEEK.
Before us and behind the curtain falls,
Forever shutting from our vision out
The secrets of the silent land beyond.
Across these borders Science can not pass;
And proud Philosophy with gathered skirts
Stops at the threshold, and with hand to brow
Peers with wide-wondering eyes and silent lips
Into the darkness that she dares not trust.

But Faith, Love's white-winged daughter, lifts the veil
That shuts the future out, and whispers hope.
The soul, with an unerring instinct that
As far transcends the utmost reach and power
Of weak and faltering REASON as the stars
Their pale reflection in the troubled pool,
Proclaims herself a thing of birth divine,
And crowns herself IMMORTAL.
                              We do live;
And it concerns us most not what is life,
But how shall we best use it, that when called
To lay this glittering pageantry aside
And, clothed in death's pale robe of night, lie down
To that long dreamless sleep that separates
Time's evening from Eternity's fair morn,
Our deeds of love, in hearts we leave behind,
May live forever; and across the gulf
That circles round the narrow shores of time

Waft their sweet perfume, borne on heavenly airs,
An incense offering to the throne of God.

He lives it best in God's sight, who but lives
To feel, to love, to wonder and adore!
*   *   *   *   *   *   *   *   *   *
Look abroad,
The precious fields are unto harvest white,
And there is lack of reapers everywhere.
Thrust in thy sickle ere the noon be past,
Or if thou hast not strength nor skill to reap,
Then follow after, gleaning; and perchance
When home thou comest, not with empty hands,
It may be thine like Moab Ruth to sit
At evening by the Master's feet and find
Sweet favor in his sight. Who dares to say
Who best fulfills His wish, or those that reap
Or those that only glean! Work, watch, and wait,
And trust His tender love whate'er befall.
Thy pathway here may not be smooth and even,
And Sorrow oft may set and sup with thee
When thou hast bidden smiling Joy along.
The vines thou'st tended with fond fostering care
May cast their fruit untimely to the ground.
Thou mayst toil with weary hand and brain
Alone through all the fiery day of life,
And looking back at evening on the fields,
See thistles growing where in tears thou sow'dst
The golden grain at morning, full of hope;
A cruel disappointment comes at last
To mock thy wasted years and helpless age.
Be not cast down! The soul her starry crown
Wins not by what the feeble hands have done,
But what the heart has suffered. 'T is God's way
To perfect His beloved and prepare
The precious in His sight to dwell with him.
The purest souls that ever blessed the earth
Have come forth from the hottest fires of pain.
The sweetest songs that ever thrilled the heart
Have by lips white with agony been sung!

Beyond some Jordan every Canaan lies.
Who will not in the wilderness abide,
Athirst and hungered for his forty days,
Shall ne'er along the palm-strewn highway ride
In triumph to be crowned a king of men.

But paths of peace the humble only find.
'T was not o'er Shinar's vain ambitious host,
Exulting in the pride of human strength,
But unto Bethel's wanderer, lone and sad,
Rock-pillowed in the desert, God drew back
The curtains of the skies, and showed revealed
The shining stairway swung 'twixt earth and heaven.

Be not a dreamer—life is not for dreams.
They live to sorrow who but live to self.
'T is God's unchanging plan and nature's law
That they shall reap not who refuse to sow.
Give, and without measure shall it thee be giv'n
Of joy and hope and happiness and love;
Give without stint, for though thy store be scant
Thou hast within the lodging of thy heart
A greater than Elijah; and fear not!
Thou canst not drain that cruse, however small,
Wherein God pours the never failing streams
Of His rich blessing.
     There is work for all.
God gems thy pathway with opportunities
Thick as the summer dew-drops on the grass,
Rich with His promises, but manna-like,
They must be gathered ere the sun is risen
And used upon the instant, else they breed
Within the heart a never-dying brood
Of worms armed with stings of vain regret,
And to a loathsome hell of torment turn
The paradise of memory.
      So from seeds
Of good, neglected, direst evils spring;
And opportunities of yesterday

Borne upward, on whose wings we might have soared
To heights immeasurable of bliss sublime,
Hang mill-stones round our necks to-day to drag
Our struggling souls beneath the unpitying wave.

Seize then the winged moments as they pass,
And, ere they speed to Heaven's record up,
Stamp each with some good deed, some gentle word,
Some holy thought, some generous action done.
So shall thy treasures be laid up in Heaven;
And where thy treasures are God says thy heart
Shall be—and where thy heart is there thou art,
For HEART IS ALL—and Heaven thus be thine.

TOM F. McBEATH.

THE BURIED HOPE.

FOLD down its little baby hands;
  This was a hope you had of old;
Fillet the brow with rosy bands,
  And kiss its shining locks of gold;
Somewhere, within the reach of years,
  Another hope may come like this;
But this poor babe is gone in tears,
  With thin white lips, cold to thy kiss.

In Summer, a little wreath of flowers;
  In Winter, a little drift of snow;
And this is all, through all the hours,
  Of the promise perished long ago;
So every heart has some dear grave,
  Close hidden under its joy or care,
Till over it breaths of memory wave
  And leave the little headstone bare.

WILL WALLACE HARNEY.

A MAY-TIME MEMORY.

WE rode adown the woodland way
  'Mid shifting flecks of sun and shade;
  Our horses' feet soft music made—
The world was wondrous fair that day.

Sweet languid scents were all around,
  A balmy softness filled the air,
  For May, a goddess past compare,
Had lately walked the enchanted ground,

And beauty sprung where'er she trod:
  A vivid green on leaf and tree,
  With whirr of locust, hum of bee,
And flow'rets peeping thro' the sod.

Green trailing branches downward hung,
  Gay birds were singing merrily.
  Dear Love! the world is fair to see
When hearts are fond and life is young!

The glad enchantment of the place
  Beguiled my secret from my breast;
  Your willing thrall I stood confest,
Made captive by its tender grace.

A benison from all things fair
  Gave sanction to my heart's desire;
  A melody of Nature's choir
Love's chorus thrilled upon the air.

Now loit'ring down the sunset side
  Of life's fair hill, I oft look 'round,
  Remembering that enchanted ground
Where the heart's whitest tents abide:

Wide morn: a shaded grass-grown lane,
  Down which we ride in pleasant talk,
  Our steeds held in to slowest walk,
My hand upon your bridle rein.

VIRGINIA F. NOBLE.

COQUETTE.

"Coquette," my love they sometimes call,
    For she is light of lips and heart;
What though she smile alike on all,
    If in her smile she knows no art?

Like some glad brook she seems to be,
    That ripples o'er its pebbly bed,
And prattles to each flower or tree,
    Which stoops to kiss it, overhead.

Beneath the heavens' white and blue
    It purls and sings and laughs and leaps,
The sunny meadows dancing through
    O'er noisy shoals and frothy steeps.

'T is thus the world doth see the brook;
    But I have seen it otherwise,
When following it to some far nook
    Where leafy shields shut out the skies.

And there its waters rest, subdued,
    In shadowy pools, serene and shy,
Wherein grave thoughts and fancies brood
    And tender dreams and longings lie.

I love it when it laughs and leaps,
    But love it better when at rest—
'T is only in its tranquil deeps
    I see my image in its breast.

The Century.   HARRISON ROBERTSON.

FRANKFORT.

SHUT in by hills, like forests hung on edges round the skies,
With rock-built stairways, spiral cut, about them as they rise.
Here on their low, broad, mossy base, close to the river's side,
This vine-like city wanders round in wild romantic pride.
Here, climbing up the cliffs apace, there, out in valleys green,
And lighting with its altar fires crag, dell, and deep ravine.
Delightful place! no one, unmoved, thy hills and plains can view,
With the Kentucky whispering and flowing softly through;
In and out and all around its waters brightly gleam,
With shadows of the cliffs and trees and houses in the stream;
So picturesque, so wildly free, so unlike any place,
We can not pluck from classic lore a symbol of its grace.
Its wayward streets, made as by chance they cut into a hill,
Or cleared by axe a bosky nook, or broken gorge did fill;
Its uncouth buildings, dark with age, of wood or massive stone,
Bespeak the wild and simple life distinctively its own.
Here forest trees grow undisturbed, and Vallambrosa's shade
Was not more deep than foliage here, of elm and maple made;
And gleaming through we see the spires of churches, great and small,
Where sweetly ringing bells proclaim the Christian creeds of all;
Here birds from bowers of the South with loving preference throng,
And build their nests, and fill the town with glory of their song;
The graceful squirrel and timid hare are not afraid to come
And play, like children, hide-and-seek, as in their forest home;
Here gabbling geese go eyeing round the strangers in a crowd,
And turkeys grace suburban homes, like people shy and proud,

And roosters lift their gorgeous wings and crow with wild
    delight—
No clock as truly tells the morn, or mid-hours of day and
    night;
These winged children nature brings, unconscious how they
    grace
The wooded homes that man has built here in this sylvan
    place,
With clang of trade and engines' screams, and busy, noisy
    mills;
These are the scenes, these are the sounds that echo thro'
    the hills.
These give the charm of ancient towns, to see that travel-
    ers roam,
Where strangers, like their citizens, feel some sweet spell
    of home
For places long inhabited here by the sons of men.
The smoke, the mist, the atmosphere of hill and dale and
    glen
Is filled with subtle sense of love—half human, half divine,
And draws us, as the pagan's drawn, to God thro' Nature's
    shrine.
Now as I gaze from topmost hill upon this city here,
Which should be, as it is to me, to all Kentuckians dear,
Imbrowned by shadows of the cliffs, o'ertopped by foliage
    grand,
With sudden distances of wood, of vale and smiling land,
With glittering mist, with sheeny smoke, that charms the
    painter's eyes,
With rainbow splendor in the clouds that deck her evening
    skies.
Endowed with life's rich blessings all, I say I know not where
A city could be found more strangely beautiful and fair.
Here from Boone's grave, surpassing all, the view that south-
    ward lies,
Where hills on hills, like giant stairs, recede into the skies,
And winding down, as from on high, thro' mist and azure
    gloom,
The river, like some spirit, comes in dress of silver bloom;

And flying on, with wave-winged feet, down thro' the heart of town,
Seems to rest beneath the cliff, where the sun, in going down,
Hangs like a broken golden wheel and slurs its shattered light
Far o'er the sky, far o'er the town, and the river in its flight.
Oh, hill-girt city! water-bound, with blue sky for thy crown—
Made lovely by a thousand charms of Nature—all thine own!
No wonder that thy people cling to thee with loving pride,
Even as thy vines and cedars cling to bank and green hillside;
No wonder that the Indians fought with savage, fearful ire,
And lit these hills and valleys fair with devastating fire,
And yelled with indignation grand that they must yield their claim
To white men and be driven from this paradise to them.
I wonder that no poet yet has given the world thy praise,
And proudly set thy beauty in immortal, glowing lays.
The English bards have one by one enrobed in their renown
Some hamlet, river, valley, plain, or quaint, romantic town
To childhood and to memory dear; but thou, sweet city here—
The most romantic of them all, to all hearts strangely dear—
Thou art not set in silver verse, and, like some precious stone,
Prized by all the world because fame makes its value known.
Here in this lofty resting place, the "City of its Dead,"
A hill of wond'rous beauty reared up from the river's bed,
Where pine and cedar, elm and oak, in forest grandeur stand,
And flower-blooms, like eyes of love, light up this silent land;
Here gleaming marble tells the tale, too long erst to record,
How many from the town below here sleep beneath the sward;

Here are the names the State has cut on monumental stone
Of those whose deeds, and words, and works are jewels all
    her own.
Here sleeps O'Hara, poet and wit, whose "Bivouac of the
    Dead"
In many a land and many a tongue with rapture has been
    read;
And though Kentucky claimed his works, his famous harp
    of song,
With all its wealth of minstrelsy, to Frankfort doth belong.
Perhaps the prophet's love of fame, unrecognized at home,
Ambition tempted him away in sunnier climes to roam;
But where his verses were invoked, and their sweet glory
    shed,
He sleeps, most honored of them all, in the Bivouac of the
    Dead;
And still here, as the past on past of ages shall be hurled,
This minstrel's lays, like music, will fore'er delight the
    world.

   *   *   *   *   *   *   *

Fair city of the hills and vales, once more I turn and gaze
Entranced upon thy beauty, robed in sundown's golden
    haze;
Here poesy could never ask a sweeter home on earth—
Her silver harp a richer song than measures of thy worth.
And when my feet shall roam no more, my life to death
    hath run,
I ask but this, to rest among my loved at set of sun,
Where singing birds, and lovely flowers, and pine and cedar
    keep
Perpetual spring above the mound that hides our dreamless
    sleep.

                            MRS. JENNIE C. MORTON.

HILLS LOOK BLUE WHEN FAR AWAY.

THE sunshine on the hill-tops
  Was sifting finest gold,
The shadows in the valleys
  Were deepening fold on fold;
To the utmost outward rim
  Of blue and purple mist,
Lightly seemed the world to swim
  In seas of amethyst.

Close to the open window,
  Worn out with childish glee,
Softly came my little boy,
  And leaned against my knee.
His brown eyes, full of wonder,
  Were gazing far away,
"Mamma, can you tell me, please,
  Why the hills look blue to-day?"

At sound of his quaint question
  I felt the sudden tears
Rise in my eyes in memory
  Of long-gone, happy years,
And tho' in sweet respondence
  I uttered not one word,
The heart within me quivered,
  Like a restless, prisoned bird.

Once I had a loyal friend—
  More than friend he fain had been—
And with eloquent appeals
  Heart of mine he sought to win.
"Take care! O, my precious girl,
  Heed thee well what I now say:
The roughest hills feet ever climbed,
  Looked blue when far away.

"Better in the Valley rest thee—
  Be unknown, but glad and free—
The low, green Valley of Delight,
  And be the world to me!
There no storms will sweep around,
  Full of coldness and of wrath;
Lay thy little hand in mine,
  I have learned to know the path."

How I laughed me at his warning!
  How I mocked me at his sighs!
And I gave but merry scorning
  For the tears within his eyes!
For the Star of Hope had risen
  Above the Goal of Fame,
And on its scroll I yearned to trace
  A grand, immortal name.

And at once my eager footsteps
  Sought to climb the far-off height,
But the clouds about me gathered
  That were darker than the night;
And many a brier and bramble
  And many a cruel stone
Beset the way in which I trod,
  Unaided and alone.

Still fearlessly I mounted
  Toward the shining goal,
Careless alike of heart-ache
  Or anguish of the soul.
What recked I of such trifles
  As weariness or pain,
When through will and self-denial
  I life's purpose could attain?

Now, with the light upon me,
  Descended from the skies,
I look across the distance
  Where the low, green Valley lies;

And I know, at last, the lesson
   Which Time alone can teach,
That the greatest of life's triumphs
   Lie always—out of reach.

Still on the distant tree-tops
   The sunshine sifts its gold,
And the shadows in the valleys
   Are deepening fold on fold;
And I hear my Julius asking
   Why the hills look blue to-day,
And thro' my tears I answer:
   "Because—they're far away."

NELLIE MARSHALL MCAFEE.

TRUE GREATNESS.

——BUT he alone whose mind is great
   And greatly dwells conjoin'd with mighty soul,
   Whose heart abounds in love, and in control
Works out the problems that to him relate,
Whether secluded deep or high in state,
   Who from the center sees the utmost whole,
   And travels boldly to the distant goal,
Nor turns regardful of reproach or hate,
   But uses powers loaned him from above
   For purposes whose aim and end is love.
All men to him as younger brothers are;
   'Tis he directs, designs, and plans and leads,
   With wisdom's high-born thoughts and godlike deeds,
And beams above them like an Eastern star.

HOWARD MILLER.

LOVE'S TRINITY.

I.

The crushed strawberry's delicate stain,
  In a tide of creamy white,
When the flesh of the luscious fruit is slain,
And plunged in the deep of a milky main,
  The daintiest tongue's delight:
This is the hue of her bosom fair
Of the roses and lilies mingled there.

II.

The radiant stars in a laughing stream,
  Tossed into scintillant spray;
Sweet silvery notes that throb in a dream,
And spangles of dew that shimmer and gleam
  In the fair tiara of May:
These are the type of her gentle mind,
The golden thoughts by the heart refined.

III.

The aroma faint which the rose exhales,
  Unseen, unfelt tho' it be,
Lading the wings of the amorous gales
That wanton in shadows of dusky vales,
  Or frolic o'er sunny lea:
This perfume hidden, this exquisite joy,
Symbols her dainty spirit coy.

DR. FRANK H. RHEA.

MY LADY SLEEPS.

My lady sleeps. No fold
  Of silken vestment stirs
On the fair bosom cold,
  Under its laces white
As that pale cheek of hers
In the dim shaded light;

Through the curved lips no breath
  Warms the chill face or breast.
Is this the thing called death?
  Then would I humbly sue
Such perfect peace; such rest
Might calm my pulses too.

Is this the end of all
  Life's sweet tumultuous thrill?
She who held hearts in thrall,
  And swayed men's destinies—
Lies she so low and still
After those victories?

Under that waxen lid
  What secret thought is veiled?
What if she heard and chid
  This futile voice of mine!
Since while she lived, it failed
To reach her heart's pure shrine.

What if her lips should break
  Death's icy seal, and move!
Would the old scorn awake,
  That I still vex her ear
With the poor tale of love
She never deigned to hear?

Peace, foolish one! Her soul
  Dwells not in this dull clay;
Heaven's height was its goal.
Haply she knows at last,
  All that I fain would say
Now hope's brief day is past.

Oh, thou majestic Death!
  As in some holy place
Kneel I with quickened breath;
Nor would I dare to press
  My lips on that dear face,
Such is its sacredness.

Sleep—while some subtle spell
  Turns brow and cheek to stone.
Would that I slept as well,
In dreamless rest secure!
  I who, unloved, alone
Live and learn to endure.

Belford's Magazine.   IDA GOLDSMITH MORRIS.

AN IDLE POET.

I.

'T IS said that when the nightingale
  His mate has found,
He fills no more the woodland vale
  With songful sound.

II.

I sing not since my love I knew,
  For, like the bird's,
My heart is full of song too true,
  Too deep for words.

HARRISON ROBERTSON.
Harper's Monthly.

CHORDS.

When love delays, when love delays and Joy
  Steals a strange shadow o'er the happy hills,
  And Hope smiles from To-morrow, nor fulfills
One promise of To-day, thy sight would cloy
    This soul with loved despair
    By seeing thee so fair.

When love delays, when love delays and Song
  Aches at wild lips regretful, as the sound
  Of a whole sea strives in the shell-mouth bound,
Tho' Hope smiles still to-morrowed, all this wrong
    Would at one little word,
    Leap forth for thee a sword.

When love delays, when love delays and Sleep
  Nests in dark eye-balls, like a song of home
  Heard 'mid familiar flowers o'er the foam,
Tho' Hope smiles still to-morrowed, thou wouldst steep
    This hurt heart over-much
    In balm with one true touch.

When love delays, when love delays and Sorrow
  Drinks her own tears that fever her soul's thirst,
  And song, and sleep, and memory seem accurst,
For Hope smiles still to-morrowed, I would borrow
    One smile from thee to cheer
    The weary, weary year.

When love delays, when love delays and Death
  Hath sealed dim lips and mocked young eyes with night,
  To love or hate locked calm, indifferent quite—
Hope, star-eyed acolyte—what kisses' breath,
    What joys can slay regret
    Or teach thee to forget!
            MADISON CAWEIN.

AT YULE-TIDE.

I.

Now upon the Soul's broad hearthstone lay the crissom brands for lighting,
With the charm of touch and whisper wake the bright warm-hearted flame
Till it, rising, kisses softly all the arches bending o'er it,
Till the wingéd sparks go singing through the night Love's holy name.

II.

Lusty mistletoe be bringing, boughs of cedar, wreaths of holly,
To each heart a cup of laughter touched by gracious vestal lips,
Now the disc of every sorrow joy shall circle with a halo,
As the sun hangs golden banners round the shadow of eclipse.

III.

Long within the soul, God's Temple, darkness, festooned, hung forbidding,
Draped the windows barred and leaden, draped the knarled and studded door;
While with fitful flare and flicker danced the Yule-light, hollow hearted
As wild Superstition, bowing, dancing on the stainéd floor.

IV.

Long the angry sparks sang "Hatred! Hate of Brother unto brother!"
Long the mistletoe was severed with a sacrificial knife
Sheathéd oft within the bosom of a hapless, human victim;
Telling of a hideous worship and the creed of life for life.

AT YULE-TIDE.   153

V.

But, at last, an oriel window set toward the hills of Morning,
Where with reverent brows uplifted pray the mighty peaks
    of Hope,
Thrilled with prescient thrills of glory as the Day-Star
    shone upon it,
Thrilled as thrills a parent watcher 'neath a blessed horo-
    scope.

VI.

Sudden dust, blown quickly downward, fell the rotten folds
    of darkness;
Through the oriel's veins, translucent, ran a ruby current
    mild;
Clusters there of roses blossomed, lilies swung their snowy
    censers
O'er a mother and a manger and the sweet face of a child.

VII.

All the Temple was transfigured, and a silent benediction
Fell on cedar, fell on holly, fell on pearl-strung mistletoe:
"God," they murmured, "and not Odin: Christ," they mur-
    mured, "and not Balder,"
And awed Superstition, kneeling, heard forgiveness whis-
    pered low.

VIII.

Swung the door upon its hinges, and the angels of God's
    Heaven
Straightway came within the Temple singing songs of holy
    cheer;
Sang they all of Jesus blessed, sang they of His peace eternal
Spanning all the broken earth-clouds like an emerald rainbow
    clear.

IX.

Stay, sweet angels, ever singing carols to the Lord and Savior,
Sing: "He oped the orient portals with a rosy, baby hand!"
Sing: "He suffered, more than martyr, marking earth with
    feet of sorrow
While, behind Him, joys and blessings bourgeoned in the
    desert land!"

CONCLUSION.

FIDE ET AMORE.

I.

Lord, we stand upon the margin of that ocean stretching outward
Far beyond the isles of Knowledge, far beyond the mount of Sight;
Only Love can hear its billows breaking on the shores Hereafter,
Only Faith can see Thy Heaven bathed in everlasting light.

II.

Then in this Thy dearest gift-time, when to us Thyself Thou gavest,
Give us Faith and Love to guide us, teaching us of Heaven and Thee;
Lest we fall to idle talking with Doubt, walking close beside us,
Lest we say, with him, "Hope never! All beyond is shoreless sea."

INGRAM CROCKETT.

AT DAWN OF DAY.

I HEARD the faint, sweet twitter of a bird,
Then all was hushed and quiet; and altho'
I hearkened with an ear intent, I heard
Naught else, save, gently waving to and fro,
The wind-swept leaves breathing soft lullaby.
Then presently on all the land there lay
A tender light that was nor night nor day;
The bird renewed his song, and murmurs broke
On the calm silence, as if all nature woke
And chanted orisons to the Most High.

VIRGINIA F. NOBLE.

TO-MORROW.

THE dying beams of setting sun
  Have touched the purple hills with fire,
And thro' the golden mists they've spun
  I see each village roof and spire;
And over where the cedarn trees
  Wrap up the earth in pungent gloom;
Where blue-flecked boughs wave in the breeze,
  I see a tinge of sunset's bloom,
And where the stream's clear waters run
  And flow on to the distant river
I see the faintest flame of sun
  Upon its wavelets fall and quiver;
It lingers here—it lingers there—
  It seems so bright—so loth to go—
Ah, well!—'tis thus with all things fair:
  We part with all we love below,
And tho' that parting gives us sorrow,
We live and love again—to-morrow.

Four years ago—four long, long years,
  We stood—we two—hand clasped in hand,
And watched with eyes filled full of tears
  The swift tide surging into land:
And as the bright waves broke and rolled
  Upon the yellow ribs of sand,
They shimmered with the sunset's gold,
  And cast their brightness on the strand;
And over rock and over shore
  They dashed their showers of pearl-white spray;
Again they turned—and yet, once more—
  Then to the deep sea flowed away.
To us they seemed full loth to go—
  And then it was he said to me:
"Dear, ere again they ebb and flow,
  Thus tinged with light to soundless sea"—

And here he sighed full drearily—
"Tho' numbered with the dead I be,
And you live on in nameless sorrow,
The tide will ebb and flow—to-morrow."

We two had met to say Farewell—
Had met there as the sun went down—
With hearts that on their every swell
    Pulsed more of love than lips might own.
I whispered low: "To part gives pain,
    And if to-morrow flows the tide
Why may not we return again,
    And stand, as now, dear, side by side?"
He smiled, yet lingered, loth to go—
    And said: "Within His awful palm
High God holds our frail lives below,
    We know not whence the storm or calm."
He spoke full well; we never know!
    We whirl like leaves in Autumn's blast,
And looking in dear eyes we know
    Not if that fond look be the last:
We parted then!—four years ago!
    I count the time with ceaseless sorrow,
For suns may set and seas may flow,
But Hope's dawn we will never know
    In Life's or Death's to-morrow!

NELLIE MARSHALL MCAFEE.

YON TINY STREAM.

My life is like yon tiny stream,
Flowing onward like a dream,
Where the meadow grasses grow
And the blue-bells brightly blow,
Softly singing, silver shining on its way,
Passing onward, swift and surely, day by day.

My life is like yon tiny stream,
Where the sunlit waters gleam,
On its wave the roses cast,
Sedge and willow gliding past,
Softly singing, silver shining on its way,
Passing onward, swift and surely, day by day.

My life is like yon tiny stream,
Rocks and brambles lost between,
Shadows brooding darkly there,
Gloom and silence everywhere—
Broken, moaning, sighing, sobbing on its way,
Groping blindly, searching for the light of day.

My life is like yon tiny stream,
Where the lightning flashes gleam,
Drops of rainfall, flakes of snow
Strike the waters like a blow,
World-forgotten, life-forsaken on its way
To the ocean and the light of perfect day.

MRS. JENNIE JONES CUNNINGHAM.

THE SWEETEST DAY.

It is not when the air is calm,
  The sky gleams softly white and blue,
And waters chant their low sweet psalm
  By maple banks of bending yew,
When flowers bloom with richest tint,
  And roses blush in wondrous pride,
And sunbeams on the grasses print
  A thousand dapples golden-eyed.

It is not when the noon is past,
  And all the green has turned to gray,
And like the sails of many a mast
  Clouds float on the air of day;
Nor when, like spirit of the night,
  The twilight in her purple gown
Moves softly o'er the day most bright
  And folds its gorgeous clouding down.

But oh! to me the sweetest day
  In any season of the year,
In dimpled spring or winter gray,
  Or autumn gold or dun or drear,
Is that fair day on whose white face
  No word or deed of mine can lie,
A cloud to gloom or stain its grace,
  This is the sweetest day to me.

JENNIE C. MORTON.

ANDALIA.

I.

Song, that did waken you,
Song, that had taken you,
Has not forsaken you;
　Still with the Spring
My mad and merriest
Part of the veriest
Season and cheeriest;
　You, who can bring
Airs that the birds have taught you;
Grace that the winds have brought you;
Mien that the lilies laughed you;
Thoughts that the high stars waft you—
　Are you a human thing?

II.

Dreams—are you aught of them?
You who are fraught with them;
You, like their thought, with them
　Beautiful too.
Life—you're a gleam of it;
Love—you're a dream of it;
Hope—you're a beam of it
　Bound in the blue
Gray of big eyes that are often
Laughter and languor; that soften
On to me sweetly and slowly
Out with your soul that is holy,
　So purer than dew.

III.

Face like the sweetest of
Perfumes, completest of
Flowers, God's fleetest of
　Months ever bear.
Sleep, who walk crisper, sleep,

Than the frost, lisper sleep,
Have you a whisper, sleep
  Soft as her hair?
Night and the stars did spin it;
Stars and the night are in it;
Let but one ray of it bind me,
And did the Fates blind me,
  Fair I should know her, fair!

IV.

Love—has it mated you?
Love, that has waited you,
Love, that was fated you
  Here for awhile.
Song, can you sing in me
Fuller, or bring in me
Peace, that will cling in me
  So through all trial
Such as her smile? like the morning's—
Fashioning luminous warnings,
Rose, of a passion unspoken;
Love, 't is your seal and its token—
  The light of her smile.

MADISON CAWEIN.

DEATH.

"Two travel-worn and weary feet—at rest
From paths of pain—now shrouded in the past;
Two cold hands folded on a colder breast
From whence the soul hath taken flight at last;
Two eyes from whose dark, vacant cells the glow
Of sunlight seems forever to have fled;
Two mute lips meeting like an unstrung bow
From which the final arrow, speech, hath sped—
This is the subtlest of all mysteries,
Some call it *Death*, and others name it *Peace*."

DANIEL F. O'SULLIVAN.

MADISON CAWEIN.

APRILLE.

She walked across the fields, ice-bound,
  Like some shy, sunny hint of spring,
And, stooping suddenly, she found
  A violet—a dainty thing,
Which shunned the chilly light of day
Until sweet "Aprille" came that way.

They knew each other, girl and flower;
  There was some subtile bond between
And I had walked, that very hour,
  The fields, and had no violet seen;
For me the winter landscape lay
All blossomless and bleak and gray.

They knew me not, blue flower, blue eyes;
  She, careless, passed me when we met;
The tender glance which I should prize
  Above all things, the violet
Received; and I went on my way
Companioned with the cheerless day.

From wintry days blue violets shrink;
  From wintry lives blue eyes will turn;
And yet if she, I sometimes think,
  Could smile on me with sweet concern,
One life so like this wintry day
Would spring-time be for aye and aye.

Harper's Monthly.   HARRISON ROBERTSON.

THE CHILD SINGER.

HE sang upon the dusty street,
  A little wandering minstrel boy,
A song of home, a song so sweet
  It checked the selfish look of joy
On many a face that passed his way,
Along the street one summer day.

I heard his heart-cry in his song
  For home, dear home beyond the sea;
His dark eye swept the heedless throng,
  His pleading tongue sang Italie;
His soul saw those he loved, and rang
In sighs along the songs he sang.

Yet we, that lecture in our halls
  Against the crime of servitude,
And hear, with pride, the voice that calls
  Us saviours of the multitude,
Will smile and call it classic art
To hear a song that breaks a heart.

The little souls that cry to God
  In prisoned song along the way,
They burn their hearts, where we have trod
  To be the pastime of a day;
In the Arena tyrants said,
"Bring in the beasts; drag out the dead."

          SALLIE MARGARET O'MALLEY.

THE OLD YEAR.

WHAT! Dying, did you say?
So soon! Why it seems but yesterday

We greeted the new-born in her christening gown,
When youth was her dower, hope was her crown.

With bright, joyous smiles life's course was begun;
Can it be, can it be, that course is now run?

Is the shroud now the mantle that suits her form best?
Must the hands be folded across her still breast?

Has the heart grown tired of traveling life's road?
Does the footstep falter because of its load?

Were pleasures too often followed by pain?
Or would it give pleasure to live life again?

The beauty of youth, the calmness of age,
Are they willingly left, as a bird leaves a cage?

Does it seem strange—the strangeness of dying—
Does it startle the soul, or still the soul's sighing?

Do the scythe and the Reaper come as in strife,
Or come they to comfort—to bring a new life?

And the river of death—is it chilly and deep,
Or only a lulling stream to rock gently to sleep?

Do the bier and the grave cause a smile or a tear?
Answer me, answer me, O dying year!

I pause, and I listen—am I unheard?
Speak to me! Speak to me! Speak but a word!

The barque is now ready, the tide's ebbing low—
Tell me, oh! tell me the things I would know!

* * * * * * * * * *

Silent! still silent! Ah! light be the tread,
Speak softly, speak lowly, the Old Year is—DEAD.

LIZZIE WALKER.

IN JUNE.

SOFT melodies that thrill with vague delight,
Faint dreamy sounds from far-off woodlands dim,
The reeds' low whisper by the brooklet's rim,
A wild bird singing from his shadowy height,
The sigh of leaves that winds have set in tune—
    These are thy gifts, O June!

Full well I know, beside the dark, blue streams,
How bend the wind-flowers in the tall, sweet grass,
How, 'mid the drooping boughs, cool shadows pass,
And thro' the vines the broken sunlight gleams
In the long stillness of thy drowsy noon—
    O tender, dreamy June!

How softly then the twilight gray and cool
Curtains with shining mists the sleeping flowers;
How, in the silence of the royal hours,
The stars are mirrored in the glassy pool,
And where the hills grow purple-dim thy moon
    Keeps mystic watch, O June!

ADELAIDE D. ROLLSTON.

THE FAITHFUL ENGINEER.

LIFE is like a crooked railroad,
   And the engineer is brave
Who can make a trip successful
   From the cradle to the grave;
There are stations all along it
   Where, at almost any breath,
You'll be "flagged" to stop your engine
   By the passenger of death.

You may run the grades of trouble
   Many days and years with ease,
But Time may have you "side-tracked"
   By the switchman of disease;
You may cross the bridge of manhood,
   Run the tunnel long of strife,
Having God for your conductor,
   On the "lightning train" of life.

Always mindful of instructions,
   Watchful duty never lack,
Keep your hand upon the throttle,
   And your eye upon the track.
Name your engine "True Religion,"
   When you're running, day or night,
Use the coal of "Faith" for fuel,
   And she'll always run you right.

You need never fear of "sticking"
   On the up-grades 'long the road,
If you've got "Hope" for a fireman
   You can always pull the load.
You will often find obstruction,
   By the cunning devil lain
On a fill, a curve, or some place
   Where he'll try to "ditch your train."

But you need n't fear disaster—
"Jerk her open"—"Let her go!"
For the King who ruleth all things
All his plans will overthrow.
Put your trust in God, the Savior,
Keep a-going—do n't look back—
Keep your hand upon the throttle
And your eye upon the track.

When you 've made the trip successful,
And you 're at your journey's end,
You will find the angels waiting
To receive you as a friend.
You 'll approach the Superintendent,
Who is waiting for you now,
With a blessed smile of welcome,
And a crown to deck your brow.

Never falter in your duty,
Put your faith and hope in Him,
And you 'll always find your engine
In the best of running trim.
Ring your bell and blow your whistle,
Never let your courage slack,
Keep your hand upon the throttle,
And your eye upon the track.

WILL S. HAYS.

NOËRA.

Noëra, when sad Fall
    Has grayed the fallow;
Leaf-cramped the wood-brook's brawl
    In pool and shallow;
When sober wood-walks all
    Strange shadows hallow:

Noëra, when gray gold
    And golden gray
The crackling hollows fold
    By every way,
Then shall these eyes behold,
    Dear bit of May?

When webs are cribs for dew,
    And gossamers
Long streaks of silver-blue;
    When silence stirs
One dead leaf's rusting hue
    Among crisp burs.

Noëra, in the wood
    Or mid the grain,
Thee, with the hoiden mood
    Of wind and rain
Fresh in thy sunny blood,
    Sweetheart, again?

Noëra, when the corn
    Reaped on the fields
Deep aster stars adorn
    With purple shields,
Defying the forlorn
    Decay death wields.

Noëra, haply then,
  Thou being with me,
Each ruined greenwood glen
  Will bud and be
Spring's with the Spring again,
  The Spring in thee.

Thou of the breezy tread,
  Feet of the breeze;
Thou of the sun-beam head,
  Heart like a bee's;
Face like a woodland-bred
  Anemone's.

Thou to October's death
  An April part
Bring, while she taketh breath
  Against Death's dart;
Noëra, one who hath
  Made mine a heart.

Come with our golden year,
  Come as its gold;
With thy same laughing, clear,
  Loved voice of old:
In thy cool hair one dear,
  Wild marigold.
                          MADISON CAWEIN.

UNCLE PETE'S PLEA.

'T was an old-time Southern darky,
   All withered and wrinkled and gray,
With the quaint and courteous manners
   Of a type fast passing away;
Convicted of robbing the hen-roost
   Of a neighbor the night before,
For the tracks in the snow discovered
   Led straight to his cabin door.

The Judge, as was his custom,
   His eye on the culprit cast,
And said: "Have you aught to say, Sir,
   Why sentence should not be passed?"
With a bow to the Judge, and the people
   Who had thronged the court-room to see,
Uncle Pete put his hat down behind him,
   And then he delivered this plea:

"'Does I hab eny thing to say,' Jedge,
   Yo' ax me, 'In my beha'f
Befo' yo' passes de sentence?'
   Why, Jedge, 't would meck dem all laugh
To see dis black ole nigger
   Stan' up heah, an' say he's say
Befo' all ub dese white folks,
   What's come to de co't to-day.

"But, Jedge, I sees I 's 'dited—
   I b'lieves dat's de way 't is said
In dat 'ar strip ob paper
   De gent'man befo' yo' has read;
Yes, suh, I sees I's 'dited,
   An' befo' de bar I stan'
For de stealin' ob some chickens
   Wid dis ole widered han'.

" For I is an ole, ole nigger,
    An' my leabin' time mos' has come;
So I's gwine to add no lyin'
    To de ebil I's 'ready done.
I 'knowle'ge I took dem chickens;
    I 'fess it wid 'fusion an' shame,
For I neber has done no stealin'
    Till dat tem'tation came.

" I wa' raised right, Jedge, I 'shure yo',
    For my folks wa' de bes' ob dar day;
An' dey fai'fully strobe wid deir darkies
    To bring dem up in de right way.
But, oh! 't is mighty rough libin',
    In dese days so hard an' so cole,
When you's got no good marster or missus
    To keer for yo' when yo' is ole.

" Dar's a little gran'daughter libs wid me,
    Her fadder an' mudder bofe dead;
De chile is puny an' sickly,
    An' long has been 'fined to her bed.
Las' night, as I sot by her bedside,
    She awoke from her sleep wid a cough,
An' 'Gran'dad,' sez she, 'I's been dreamin'
    Dat de angels had brought chicker-broth.'

" Den my ole eyelids 'gan to tremble,
    An' de big tears dropped down to my feet,
For I knowed dat de cubboard wuz empty,
    An' dar wuz nuffin' for de po' chile to eat;
An' dar wuz none to help in my trouble,
    For de folks I had knowed in my day,
War all ob 'em now dead an' buried,
    Or else dey had done moved away.

"'Yes, gran'dad, 't war brought by de angels;
    Dey sot it down heah 'tween us two.
Oh, I is so weak an' so hongry;
    How I wish dat my dream had been true!'

Den ober she turned on her piller,
   An' sank into slumber again;
While I stood dar weepin' an' gazin'
   On her form pinched wid honger an' pain.

"Den I think 't wa' de debil dat whispered,
   'Da'r' chickens dat's roostin' nigh;
Yo' kin coch 'em, an' dress 'em, an' stew 'em,
   'Fo' she wakes, Uncle Pete, ef yo's spry!'
An' I nebber stopped to lis'n
   To de warnin' voice widin;
But I stole out into de darkness—
   An', Jedge, I committed dat sin.

"I took from dar roost dose chickens;
   I sneaked dem into my home;
An' befo' dat little chile 'wakened
   Dat good chicken broth was done.
I took it, all steamin' an' 'licious,
   An' sot it down close by her side;
When she got a good whiff o' its fragrance,
   Her big brown eyes popped open wide.

"'Oh, de dream, it has come true, dear gran'dad!
   Fo' de angels dey brung it, I know.
When dey entered de room din yo' see dem?
   Had dey wings, as de picture-books show?'
Sez I: 'Little Honey, we mus n't
   Pry into sich mysturious things;
No, I did n't see de angels. I'm sartin
   Dat I did heah de rustlin' o' wings!'

"But dat's jes' de way wid de debil,
   Yo' trus' him an' he'll trick yo', dat's sho';
An' he done let dat light snow-fall happen
   Jes' to show dem tracks up to my do'.
So, as we sot dar so cheerful,
   De officers came to my home—
Dey came an' dey 'rested Ole Peter,
   An' dey lef' dat dyin' chile all alone."

Every eye in the court-room was moistened;
The Judge, with a tear on his face,
Said, "You're free, and can go, Uncle Peter;
I've decided to dismiss the case."
When out of the dock he shuffled,
And reached for his battered hat old,
Uncle Pete found he scarcely could lift it,
'T was so heavy with silver and gold.

JOSEPH ALLGOOD.

"WE FADE AS A LEAF."

ON the wings of a moment the summer flits by;
We gather its blossoms, they wither and die;
The leaves wave around us, then silently fall,
And the year is enwrapt in the shroud and the pall.

"We fade as a leaf"—wherever we stray
Time scattereth o'er us the seeds of decay;
Though the cordial of health in our veins may abound,
We are broken from life and fall to the ground.

"We fade as a leaf"—then let the rich wine,
The nectar of truth, our life in the vine,
Flow through us and make us so radiantly bright
That, fading, we fill all around us with light.

"We fade as a leaf"—but sure we shall feel
The life-giving touch of a hand that doth heal,
Wondrously glorified, tinged with no grief,
Nevermore after to fade as a leaf.

INGRAM CROCKETT.

TWO TRIOLETS.

I.

WHAT HE SAID.

THIS kiss upon your fan I press—
Ah! Sainte Nitouche, you do n't refuse it?
And may it from its soft recess—
This kiss upon your fan I press—
Be blown to you a shy caress,
By this white down, whene'er you use it.
This kiss upon your fan I press—
Ah! Sainte Nitouche, you do n't refuse it!

II.

WHAT SHE THOUGHT.

To kiss a fan!
What a poky poet!
The stupid man,
To kiss a fan,
When he knows that—he—can—
Or ought to know it—
To kiss a *fan!*
What a poky poet!

The Century. HARRISON ROBERTSON.

CUPID'S ARROW.

The little god stood at my door,
　Whom I had turned so oft away;
But Friendship's harmless guise he wore
　And sweetly stole my heart away.

Of all the masks that he can wear,
　Of all the pranks that he can play,
None better hide his fatal snares
　Than friendship—as I know to-day.

I could not think—I did not dream
　Of danger from my sober guest;
But gods, nor men, are what they seem—
　The arrow quivers in my breast.

Mrs. Jennie Jones Cunningham.

TIME.

What is time?　A priceless thing;
　Nor gems, nor gold,
Nor all the pleasures earth can bring,
　Or seas unfold,
Can tell its wondrous worth, or stay
The moments as they fleet away.
Time? 't is a swiftly gliding stream
　That bears us on
To the dark, lonely tomb—a dream
　Scarce told ere gone.
Mortal! a warning voice to thee—
The prelude to eternity.

Sarah Campbell Thornton.

LATE AFTERNOON IN NOVEMBER.

Woods, leafless, fringe the tawny fields
  With mingled black and gray;
The wind is as one walking through
  A tear-marked way.

O'erhead, on lazy, loitering wings,
  Against a far, cold sky,
With out-craned necks and mocking caws
  The crows flock by.

The tented regiments of corn
  Camp in the lowlands brown;
The sun drops hazily behind
  The smoke-wreathed town.

Now Quiet hushes with mute touch
  The whispering grasses tall,
Lest haply she should fail to catch
  Night's first footfall.

A bar of red gold gleams athwart
  The west, and groweth dim
And fades, and darkness overflows
  The twilight's brim.
              INGRAM CROCKETT.

ACROSS THE WAY.

Across the way her face I see, but dimly;
   'T is white and fair thro' mists of long-gone years;
Alas! to-day it only lives in mem'ry—
   In vain regrets and useless, bitter tears.

'T was years ago I saw her at the window,
   While autumn hours passed, all too fast, away;
Her eyes spoke love that ever was unspoken,
   Or voiced in needless words—across the way.

And it may be that in the fairer sometime,
   When earth's sad night has broken into day,
Her face I'll see, in smiling, tender greeting,
   Again, in sunnier lands—across the way.

ARCH POOL.

ANTITHESIS.

Death is like the lily,
   Life is like the rose;
The one awakes the soul to strife,
   The other grants repose.

And death in life it is
   To love—O bitter lot!—
To love thro' all one's days,
   And know we are forgot.

And life in death it is
   Nevermore to weep,
Only to lie down in the grave,
   And sleep—and sleep—and sleep.

NELLIE MARSHALL MCAFEE.

LIZZIE WALKER.

ENCELADUS.

I SHALL arise; I am not weak; I feel
A strength within me worthy of the gods—
A strength that will not pass in utter moans.

Ten million years I have lain thus, supine,
Prostrate beneath the gleaming mountain-peaks,
And the slow centuries have heard me groan
In passing, and not one has pitied me;
Yea, the strong gods have seen me writhe beneath
This mighty horror fixed upon my chest,
And have not eased me of a moment's pain.

Oh, I will rise again, I will shake off
This terror that outweighs the wrath of Jove!
Lo, prone in darkness I have gathered hope
From the great waters walking speaking by.
These unto me give mercy, thus foreshown:

"We are the servants of a mightier lord
Than Jupiter, who hath imprisoned thee;
We go forth at his bidding, laying bare
The sea's great floor and all the sheer abysms
That drop beneath the idle fathoms of man,
And shape the corner-stones, and lay thereon
The mighty base of unborn continents.
The old earth, when it hath fulfilled his will,
Is laid to rest, and mightier earths arise,
And fuller life, and liker unto God,
Fills the new races struggling on the globe.

"Profoundest change succeeds each boding calm,
And mighty order from the deep breaks up
In all her parts, and only night remains
With all her stars that minister to God,
Who sits sublimely shaping as he wills,
Creating always." These things do they speak.
"The mountain-peaks, that watch among the stars,

Bow down their heads and go like monks at dusk
To mournful cloisters of the under-world;
And then, long silence, while blind Chaos' self
Beats round the poles with wings of cloudy storm."

These things and more the waters say to me,
How this old earth shall change, and its life pass,
And be renewed from fathomless within;
How other forms, and likelier to God,
Shall walk on earth and wing the peaks of cloud;
How holier men and maids, with comelier shapes,
In that far time, when he hath wrought his plan,
Shall the new globe inherit, and like us
Love, hope, and live, with bodies formed of ours—
Out of our dust again made animate.

These things to me; yet still his curse remains,
His burden presses on me. God! thou God
Who wast before the dawn, give ear to me!
Thou wilt some day shake down like sifted dust
This monstrous burden Jove hath laid on me,
When the stars ripen like ripe fruit in heaven,
And the earth crumbles plunging to the void
With all its shrieking peoples. Let it fall!
Let it be sown as ashes underneath
The base of all the continents to be
Forever; if so rent I shall be freed!

Shall I not wait? Shall I despair now Hope
On the horizon spreads her dawn-white wings?
Ah, sometimes now I feel earth moved within
Through all its massive frame, and know his hand
Again doth labor shaping out his plan.
Oh, I shall have all patience, trust, and calm,
Foreknowing that the centuries shall bring
On their broad wings release from this deep hell,
And that I shall have life yet upon earth,
Yet draw the morning sunlight in my breath,
And meet the living races face to face.

The Century.   CHARLES J. O'MALLEY.

MARGERY.

The poem which follows here has a little history which may be
of interest. An argument was being carried on one evening in one
of the upper rooms of the *Courier-Journal* building between Mr.
O'Sullivan and some newspaper friends. It was the old subject—the
effect of attaching some well-known name to the work of some
unknown author, Mr. O'Sullivan contending that it would carry
it through—that it would be copied by the press for that reason.
Finally a wager was arranged. A fictitious interview with some noted
personage (an actress, I believe) was planned. The poem in ques-
tion was to be introduced as belonging to this person, having been
written for her by William Winter, and was to be reluctantly given
up to be printed as part of the supposed interview. All was carried
out as arranged. O'Sullivan wrote the poem, and introduced it in
due form, etc. It was published, and was extensively copied, as pre-
dicted, and Mr. O'Sullivan won his wager. Nevertheless, I do not
believe in it. I think the poem would have been copied on its own
merits alone. Most likely it was because of its merit that it was
copied, and not because a well-known name was signed to it. How-
ever, it is given here an honest presentation. It is a simple and
beautiful picture, and, considering how it was written—on the spur
of the moment (interview and poem were written within thirty min-
utes)—it is a very interesting performance, as showing what the
author could do under pressure. The subject is handled deftly and
daintily, and the artistic proprieties admirably preserved.

MARGERY came to the crowded town,
Into the busy, hurrying street;
She came from where the green fields meet,
And the apple blossoms are drifting down
To their beds in the clover sweet.

Pure as the lily which leans to her throat—
Look on her sculptured queenliness
And tell me, must I not confess
That never minstrel knew a note
Could picture half her loveliness?

How modestly her way she plies
Through all the crowd. I fain would swear
That Love walked with her everywhere;
It seemed that Cupid kissed her eyes
And nestled in her clustering hair.

Quick blushes came to her cheeks so brown
When I said a simple word of praise.
She heeded not, she went her ways,
She lifted not her eyes to crown
The rarest of my joyous days.

So Margery went from the crowded town,
Out of the busy, hurrying street,
Away to where the green fields meet,
And the apple blooms are drifting down
To their beds in the clover sweet.

DANIEL E. O'SULLIVAN.

CASTLES IN THE AIR.

Is it wise, I have wondered, to build them,
  Those castles so bright and so fair,
With nothing on earth to support them,
  The castles we build in the air?

They are lofty, magnificent structures,
  As grand as our fancies can build,
And their rooms are all filled with our treasures,
  Our hopes that may ne'er be fulfilled;

The dreams and the fond aspirations,
  The good deeds we think we will do,
All the last New Year's good resolutions,
  The heart secrets tender and true.

Ah, yes, let us build and enjoy them!
  Reality comes all too soon;
And if Time with his touch must destroy them,
  Let memory dwell in the ruin.

ALLINE BROTHER.

WORTHINESS.

WHATEVER lacks purpose is evil: a pool without pebbles
    breeds slime;
Not any one step hath chance fashioned on the infinite
    stairway of time;
Nor ever came good without labor, in toil, or in science or
    art;
It must be wrought out thro' the muscles—born out of the
    soul and the heart.

Why plow in the stubble with plowshares? why winnow
    the chaff from the grain?
Ah, since all of His gifts must be toiled for, since truth is
    not born without pain!
He giveth not to the unworthy, the weak, or the foolish in
    deeds;
Who soweth but chaff at the seed-time shall reap but a
    harvest of weeds.

As the pyramid builded of vapor is blown by his whirl-
    winds to naught,
So the song without truth is forgotten: His poem to Man
    is man's thought.
Whatever is strong with a purpose in humbleness wrought
    and soul-pure,
Is known to the Master of Singers: He toucheth it saying,
    "Endure."

CHARLES J. O'MALLEY.

A HAPPY WOMAN.

"I SHALL be happy!" she said,
As she gathered the poppies white and red;
"I will pull the blue grapes over the wall,
And sit in the shade and eat them all,
And count the butterflies, one by one,
As they fly along in the morning sun;
   I shall be happy!" she said.

"I shall be happy!" she said,
As they placed the orange-wreath on her head;
"Life will be lovely, and love will be true;
I shall drink the wine without the rue;
I will share my joy with the poor and sad,
And help to make the world more glad;
   I shall be happy!" she said.

"I shall be happy!" she said.
*   *   *   *   *   *   *
And they strewed white lilies over her—dead.
They closed the eyes and smoothed the hair,
And one who stood there dropped a tear;
They folded the hands on the quiet breast—
Poor empty hands—and what was the rest?
   "And she was happy," I said.

EUGENIA PARHAM.

WHERE THE BEAUTIFUL RIVER.

WHERE the Beautiful River smooth wanders along,
Lives the maid that I love, the theme of my song,
Her eyes are as bright as sunbeams in rain,
And light is her heart as the spray on the main.

When twilight comes forth and mellows the hour,
Away speeds the maid to gather the flower,
Which in the bright vale in its earliest bloom,
Gently throws on the air its fragrant perfume.

Her ringlets of gold sweetly wave in the air,
As if glad that they hung 'round a bosom so fair,
Her cheeks are like roses that bloom in the Spring,
Her step is as light as a bird on the wing.

Her tones are as sweet and her fancy as free,
As the wild forest bird, or the bird of the sea,
And oft has she told me her soul's only dream
When she dies is to sleep by Ohio's bright stream.

Then Beautiful River, as onward you roll,
Let no darkling murmurs arise from your soul,
But ever as now let your mirroring tide,
Flow gently when Laura shall sleep by your side.

ALEXANDER EVANS.

HOW SPRING COMES IN THE BLUEGRASS.

MARCH lions ramping, with snow-brindled manes,
Leap with the storm along the airy floors
Whereon the mad winds roll, and with loud roars
  Bound, with soft-padded feet, across the plains—
  Sere from the frost and beaten by the rains—
Denting the tufted grasses by the shores
Of shuddering, shallow pools which dot the moors;
  Wherefrom, in driven loops, like hurtling chains,
  Scared birds swift-wing'd outfly the speeding gale.
The battling clouds, above the woodlands gray,
  Flaunting dim banners, pass in hurrying flight
Like some tumultuous dream. A nightly wail
Comes from the writhing trees; and, far away,
  The billowy landscape meets the coming night.

  And when night comes—behold! the winds are still!
Like floating mountains the great clouds divide
And in the space, with one star at her side,
  Floats the bright-mantled moon. The dripping hill
  Looms in dark silence, and the little rill,
Pleased with its own soft music, threads the wide
Faint-glimmering lands where broad cloud-shadows glide,
  Changing the features of the fields at will.
The fields—they may be bare or matted deep
With tawny grasses, brown with weeds, or green
  With winter wheat; or lands whereon they fling
The weathering hemp, or maize-camps, fast asleep—
All, now, are blent in one fantastic scene
  Made for the moonlight's noiseless reveling.

  The moonlight's noiseless revel! Does she know—
You princess of the ever-changing sky,
Floating serene amidst the clouds on high—
  That, where the woven shadows come and go
  Among fine-lacing twigs, and on the flow

HOW SPRING COMES IN THE BLUEGRASS.

Of chilly streams, while the slow night goes by,
There is uplifted many a tearful eye?—
Pale blooms, close-nestled in the dappled snow,
Fair woodland spirits, tremulous and frail,
 Clad in soft garb—in timid loveliness
Through dead leaves peeping, and by rugged rocks;
Ill can they bear the unfriendly time, the shocks
And buffets of the storms, the ruthless hail,
 The whirling snows and drenchings merciless.

The whirling snows! With morning comes the sun,
Spangling the air and earth with glinting spears;
From emerald knolls the white vail disappears,
 And merrily the snow-fed rillets run
Their sparkling, transient courses. One by one
The deeper streams grow loud with song that cheers
The listening vales; the preening field-lark hears,
 And pipes for joy of days not yet begun.
Uncertain are the skies; precarious mirth
 Rings from the drying thickets; on the peach,
Whose pink buds bloomed amidst the falling snows,
The robin tries his note; far off the crows
Call down through films which float from the moist earth
 Towards the blue, which they will never reach.

Towards the flashing blue—the crystalline,
Unfathomable sea of dazzling light
Where rides the sun. Soon are they vanished quite,
 And only winds, low-breathing, intervene
'Twixt the miraculous heavens and the scene
Of earth's enchantments. Every moment's flight
Brings the immortal wonder of life's might;
 Within the hour the banks are tinged with green.
One knows not how it came; a quickening flame
Stole past the woodland, down yon slope of gray
 Among the russet leaves. Anon, there came,
Though all was silent there but yesterday,
 Soft-echoing by the stream, a carol clear—
The bluebird's note! 'T is past, the Spring is here.

ROBERT BURNS WILSON.

TO A PIN.

At the fancy dress ball given at the Athletic Club many beautiful women congregated. One in particular attracted general attention, not only by the historical accuracy of her costume, but by the rare charm of her face and form. Her shoulders and her throat gleamed like polished marble. She was physically perfect, but across her bust was a long and angry pin scratch, as if Pygmalion had, in a fit of temper, drawn his sharpest chisel across Galatea's bosom. The incident was sufficient to drive *The Critic's* poet to a production of the following lament:

I.

WHY, luckless wight,
Didst thou indite
Upon her bosom white and fair,
In thy carouse,
Such carmine vows,
And leave thy words forever there?

II.

Upon the brink,
(If pins do think)
Thou viewed that virgin page below,
As if to say,
"I'll plow my way
Across that trackless waste of snow."

III.

Thou might have crept,
And softly slept
Upon her breast, her heart above—
But, saints anoint!
Thou turned the point
Of thy poor joke against thy love.

IV.

O foolish pin!
Thou can not win
Thy love by such caresses;

To win the prize,
The swain who's wise,
His passion suppresses.

V.

Farewell, fool pin,
Thy mortal sin
Can not be lightened by a laugh—
And yet, and yet,
I can't forget
How well thou wrote thy autograph.

DANIEL E. O'SULLIVAN.

THE KISS I STOLE.

A RONDEAU.

THE kiss I stole when Mary closed her eyes
(The day was hot beneath those Southern skies)
And sat there dreaming 'neath a great pine tree,
Her dark brown curls the Gulf wind blowing free,
I treasure yet, a memory—and a prize;
She sought from me her feelings to disguise
(But showed too plain a sense of glad surprise),
And blushed me welcome to the kiss, did she—
    The kiss I stole.

A memory only I may idolize,
For Mary no more glads me with her eyes;
Oh! no, her sweet smiles are no more for me;
She's married, and her husband—a clever fellow he—
Owns all and guards them well—except one prize—
    THE KISS I STOLE.

JO. A. PARKER.

HIS BIRDS.

I.

How doth He shelter them, His birds
That call among the brakes and fens
At twilight when the snowy herds
   Stray down within the hollow glens?
     Ah, whither do they rest
     When, from the stormy west,
   Fierce-blown the flakes are hurled
   Like ashes across the world,
Covering the earth and every helpless thing?
   Do they cower with piteous wing
   Under the leaves that rattle in the sleet?
     Or grasp with cold, bare feet
The swaying branches of the forest trees
That all night moan regretful threnodies?
Snowy and bent is every leaf and stem:
   Where doth He shelter them?
How doth He shelter them, His birds?
     Lo! now it is the night!
     The woods are spongy white;
     The twilight crofts are still;
Frozen the little stream below the hill,
That sang thro' summer all His poet-words;
     Stark-stiff the marsh-pool lies
     Gazing with icy eyes
Up to the hurrying clouds that ride in troops;
     Lost in the blinding snow
     The shelterless cattle low
Over the bleak, bare fields in shivering groups;
Nature her gates hath shut on Day's vast brim,
And great Night sits perched on Dusk's blue rim—
   Where doth He shelter them?

II.

As one who from a lighted chamber goes
   Suddenly out seeth nought but darkness quite,

HIS BIRDS.

Later beholds across the lifting snows
   All things take shape in a serener light;
So, when the heart walks outward from base glare
      Into a purer air,
Shot is the arrowy soul thro' planes of vaster height,
And things before unseen themselves to us disclose.
   How doth He shelter them? Behold,
Housed 'neath its roof, the brook with life sings warm
Under its ice, shut from the whirling storm;
   The timid rabbit, trembling with the cold,
At twilight creeps into his nest of weeds;
      Under his thatch of reeds
And warm marsh-grasses steals the shivering hare;
The sleek, brown field-mouse silent doth repair
Under the grass-tufts and the hillocks bare;
Yule-nuts the squirrel cracks within his oak,
Like a rough yeoman with his jest and joke,
By the last embers of the smouldering year,
Sitting a-gossip with his nuts and beer,
   Drunk with the music of the dripping eaves.
Nothing of His doth He leave shelterless,
   None whom His pity seeks not and relieves;
      Behold,
      Out of the storm and cold,
The warm-fleeced sheep are gathered in a fold
   Under His beechen boughs; in quietness
The patient kine lie sheltered in a croft,
      While the thick snows aloft
Are whirled in gusts to the adjacent hill,
Where now the garments of the dusk hang chill
And dim in the pale splendor of a day
Poured from the peaks of morn on twilight's vestments
   gray.
Nothing of His does He leave shelterless;
   Even the toads have holes wherein to bide;
By nooks and crofts in the white wilderness
   He spreadeth couches on the bare hillside
      Where his wild flocks may lie;
      Shall then His pitying eye

Unseeing pass those humblest watchers by
Who trust and wait His coming patiently,
   When the white feet of Light
With slow steps walk the hill-tops silently,
   And from the mournful north
   The sexton winds start forth
Plowing black graves thro' the swart sands of Night!

III.

Nothing so low but His care reacheth it,
Mild as a day-flush on eve's twilight rim.
Groping in darkness, stained of soul, unfit,
Oft clasp we hands unknowingly with Him,
   And He doth lead us in
Out of the snow-gusts to His shepherd tents
That lowly rise 'yond the high domes of Sin,
Unseen at dusk by our thick eyes of sense:
In reverence knock; the Master waits within;
O Soul! my Soul! go out in thy distress
And seek His tents, and rest in lowliness!
Beneath thick clouds that overhang the plain,
Between white gusts that seek the broken pane
In yon poor hut where shivering Poverty
Stirs his last coals, I look and see again
Visions of warmth, such as they fail to see
Whose bleeding feet touch not life's high Gethsemane:
Under the warm ricks and the byres
That lie a-field, white with the frost's keen fires,
In hedges, hay-mows, fodder shocks that stand
Like ghosts thick-dotted on the broad, white land,
Or housed in barns beneath the roof's great boards,
Robins and linnets, birds of snow in hordes,
Or warm in grass-tufts where the snows fall dim,
Fill they those homes which He hath ordered them,
Thatched with His care which shields night's bitter cold:
   Thus doth His love enfold
All things of His that life hath upon earth.

CHARLES J. O'MALLEY.

MY LUTE SO LOVED IS NOW UNSTRUNG.

My lute so loved is now unstrung,
    Its music tones have fled,
The plaintive air that once it sung—
    That touching air is dead.
No fingers round its cords entwine
    To wake the charming strain,
The hand that once had touch divine
    Can not that touch regain.

If then my lute is silent now,
    And tuneless hangs in hall,
Let her who wears the marble brow
    Our fondest love recall.
When maiden shall her first love own,
    To former vows be true,
My heart shall grace a royal throne,
    My lute be strung anew.

Then lute and maid, a fond adieu,
    Our morning love was bright,
But ere the twilight wept its dew,
    Our hopes were veil'd in night.
If on the shore beyond the grave,
    Our souls shall meet again,
Beside the lake, life's silver wave,
    We'll weld love's broken chain.

                    ALEXANDER EVANS.

A THOUGHT.

I HEARD a little maiden call
　Her pretty pigeons three,
"Reality, and snowy Art,
　And sweetest Poetry."

"Reality" flew to her hand;
　"Art" found a golden rest
Amid her curls; while "Poetry"
　Was clasped unto her breast.

* * * * * * *

I clasp hands with *Reality;*
　My head bows down to *Art;*
While *Poetry* is fondly clasped
　Forever to my heart.

MRS. W. LESLIE COLLINS.

VANISHED.

WHEN suddenly there passes from your sight,
　And from the life around you, some sweet face
　Which you have looked to as the ideal grace
Of your best being, and the guiding light
Of each and every common day and night,
　By which to measure your ambition's pace,
　Your soul's high aims, your hopes for nobler ways,
Your love of truth, your purer sense of right
　And better faith in men; and when missed so,
You realize that, as the years unfold,
　You shall not greet it in the ebb and flow
Of all the human faces, nor behold
　It in your loneliest hour, then you may know
How great a void so small a world may hold.

EUGENIA PARHAM.

A KENTUCKY TWILIGHT.

I.

TAWN as the yellow gold
Cheeks of the panther
Stormeth the restless flame
Of the great twilight
Under the oak boughs.
Horses neigh and plunge,
Cattle low and call,
Sheep in the dusk outbleat
On the deep meadows,
Children laugh and cry,
Voices rise and fall,
Heard, thro' the gray dusk
In the white village,
Over which lean the stars
Like pale maidens,
While the moon rushes on
Over the steep roofs.

II.

Thick, on the quiet hills
Eastward out-kneeling,
Gather the purple leaves
Under the nightfall;
Carols the little wren,
Twitters the red-bird,
Low pipes the russet quail
On the dark upland,
And the brown robin
Hymns to the twilight fields
Of late November;
Purpler the hills become,
Slower the streams run on,
Dusker the valleys,
And on the shocks of maize,
Dotting the lowland,
Like a brown garment loosed
Falleth the darkness.

III.

Now like a purple flame
Under the oak boughs
Hushed are the meadow-fields
In the gray nightfall—
Silent the pastures.
Far in the village
Lamps like red stars gleam out
From the deep windows,
Pendulous icicles
Under the shadowy eaves
Gossip and gabble,
While, a great sheaf of gold
Blown thro' the heaven,
On flies the rushing moon
Over the house-tops.

CHARLES J. O'MALLEY.

Round Table.

A SONG.

A BIRD sang in the orchard trees,
  Sang every nodding flower awake,
  Sang on as if its heart would break:
The music rippled down the breeze,
  And laughed across the clover bloom,
  And seemed to bring the sweet perfume.

Within the shadows, on my wall,
  Imprisoned in a golden cell,
  Another bird sang just as well:
It answered every joyous call
  And flooded all the house with song
  In mellow measures—loud and long.

Ah!—longing—still seem echoing
The gladdest songs that Joy can sing.

DANIEL E. O'SULLIVAN.

I SHALL FIND REST.

"A LITTLE further on—
There will be time—I shall find rest anon:"
Thus do we say, while eager youth invites
Young hope to try her wings in wanton flights,
And nimble Fancy builds the soul a nest
On some far crag; but soon youth's flame is gone—
Burned lightly out—while we repeat the jest
With smiling confidence, "I shall find rest
A little further on."

"A little further on
I shall find rest"—half-fiercely we avow,
When noon beats on the dusty field, and Care
Threats to unjoint our armor, and the glare
Throbs with the pulse of battle, while life's best
Flies with the flitting stars: the frenzied brow
Pains for the laurel more than for the breast
Where Love soft-nestling waits. Not now, not now,
With feverish breath we cry, "I shall find rest
A little further on."

"A little further on
I shall find rest"—half-sad, at last, we say,
When sorrow's settling cloud blurs out the gleam
Of Glory's torch, and to a vanished dream
Love's palace hath been turned, then—all depressed,
Despairing, sick at heart—we may not stay
Our weary feet, so lonely then doth seem
This shadow-haunted world. We, so unblest,
Weep not to see the grave which waits its guest;
And feeling round our feet the cool, sweet clay,
We speak the fading world farewell and say:
"Not on this side, alas!—I shall find rest
A little further on."

ROBERT BURNS WILSON.
The Century.

THE MODERN TITHONUS.

THE rose that blessed the balmy air of June
  Is but a fragrant reminiscence now,
The leaf that mocked the sultry summer noon
  With grateful shade has fallen from the bough;
But oh! the blood is warm, the heart is young,
And still of all the songs the sweetest are unsung.

For Love is Love, although the roses fall,
  And lips are luscious, though the leaf be dry,
And still my voice unto thy cheek can call
  Its crimson flush, although the summer die:
Then let it die! so thou and I can live,
And I have aught to ask, and thou have aught to give.

The Past is Past, the Future is not yet;
  To-day we are—let that content us, Sweet;
The wild winds roar! aye, let them sob and fret,
  While I lie prostrate at thy dainty feet,
And still consume thy love in my great need,
And feed on thee, and hungrier grow the more I feed.

The rose of Spring blooms for me on thy cheek,
  The balmy breath of May is in thy sigh;
Thy arms are soft as June, and who would seek
  A sweeter summer than thy melting eye
Bestows upon him! Oh! my Love, my Life,
Thou art my Spring, my Summer; thou, my bride, my
    wife!

J. SOULE SMITH.

A MADONNA.

She does not dwell in sheltered nook apart,
  In gloomy cloister or cathedral shade,
Where priest and people come with prayer and song
  To do her homage or implore her aid.

Nor from the wayside shrine look helpless down,
  As rolls along the sad, salt tide of life,
Bathing her hallowed feet with bitter tears,
  Filling her ears with sounds of hopeless strife.

Nor does she stand in calm and perfect grace,
  Where eager pilgrims crowd from every clime,
The rare fulfillment of a poet's dream—
  Immortal Beauty wed with Art divine.

She is a woman, one whose heart is filled
  With love of her own kind, whose simple creed
Holds pure uprightness in her daily life,
  And help, where'er she may, for others' need.

Meekly she serves, nor does her right hand e'er
  Unto the left its mission blest reveal;
Humility, like green about a flower,
  But makes the fairer what it would conceal.

Her shrine is in our hearts, which she hath healed;
  Ever our love and prayers like incense rise,
And bear a tribute to this holy soul,
  Where it at last must dwell, beyond the skies.

And so she treads the world's most crowded ways—
  Hands strong to help, eyes quick to see, its needs;
And so we praise and bless her evermore,
  Our Lady of Kind Words and Gentle Deeds.

Patty Blackburn Semple.

GEORGE MOORE.*

Down where the waters of the Golden Gate
  Kiss San Francisco's story-haunted shore,
With wail as dreary as his mournful fate,
  Doth sleep the pride of rugged Amador.

When on his brow the cruel hand of Death
  Did leave that summer night his impress pale,
His ermine was, until his latest breath,
  As spotless as the robe of mighty Hale.

And his big heart as gentle as the boy's
  Whose childish lips have never breathed his name—
That heart that felt for others' griefs and joys,
  And loved the right far more than wealth and fame.

Great Matthew Hale! Aristides the Just!
  I bare my head before you both,
But yet I dare to tell you, mighty dust!
  You did no grander thing than he whose oath

To be an upright judge did lead him on,
  Through fields of honor, to an early grave;
From lofty place, by splendid genius won,
  To rest beside the most ignoble slave

That e'er was food for worms. He spurned the gold
  Laid at his feet by devilish tempter hands;
He lived, he died with honor yet untold,
  And now he sleeps 'neath fair Pacific sands,

That are not whiter than his soul. O stricken ones,
  That weep for him an hundred times a day,
You oft have seen those daily dying suns
  That live again with morning's earliest ray.

*A native of Kentucky; a Judge of the Supreme Court of California; assassinated August, 1884.

Take solace from the lesson, night is now—
But night must fade and morning soon must break,
And then will come a day for such as thou,
When sorrowing hearts shall ever cease to ache.

San Francisco, thou of Asis! thou
Whose feet the paths of endless penance trod,
Whose pious lips did waft on high a vow,
That all who asked it for the love of God

Should have thy blessed care, guard tenderly
The well-loved ashes of our vanished friend
In their long sleep beside the Western Sea,
Which seems to moan o'er his untimely end.

And thou, the Saint upon whose natal day
I write for love these poor memorial lines,
Is not this the saddest, tell me, pray,
The saddest and the oddest of all Valentines?

STUART MURRAY.

YESTERDAY.

AT dawn a white-sailed vessel touched the pier,
  Laden with gold and jewels rare for me;
All day she lay in port, but in the clear,
  Calm even with her gems she put to sea.

And mingling with a fleet, with bitter tears
  I see her white tops glimmer far away,
Sailing across the sea of wasted years,
  And know my gems are lost fore'er and aye.

W. H. FIELD.

THE CRICKET.

A CHRISTMAS IDYL.

I.

WHERE the wild rose dangles
 O'er the half-hid brook;
Where the fisher angles,
And the white perch wrangles
And tangles
 In the coil about the hook;
As the twilight closes,
And the bosky roses
 Blossom sweeter round the nook;
And the moonlight, dreaming moonlight,
Points the tardy rising June night—
Comes the spider from his web,
Hums the bee into the hive,
Flows the hawk across the sky,
Glows the fire-fly in the grass,
Hies the swallow home to roof,
Sighs the gray frog in the marsh,
Creeps the brook rat from his lurk,
 And the nook bat from her den—
Oh, there tinkles, tinkles, tinkles!
Chirp! Chirp! Chirp!
One jolly, unseen visitor,
 In the thicket
 By the wicket—
  Cricket! Cricket! Cricket!
  Chirp! Chirp! Chirp!

II.

When the noisy kettle
 Sings, like a humming bug,
And the kittens settle
 Close in the hearth-hold rug—

THE CRICKET.

        When the faggots sparkle,
        And the corners darkle,
        And the wainscot panels,
        (Full of mice and annals)
        Do begin a cricking,
        Like the clock a-ticking,
        And the low of cattle,
        And the tattling rattle
        On the pane—and prattle
Of the little ones in cozy chairs close by the chimney lug—
        Come a thousand unheard voices,
        With these mellow, snow-sent noises,
        Mingling with our Christmas fancies,
        As we dream of old romances,
        In the days of sighs and dances,
        Ere we were thus one and snug;
        But above them each and all,
        Thrills that fireside Christmas call,
        For from chimney, hearth and wall,
          Sings the cricket, cricket, cricket,
          Chirp! Chirp! Chirp!
        As by wicket,
        Under thicket,
                Cricket! Cricket! Cricket!
                Chirp! Chirp! Chirp!

                            HENRY WATTERSON.

IN THE AIR.

Who is it singing, a maid or lover,
  Waifs of a song so near?
Form of no human can I discover,
  Whose is the voice I hear,
Sudden as laughter, as clear and strong,
Bantering the birds for a burst of song?

Is it some sprite of the waterfall,
  Some spirit the warm wind frees,
Ranging the bounds of the forestwall,
  Joying among the trees,
Under concealment of reed and vine,
Charming the dwellers of oak and pine?

Is it a Peri, some fair outcast,
  Mantled in pink and gold,
Vailed in yon cloudlet just floated past,
  Filling with memories old,
Chanting, as idly the airship strays,
Dreamful refrains of her Eden-days?

April it is! As the soft air clears,
  Sweet is the joy of her,
Tripping as wont down the columned years,
  Setting earth's heart astir,
Making the woods and the welkin ring,
Filled with the praises of God and spring!

RUFUS J. CHILDRESS.

THE LEVEL AND THE SQUARE.

WE MEET UPON THE LEVEL, AND WE PART UPON THE
    SQUARE—
What words of precious meaning those words Masonic are!
Come, let us contemplate them; they are worthy of a
    thought—
With the highest and the lowest and the rarest they are
    fraught.

We meet upon the level, though from every station come,
The king from out his palace and the poor man from his
    home;
For the one must leave his diadem without the Mason's
    door,
And the other finds his true respect upon the checkered
    floor.

We part upon the square, for the world must have its due;
We mingle with its multitude, a cold, unfriendly crew;
But the influence of our gatherings in memory is green,
And we long, upon the level, to renew the happy scene.

There's a world where all are equal—we are hurrying to-
    ward it fast—
We shall meet upon the level there when the gates of death
    are past;
We shall stand before the Orient, and our Master will be
    there
To try the blocks we offer by His own unerring square.

We shall meet upon the level there, but never thence de-
    part;
There's a Mansion—'t is all ready for each zealous, faithful
    heart;
There's a Mansion and a welcome, and a multitude is there,
Who have met upon the level and been tried upon the
    square.

Let us meet upon the level then while laboring patient
   here—
Let us meet and let us labor, though the labor seem se-
   vere;
Already in the western sky the signs bid us prepare
To gather up our working tools and part upon the square!

Hands 'round, ye faithful Ghiblimites, the bright fraternal
   chain;
We part upon the square below to meet in Heaven again.
Oh! what words of precious meaning these words Masonic
   are—
WE MEET UPON THE LEVEL, AND WE PART UPON THE
   SQUARE!

ROBERT MORRIS.

TO POESY.

SWEET POESY! divinest of the arts
   Which man has framed to soothe his restless soul,
   When genius weds with thee and takes control,
Thou by most potent spells doth bind all hearts;
And when thou fliest far thy shining darts,
   Be their alighting near to either pole,
   Where liveth not so cold and dense a soul
But thou to it some heart-warm heat imparts,
   Kindling therein some smothered sense of beauty,
Awakening mind and heart to emulate
   The grand achievements of his fellow-men,
   And cause him wish to see arise again
The trenchant thoughts and deeds which make men great
   And raise their souls to more ennobling duty.

HOWARD MILLER.

MARBLE HEART.

[MARCO AND RAPHAEL.]

"I've gazed upon thy matchless grace,
The peerless beauty of thy face,
    Dear Marco fair,
    With golden hair
And luster beaming from your eyes
That vie in shadow with the skies."

"And I too, Raphael, often sigh,
Darling one, when thou art nigh,
    I know not why,
    Unless 't is I
Am like a statue in thy eyes—
A statue that you will despise."

"Aye, I would bow at beauty's shrine
If I could call Queen Marco mine;
    But I 'll go home
    And live alone.
Marco, we should dwell apart;
They say you have a marble heart."

"Then fare thee well, brave King of Hearts;
Our lives are filled with phantom starts—
    'T is gold I crave,
    And gold I 'll have;
Go chisel on your statue—arts—
The world is full of marble hearts."

"Aye, Marco, I would die for thee,
And from this mental trouble free,
    Oh! Marco fair,
    With golden hair,
A light to me from heaven gleams;
I leave the statue of my dreams."

                        ALICE HAWTHORNE.

WEDDING BELLS.

WEDDING bells! wedding bells!
Now their merry, silvery chime
Seems to tell of naught but gladness;
How it wakens into rhyme
All that's fairest, all that's brightest,
All that's tend'rest, all that's best,
All that's dearest, all that's truest
In the heart within our breast.

Wedding bells! wedding bells!
What a soft and rosy haze,
What a rainbow-tinted glamour
Cast they o'er our coming days!
Life seems all one summer garden—
Endless bloom without decay;
Grief and care but empty shadows
That a breath can trace away.

Wedding bells! wedding bells!
Oh! how broad the path appears,
Flower-crowned and bright with sunshine,
Down the mystic vale of years!
And the thorns amid the roses,
And the rocks we fain must meet,
Know no terrors, and detain not
Our unwearied, untried feet.

Wedding bells! wedding bells!
Must their echoes die away?
Must the clamor and the tumult
Of life's still advancing day
Drown the sweetness and the music
Of their distant, gladsome chime,
Break the charm and pierce the brightness
Of our early morning time?

WEDDING BELLS.

Must the slowly dawning wisdom
  Of the ever-passing years
Bring to eyes unknown to weeping
  Dreary shadows, bitter tears,
As we catch the saddened cadence
  As it rises, as it swells,
That is mingled with the chiming
  Of the bells—the wedding bells?

Wedding bells! wedding bells!
  Is there nothing that survives
Of the beauty and the freshness
  Of the morning of our lives,
Nothing that when youth has left us,
  And our heads are bowed and gray,
We can claim of all the brightness
  That shone o'er our bridal day.

Ah! we know our steps shall falter,
  And our sparkling eyes grow dim,
Hope shall fade and Death shall gather
  Many dear ones unto him;
But within our hearts, perennial
  In its beauty, ever dwells
Love, the changeless, the immortal,
  Of the bells—the wedding bells.

Love! the burden and the cadence
  Of their ever joyous strain,
Sometimes faint; but in its fullness
  Do we catch the sweet refrain
When, the tumult and the striving
  Of life's noonday conflict past,
Battle-scarred, we turn our faces
  To the evening shades at last?

Wedding bells! ah, then, all golden
  Shall the mighty touch of Time
Wake the ever growing brightness
  Of their chime—their silvery chime,

Golden with the fair effulgence
Of that holy, heavenly place,
Where in all His dazzling glory
We shall see God "face to face."

CLARA L. MCILVAIN.

AS IN THE LONG AGO.

SWEETHEART, I love thee still, as when
Amid the flowers and showers of June,
We strolled through many a shaded glen,
And climbed o'er many a rugged hill,
Or praised the silvery beauty of the moon,
Which threw its light—
A shower of star-rays scattered free
Upon the waters wide and white—
Upon the dear old Tennessee.
* * * * * *
Still flowers bloom and showers fall;
The hills and glens have shade for all—
The silvery summer moon is still as rare
As when it crowned you with its halo fair.
The star-beams light the Tennessee;
All, all are there—save only me.
But still I dream of dear old Yore—
Of flowers and showers and shade—and more—
And still I tear in my impatient way
The thick'ning veil of gray old Time away.
Once more I stroll beside the Tennessee
In Paradise, my Southern maid, with thee!

JO. A. PARKER.

MATTIE PEARSON SMITH.

THE IMMORTAL THREE.

'T IS thought by many to this day
That spirits, disembodied, may
Revisit scenes below at will
Throughout the world and—Louisville.
The thought is dear to every one
That we poor mortals, as we run,
Are watched and tended on our way
By loved ones who have passed away.

In this connection I have dreamed
Of things that to my memory seemed
As clear as if they'd surely passed
Before my eyes, and never asked
To have them fully verified
By evidence from o'er the tide
Which separates this world of ours
From that where dwell diviner powers.

It seems to be my pleasing fate
To have such dreams quite oft of late.
The other day, in musing mood,
I dreamed an angel near me stood—
(Or something of angelic kind,
For it had little wings behind);
He, tipping me a smile and bow,
I asked of him, "What news hast thou?"

He said he'd been to Saturn sent
On mission of some high portent;
But, having thirty minutes leisure,
He'd dropped around this way for pleasure.
From what he'd heard of it—the Earth—
He thought it full of joy and mirth,
He said, though he had ne'er before
Set foot upon its beauteous shore.

His talk I could with ease distinguish
(The language taught up there is English)—
Long time ago the language used
Was quite mixed up, and much confused
With Dutch, and French, and Welsh, and Greek;
But Shakespeare taught them all to speak
By trumpet, wire, and telephone,
The grand old Anglo-Saxon tone.

I asked him if he knew Shakespeare—
The one who one time lived down here?
At mention of that name he spake,
And, reaching out his hand, said: "Shake?
I know him well—have heard him talk
Of this great actor, of that 'gawk;'
And since he's been in realms above
He's ne'er forgotten his first love."

He said a court had lately sat,
A sort of high commission, at
Which Shakespeare, Goethe and Lord Byron
(That all-bewitching earthly siren)—
Had full instructions to report
As to which actor this high court
Gave greatest fame—who'd had no peers
Within the current hundred years.

The claims of Couldock were discussed:
In him they all held quite high trust.
When Byron named young Billy Florence
Applause came down in perfect torrents.
John Owens, too—old ducky dear!—
Was praised quite warmly by Shakespeare;
But when it came down to the test
No one could show which was the best.

They argued long, both *pro* and *con*,
As to which actor they'd place on
The royal badge of "First in Art."
So well had each one "played his part"

That Shakespeare, who was in the chair,
Arose and said he thought it fair,
As they could not on one decide,
To "move" the honors to divide.

This grand commission then arose,
As their proceeding neared its close.
When Shakespeare spoke—the mighty chief—
They all joined him in his belief,
That Owens, Couldock, and young Florence
Should each one hold their royal warrants
That none of them have had their peers
In mimic art these hundred years.
OLIVER LUCAS.

TO ADELINA PATTI.

I'VE seen the empress of a summer's night,
  Swinging her amber censer up and down,
And all so lavish was her regal light
  The diamond splendor of the stars did drown;
While shower on shower of moonlight rare
Made every changing current of the air
Rich with the treasure trembling in its hold,
As though the miser heavens had spilled their gold.

So I have heard the priceless fount of song
  Gush from thy golden throat so joyously,
As if great Pan piped once more to the throng
  Of shepherds 'midst the meads of Arcady;
Its music quells the tumult of the mart
And drives the tenant care from every heart;
I know the "morning stars" sang not more true,
When all the virgin world was sweet and new.
DANIEL E. O'SULLIVAN.

A BALLADE OF POETS.

SINCE bold Admetus reigned a king,
  And blond Apollo was his thrall,
Song seems a less immortal thing—
  Some earthly leaven degrades it all.
Aye, since the lord of music's fall
  From the bright gods' resplendent palace,
Do n't swear by news the poets bawl,
  Take what they say *cum grano salis*.

Once poesy was in its spring,
  But now, close-driven to the wall,
It loses its celestial ring—
  Some earthly leaven degrades it all.
Our lutes are out of tune; we drawl
  Some hackneyed song to Nan or Alice—
Poets will fib and steal and brawl;
  Take what they say *cum grano salis*.

No more the gods to earth we bring,
  Sweet Fancy's heroes seem less tall,
And song, alas! to which we cling—
  Some earthly leaven degrades it all.
There is no David now for Saul,
  There is no wine in Music's chalice,
And poets get their goods from Gaul;
  Take what they say *cum grano salis*.

Base rhyme poor Pegasus must haul,
Some earthly leaven degrades it all,
And poets?—ah, in jest or malice,
Take what they say *cum grano salis!*

ELVIRA SYDNOR MILLER.

TO A ROBIN.

Thy song with morning breaks,
Sweet robin, and its short refrains
Soft on my casement splash like sudden rains
Of flowers which shatter into flakes;
All unaware my soul from slumber wakes
　　Full of thy cheery strains.

Thou dost not skyward soar
Nor thy song bubble through the trees
Swelling with mortal pain; but on the breeze
Borne leaf-arousing, dancing o'er,
What time the dawn begins to pour
　　Its glory o'er lands and seas.

No keen wound subtly pains
Thy heart, no woe that inly grieves
Into my spirit, crying, wanly weaves;
Which, when thou ceasest, still complains
O robin, pouring ever-joyous strains
　　Amid the dewy leaves!

Oft in my deeper dreams
I hear thee dwindled to a tone
Like Love's own lute ere Love has sorrow known,
Or flutings wound along the streams
Of fairy-land by stilly twilight gleams,
　　From elfin pipers blown.

Thin flageolets and veins
Of music faint and far away,
Which lure me forth from Sleep's oblivious sway
Wherein the woeful present wanes,
And lead me laughing into rosy lanes
　　Where feet of childhood stray.

Bird of melodious powers,
Before thee what green valley swells,
What fountains blue, that from thy full throat wells

But gladness only?—fadeless flowers,
Unclouded sky and scented Summer bowers
    Where Joy forever dwells!

To woo and win from Death
Shows thee a wondrous conjurer;
Thy song creeping into the dreamful ear,
The Heart's red blossom shattereth;
Once more I feel the fresh and fragrant breath
    Of hopes about to stir.

The dainty germs that gem
With light the cloud that shields the whole,
The young hopes nested in the sinless soul,
O soon to be, blest brood of them,
Like winged flowers in ruby seas a-swim
    With Heaven for their goal!

These years with all they hold
Of weary burdens that increase,
Annihilated, melt away and cease;
Once more around me as of old,
The bloom-bewildered orchards are unrolled
    In breezy joy and peace.

With self-same look it wore,
Looms the old homestead green and grand!
Now happy voices reach me where I stand,
And oh! I see once more, once more,
My youthful mother in the open door,
    The distaff in her hand.

O house where I was born—
Where I was reared and reached the goal
Of manhood, free from ills that now control;
Where I, amid the flowers and corn,
In boyhood romped with ne'er a dream forlorn
    Preying upon my soul!

Your scenes before me laid
Are all familiar: glad and bright
The wavering landscape broadens in my sight;
Here first I yielded undismayed,
Then felt my young soul stir within me, swayed
By song and sorrow's might!

Alas! I do not err!
I felt it in a mournful thrill
Among my spirit's leaves, like winds that fill
The murmurous groves of pine and fir;
The spirit's leaves that Song hath set a-stir
Can never more be still!

What wonder that I said,
In touch with things that made me weep,
"Love lift thy wing and let me safely creep
Thereunder—I am so afraid;"
The red dawn blushing, like the sky had bled,
Did all earth oversweep!

RUFUS J. CHILDRESS.

AT SET OF SUN.

THE soft'ning twilight creeps apace
The after-mood of stormful day,
And close within its fond embrace
The yielding shadows fade away,
    At set of sun.

The heart's soft twilight creeps apace
The after-mood of stormful day,
And hides within its calm embrace
The pride that held imperial sway,
    At set of sun.

ANNA J. HAMILTON.

TOPPING THE LOCUSTS.

The author's father in his advanced years found it necessary to top two locust trees which stood near the old family residence. He wrote to his son that he had "topped the Locusts," though he did it with great reluctance, adding, "Now they may put out new tops and give shade to a new generation." The sentiment expressed suggested the lines below.

Two Locusts, in a grove of beech,
Their giant arms up skyward reach,
Four yards their ancient trunks are 'round,
Their tops with leaves and branches crowned.
A hundred years their ages tell,
They've kept their vigor wondrous well,
They've stood a hundred winters' rage,
As often spread their foliage.

Oh, these are trees for axe to spare,
For many a tale could they declare,
How first they grew for him whose hand
Upreared the house, and cleared the land,
And made the home for them to shade,
Whilst 'neath their boughs his children played.

To kinsfolk, neighbors, strangers, friends,
Their hospitable shade extends;
Here lovers whispered happy dreams,
'Midst silvery sprays of soft moonbeams,
And at the close of Sabbath days
Through arching boughs went up God's praise,
While sweetly borne on evening's breeze
The church-bell chimes sang through the trees;
Oh, let the axe these old trees spare,
Is memory's earnest, pleading prayer.

But now these skyward reaching arms
Have grown so tall their height alarms,
Lest storms may bring them crashing down
The old paternal roof upon;

So keen-edged axe and cruel saw,
Strong arm to wield and a rope to draw,
Soon send the grand old tops below
To kiss the ground they've shaded so.

No more a grateful shade they'll cast,
No more defy the winter's blast;
But though no graceful top remains,
Each trunk a mighty life retains,
And spreading glories yet will crown
The locust trees whose tops are down—
Glories of leaf and fragrant bloom
For generations yet to come.
THOMAS SPEED.

NOVEMBER.

CHILL-BROWED elf, November,
  Casting your shadow and frown,
Lending a touch of amber—
  Shading it into brown.

Hiding the smile of the sun,
  Chasing Summer away—
Turning green into dun,
  Then curtaining it in gray.

Robbing the grim old oaks
  Of their summer frond,
Stopping the froggish croaks,
  Stilling the meadow pond.

Hushing the hum of the brook
  That waded through the vale,
Stealing into every nook
  Whispering your autumn tale.
CLINT RUBY.

LOVE.

OH! what is love? a fading flower,
The fleeting vision of an hour,
The bow that decks the summer sky,
The passing breeze that flutters by,
A meteor flash across life's heaven,
A word, a promise idly given,
A strain of music come and gone,
Whose memory passeth with its tone,
A star that kindly beams awhile,
Then leaves us darker for its smile;
    Say, is this love?

Ah, no! Love is a quenchless flame,
Forever burning, still the same;
A fire that angel torches light
To cheer our life's long, gloomy night;
A sun that will around us cast
A flood of brightness to the last;
The dearest boon to us is given,
The radiance of reflected Heaven,
Which when death comes will brightly shine,
Losing the Human in Divine;
    Oh! this is love!

CLARA L. MCILVAIN.

EDGAR ALLAN POE.

POET, whose heritage was dreams and tears,
  Blue are thy loved Virginia skies to-day;
  Amid the leaves the lutes of spring-time play
Sweet strains of ecstacies and hopes and fears;
  But thou, whose lyre was swept by heaven's own breath,
  Hast rendered all thy minstrelsy to Death.

Canst thou not hear beneath the veiling sod,
  The warm earth breaking o'er the daffodils,
  In whose green stalks the pulse of April thrills?
Canst thou not hear young grasses grow? Dear God,
  Hard must it be to leave the glorious light,
  Aye, all fair things, and bid the world good night.

Poet, thy dear South bears a rose for thee
  Far fairer than unfading asphodels,
  From fields beyond the region of farewells,
Washed by the white waves of eternity.
  Behold, this rose of love, whose bloom divine
  Is a censer and thy grave a shrine.

Sweet be the silence of these fleeting years
  To thee who left us, ere Fame's sunshine came,
  The heritage of thy immortal name,
Whose bread was sorrow, and whose wine was tears;
  Sweet be it, oh thou lord of language rare,
  Mad minstrel of a most divine despair.

The pulse of trade now falters in the mart
  At breathing of thy name, and love forgets
  The lips, the kisses, so this sorrow sets
All crowned and sceptered in each feeling heart,
  Yea, deep in mine, for singer I would be
  E'en as a strain of music praising thee.

For thee the dream-gods poured rare draughts of wine,
  The splendid drink of immortality,
  Till drunken with such nectar thou didst see,
Beyond the sunsets, lands that are divine,
  And o'er earth's clamor heard weird voices call
  From parapets cut in the sky's blue wall.

The tears of fallen angels sadly smote
  Upon thy trembling lute-strings, and soft blown
Through golden portals fell the raptured note
  Of seraph's song and mingled with thy own,
So thus unto each earth-born strain was given
  The sigh of Hell, the ecstasy of Heaven.

Endowed with visions of mysterious things,
  Upon a ship of song thyself didst stand,
  And like Columbus hailed a grand new land.
Oh! dweller under Fame's outstretching wings,
  Alas, alas! that in thy prime of day
  Death's darkness fell, like frosts on blooms of May.

Perchance life's sorrow made thy heart grow old;
  The sight of haggard faces and sad eyes
  Made dim the brightness of thy paradise,
And on thy music jarred the clink of gold;
  So thou didst faint beneath the heavy cross,
  While all the world laughed, knowing not its loss.

Though thou hast stood a beggar at the gate
  Of splendor, asking for a bit of crust,
  Thy hot tears falling thickly in the dust
Of rich men's chariot wheels. Oh, cruel Fate,
  Why e'er delaying? Better wine and bread
  For genius living—laurels mock the dead.

Ye statesmen weaving webs for souls of men,
  Ye victors from the glory-giving fray,
  Take back your honors; 't was but yesterday
He asked for bread, and silence answered then.
  Poor singer! even Beauty would not spare
  One gem for thee from out her scented hair.

Now, glorious is thy resting-place, thou king
Of songs and dreams. The splendid lights of Heaven,
Sun, moon, and stars, for lamps to thee are given.
Red leaves of autumn and green mists of spring
Fold softly o'er thee; for thy music, hear
The psalm of nature waking ever near.

Mute poet, as the burning west grows cold,
Lo, I will write upon this fair head-stone
(The mocking gift Fame gave thee for thine own):
"Here Genius lies, that died for lack of gold;"
And, passing by, the laughing world shall see
Its baseness and thy immortality.
                                    ELVIRA SYDNOR MILLER.

TOBOGGANING DOWN THE HILL.

UPON the summit of Life's slope,
We stand in vigor, full of hope,
With beauteous snowdrifts all around:
What grander scene could e'er be found?
Let's get aboard of Life's swift sleigh
And grandly down pursue our way,
Enjoying each delicious thrill
As we toboggan down the hill.

But, ah! this charming thrill can't last!
The gait is pleasing, but too fast;
Too soon we'll reach, so swift we sail,
The gloomy shadow of the vale.
But take the sleighing as it goes,
And make the most of winter's snows—
Enjoy the ride, let come what will,
As we toboggan down the hill.
                                    OLIVER LUCAS.

AUTUMN LEAVES.

WHEN Autumn's breeze fans through the trees
  And leaves begin to fall,
The leaves and wind bring to the mind
  The certain fate of all.

The breeze of time which constant blows
  On man with potent blast,
Though one by one it overthrows,
  Still all must fall at last.

With men it is as with the leaves,
  Each springs from mother Earth,
They rise and grow, and fade and fall
  To where they had their birth.

On the oak you'll see—the stateliest tree
  In all the forest 'round—
Some leaves of humble, modest height,
  And scarce above the ground,

Whilst others rise almost to skies
  Upon the topmost bough,
Yet when they fall they're scattered al
  Promiscuously below.

Thus 't is with man, do all he can
  To elevate his head,
In earth at last with millions past
  He mingles with the dead.

Gay scenes adorn man's vernal morn
  In fancy's pleasing views,
One object gained, another feigned
  He ardently pursues.

Then come his cares in riper years,
  The Summer of his day
With toil and strife, in future life
  His labors to repay.

His end attained, fruition gained,
  His Autumn more serene,
But wealth nor ease here long can please,
  For he must quit the scene.

As years prevail his pleasures fail,
  His strength declines apace,
And Winter's bleak and chilling gale
  Shall end his mortal race.

Then pause, Oh man! an emblem see
  In every falling leaf
Of that frail body given to thee,
  Ponder, but not with grief.

Thy noble past, thy Heaven born mind,
  If virtuous it be,
Enjoys when free and unconfined
  A blest eternity.

THOMAS SPEED.

A SEA SHELL.

IT tells in its lonely sighs,
  In its *misere* wild,
Its love for its far-off ocean home,
  This exiled ocean-child.

I send it unto thee,
  Type of my own full heart,
That sings and sighs for its native land
  Though doomed to dwell apart.

And when in thy listening ear
  Its plaintive music rings,
Let it tell of love for thee and thine
  That flows from my heart's deep springs.

ANNIE CHAMBERS KETCHUM.

THE BORE.

'NEATH every sun, in every land,
Th' impartial breezes e'er have fanned
The cheek of modest merit and
    That other cheek,
'Gainst which a hurricane might dash
And tempests rave and lightnings flash,
They would n't harm or e'en abash
    The bore's dread beak.

In fact, the storm that sweeps the main
And plays sad havoc on the plain,
Might beat upon the bore in vain—
    He'd face the breeze,
And, with his never-ceasing tongue,
Backed by a wondrous strength of lung,
He'd blow a "Norther" back among
    The Arctic seas.

The bore he boreth every soul
Who yieldeth him a button-hole,
And then in his obnoxious role
    Begins to blow;
The while his victim, in distress,
Hearing but little, heeding less,
Murmurs "I reckon," "no," and "yes,"
    In tones of woe.

Now, Noah's ark contained a pair
Of all things breathing God's pure air
Except the bore—he wasn't there,
    Or else the "crew,"
Through forty days and nights of rain,
Would surely have been talked insane,
And 'neath the waters eased their pain,
    With Noah, too.

You recollect that Babel's rise
Was checked before it reached the skies
By too much talk, and I surmise—
  (I may be wrong)—
That Lucifer, chagrined and sore,
Then, out of gas, evolved the bore
To torture man forevermore
  With stories long.

In t'other land we'll gladly miss
The bore who tortures us in this;
In that bright land's antithesis
  He'll sit and sigh
To even feel the humid breeze
From an old-fashioned, healthy sneeze,
Or on his blistered tongue to squeeze
  A dish-rag dry.

                                A. W. KELLEY.

GOD'S POEM.

PATCHES of shimmering sunlight everywhere
  Filtering through clouds white, airy, opalescent—
  Skies to the eastward glowing, iridescent;
A restful, holy calm, unwonted, rare,
  Like that which in our fancy broods above
The peaks of Paradise; a drowsy glory
That radiates from regions fresh with flora,
  Enshrouding all; a sense of that vast love
(Illimitable, infinite as Heaven),
  That fashioned all, alike pervading all;
  These are thy revelations, June, thy call!
O! may they not in vain to us be given;
  Written on sea and sky, on leaf and sod,
  Thou art an idyl from the hand of God!

                              MATTIE N. BROWN.

THE NIGHT DISPLAYS THE STARS.

THE storm displays the rainbow,
  The night displays the stars,
And twilight's gathering darkness
  The sunset's golden bars.

The rain begems the meadow
  With shining rills of light,
And fills the flowers' dew-cups
  With honey clear and bright.

The winter fills the world
  With winds of wailing woe,
But clothes the moon-lit valleys
  With glist'ning robes of snow.

'Tis thus, when gloomy shadows
  O'erspread us and combine,
The hidden virtues in us
  Like stars begin to shine.

And as the starry heavens
  Of night surpass the day,
So noble souls in sorrow
  Their loftiness display.

But if, when sorrow-smitten,
  No virtues in us shine,
Then we are full of darkness,
  And void of light divine.

THOMAS WALSH.

THE OLD SCISSORS' SOLILOQUY.

The following poem, bright in humor and tender in sentiment, was written several years ago by A. W. Kelley (Parmenas Mix), and first published in *The Century*, then *Scribner's Magazine*.

I AM lying at rest in the sanctum to-night—
    The place is deserted and still—
To my right lie exchanges and manuscripts white,
    To my left are the ink and the quill—
Yes, the quill, for my master's old-fashioned and quaint,
    And refuses to write with a pen;
He insists that old Franklin, the editor saint,
    Used a quill, and he'll imitate Ben.

I love the old fellow—together for years
    We have managed the *Farmers' Gazette*,
And although I am old, I'm his favorite shears
    And can crowd the compositors yet.
But my duties are rather too heavy, I think,
    And I oftentimes envy the quill
As it lazily leans with its nib in the ink
    While I'm slashing away with a will.

But when I was new—I remember it well,
    Though a score of long years have gone by—
The heaviest share of the editing fell
    On the quill, and I think with a sigh
Of the days when I'd scissors an extract or two
    From a neighboring editor's leader,
Then laugh in my sleeve at the quill as it flew
    In behalf of the general reader.

I am being paid off for my merriment then,
    For my master is wrinkled and gray,
And seldom lays hold on his primitive pen
    Except when he wishes to say,

"We are needing some money to run this machine,
  And subscribers will please to remit;"
Or, "that last load of wood that Jones brought us was
    green,
  And so knotty it couldn't be split."

He is nervous and deaf, and is getting quite blind
  (Though he hates to acknowledge the latter),
And I'm sorry to say, it's a puzzle to find
  Head or tail to the most of his matter.
The compositors plague him whenever they see
  The result of a luckless endeavor,
But the darling old rascal just lays it to me,
  And I make no remonstrance whatever.

Yes, I shoulder the blame—very little I care
  For the jolly compositor's jest,
For I think of a head with the silvery hair
  That will soon, very soon, be at rest.
He has labored full long for the true and the good,
  "'Mid the manifold troubles that irk us;"
His emoluments, raiment and food,
  And—a pass, now and then, to the circus.

Heigho! from the past comes a memory bright
  Of a lass with the freshness of clover,
Who used me to clip from her tresses one night
  A memorial lock for her lover.
The dear little lock is still glossy and brown,
  But the lass is much older and fatter;
And the youth—he's an editor here in the town—
  I'm employed on the staff of the latter.

I am lying at rest in the sanctum to-night—
  The place is deserted and still—
The stars are abroad and the moon is in sight
  Through the trees on the brow of the hill;
Clouds hurry along in undignified haste,
  And the wind rushes by with a wail—
Hello! there's a whopping big rat in the paste—
  How I'd like to shut down on his tail!

A. W. KELLEY.

AMABERE ME.

When the white snow left the mountains,
When the spring unsealed the fountains,
When her eye the violet lifted,
Where the autumn leaves had drifted
  'Neath the budding maple tree,
    Amabere Me.

Now the summer flowers are dying,
Now the summer streams are drying,
Yet I cry, though lone I linger
Where the autumn's wizard finger
  Burns along the maple tree,
    Amabere Me.

As the wild bird, faint and dying,
Follows summer faithless flying,
So my heart, doubt's blank air beating,
Broken-winged, is still repeating
  While it follows, follows thee,
    Amabere Me.

Soon will winter, gaunt and haggard,
Shroud a new grave, sodless, beggared;
Still, though not a flower be planted,
Not a requiem be chanted,
Not an eye with tears be laven,
On a gray stone will be graven
  'Neath the leafless maple tree,
    Amabere Me.
                    ANNIE CHAMBERS KETCHUM.

MIDNIGHT MUSINGS.

There is a beauty on Night's queen-like brow,
With her rich jewelry of blazing stars,
That to the heart, which yearns for purer scenes
And holier love than greets it here, appeals
With a resistless force. Great Nature then
Asserts her empire o'er the souls of those,
Ne'er favored children, on whose eager ears
There falls no wind which hath no melody,
And to whose eyes each star unfolds a world
Of glory and of bliss. The poet feels
The inspiration of an hour like this,
When silence like a garment wraps the earth,
And when the soundless air seems populous
With gentle spirits hovering o'er the haunts
Which most they loved while prisoned in their clay.
The mysteries of the universe then woo
His mind, and lead it up from height to height
Of lofty speculation to the Throne
Round which all worlds and systems roll.
The Past for him unlocks her affluent stores,
And human crowds, long gathered home by death
To his dark kingdom, people earth again.
* * * * * * *
Such is the talismanic power divine
Of Genius over death and time and space.
It reads the dim memorials on the tombs
Of buried empires—peoples solitudes—
And sways its scepter o'er the realms of night.
In its blest missions to the homes of men
It turns aside from palaces and pomp,
And gently stoops to kiss the pearly brow
Of the boy peasant 'neath the humblest roof.
With eye anointed it hath read the stars,
And traced out on the boundless blue of heaven
The wanderings of worlds. Its voice goes forth,

And o'er the billows of Time's wasteful sea
It rolleth on forever. It hath sung
Old Ocean's praise, and with his surges' roar
Its song will ever mingle.

THOMAS H. SHREVE.

THE PASSING OF MARCH.

THE braggart March stood in the season's door
  With his broad shoulders blocking up the way,
Shaking the snow-flakes from the cloak he wore
  And from the fringes of his kirtle gray.

Near by him April stood with tearful face,
  With violets in her hands, and in her hair
Pale wild anemones; the fragrant lace
  Half-parted from her breast, which seemed like fair,
Dawn-tinted mountain snow, smooth-drifted there.

She on the blusterer's arm laid one white hand,
  But he would none of her soft blandishment;
Yet did she plead with tears none might withstand,
  For even the fiercest hearts at last relent.

And he at last, in ruffian tenderness,
  With one swift, crushing kiss her lips did greet;
Ah, poor starved heart—for that one rude caress
  She cast her violets underneath his feet.

ROBERT BURNS WILSON.

SPRING THUNDER.

We know by the breath of the balmy air,
The springing grass and the sunshine fair,
By the soft rain falling—as if in love
The sleeping blossoms and bulbs above—
By the tint of green on the forest brown,
By the fallen tassels of aspen down,
By the lilac-bud and the tufted larch,
That we have done with the wayward March.

We know by the call of the nestling bird
When she feels her mother impulse stirred,
By the venturing forth of the lonely bee
Like the dove sent out o'er the olden sea,
By the croak of the frog in his willowy pond,
By the dove's low moan in the copse beyond,
By the quickening pulse and the thrilling vein,
That April laughs into life again.

But not the sunshine, the breeze, the showers,
The tender green on the embryo flowers,
The voices of birds or the quickened sense,
Appeal with such startling eloquence
To the heart that yearns for the Summer's reign,
Weary and earth-sick from Winter's chain,
As that sound which seems through space to ring,
The first low thunder of wakened Spring.

O marvel not that the men of old
Deemed its deep music by gods controlled,
And, by the power that within them strove,
Called it the wrath of the mystic Jove—
For we are stirred with an awe profound
By that mysterious and sullen sound—
Nor give we faith to the birds and bloom
Till we hear that fiat of Winter's doom.

So in the Spring of our life's career
We stand and gaze on the opening year,
We feel the sunshine, we drink the breeze,
But no source of feeling is stirred by these;
Not till the voice of the stormy soul
Swells like the sound of the thunder's roll—
Not till the flood-gates of sorrow break
In passionate tears—doth our Summer wake.

CATHERINE A. WARFIELD.

THE LEAF.*

So rudely torn from thy support,
   Where goeth thou, poor withered leaf?
I do not know. The tempest's sport
   Is the dire cause of all my grief.

It felled the oak, upon whose bough
   My slight form clung since early spring;
And from that dreadful day till now
   The fickle wind upon his wing

Hath borne me o'er the spreading plain,
   And through the forest's shady nooks,
And o'er the rugged mountain chain,
   And by the valley's babbling brooks.

Without complaint, and without grief,
   I go where every thing else goes,
Where goes the slender laurel leaf,
   Where goes the soft leaf of the rose.

MRS. W. LESLIE COLLINS.

* Translated from the French of Fenelon.

A WILD VIOLET IN NOVEMBER.

ALAS, dear flower! child of the morning sun,
  Of April showers and spring-time's kindly breath,
Against what odds hath thy sweet life begun!
All nature bodes thee ill. Thou mayst not shun
  The hard mischances of this changing world,
  Nor 'scape the sad presaging of this sky.
To-day thy gentle beauty is unfurled,
To-morrow in the lap of sleep to lie.
All cheerfully the wonder of thine eye
  Looks upward, smiling in the face of death.

Is nature then forgetful and unkind?—
  Unknowing of her time to send thee forth
Uncared for, unprotected from the wind,
  Whose threat'ning voice stirs from the pallid north?
Or hath the sun, made fierce with Autumn's wine,
  Too fondly wooed, too soon, the drowsing earth,
So that she stirs uneasy in her rest,
  And dreams she must put forth some tender sign
Of love's sweet troubling in her yearning breast,
  And so, unwitting, gives thy beauty birth?

Hast thou no fear? Ah, poor unconscious waif!
  No dew-drop hast thou but compassion's tear.
Would that an angel now might bear thee safe
  To some sure hiding place! Dost thou not hear
The anger of the coming storm, that fills
  The sky with gloom and shakes the earth with dread,
Voiced in the deep mouths of the bellowing hills,
  Wherefrom bright Autumn in despair hath fled
And left the gray trees naked to their ills,
  Each holding mournfully some farewell shred
Torn from the rich robe of the passing year?
No help of mine, alas! can bring thee cheer.

A WILD VIOLET IN NOVEMBER.

Here will I heap the leaves about thy bed,
That I may leave thee, when the storm draws near,
A friendly shelter for thy drooping head.
Soon will thy life be done, and mine more drear,
That I shall seek for thee and find thee dead.

Now from the far horizon sweeps the blast,
Distress and desolation in the sound,
Swift through the moaning forest, driving past
The frantic leaves along the rustling ground.
Now on the drear fields night is closing fast,
The shadows and the darkness fill the air;
Dun Melancholy leaves her haunts at last,
And wails along the hillsides in despair.

Far from the fading valley bursts the boom
Of distant echoes, and the darkness reels
Where sightless chariots, thund'ring through the gloom,
Bear down the tree-tops with their crackling wheels.
Sheer down the shattered silence of the sky
The fierce, white steeds of Winter plunging go;
Swift on the level of the storm they fly,
And from their gleaming manes, as they rush by,
They shake the hoar-frost out, like moon-lit snow.
Now is the summer as if it had not been;
The autumn but a fancy and a jest;
All is but night, and phantoms come again.
The rounded moon sinks in the tangled crest
Of yon dark hill. Are all but shadows then?
And what should I do other than the rest—
A dreamer of the whisp'ring fields at best?

Why am I grieved? What matter should it be
That flowers must fade; that every joy should fly;
And all things change? Why am I pained to see
That good can fail and gentle beauty die?
One violet less on earth! What's that to me?
Alas! I know not; no, in truth, not I.

Farewell! I draw my cloak about me now;
   Far hence upon the midnight fields I go;
Cold is the whistling gust upon my brow;
   Crisp is the frosted grass and white as snow;
Gone is the moon, deep darkness and the stars
   Gird now the sleeping earth; and I alone
Must go to battle in the silent wars
   That rend the soul with thought's unuttered moan.

Still shall I seek the dawning and the light,
Loth to believe that Nature was designed
   To be but cruel. Though her ways may thrill
My soul with doubts, and though her front may fright
   My longing with a grave which I must fill;
Yet shall despair not mount on hope resigned;
Her beauty and her love are life. I find
   More cheer and comfort in her worst of ills
Than in the choicest babbling of mankind.

From thee, frail creature of the mind divine,
   My soul is loth to part. I linger near,
Vexed with a boding that is not, and is—
   A contemplative sense of wounding fear,
Where fain I would find comfort and repose.
Hath God made man a gentler heart than His?

There is a nameless agony that grows
   Too burdensome to melt with pity's tear;
   And I, who bend in helpless sorrow here,
Pained with regret and longing, that, God knows,
   I got not of myself—a wild despair
That death should ride upon the breath that blows
   Fresh from the sky's far solitudes—I get
   No answer. Silence mocks my cry. And yet
   Thy faith-face bids my doubting soul forget
The cloud of gloom that closes over me
With thinking why so hard a thing should be.
   Thus am I lessoned by this trust of thine,
Thy beauty's charm and sweet content, which shows
   Thy life is sheltered from the blight of care
   As though a guard of gods encircled thee.

Farewell, sweet flower! We yet perhaps shall meet
  At some time, somewhere. God, He knows; not I.
But if this life be not a useless cheat—
  A farce for fiends to laugh at, and a lie—
Then sure I know that in some land unknown
  To which we journey, we shall meet again.
And if there be not this—if life be grown,
  Heart, soul and mind, a fleeting dream and vain,
Born of the earth and nurtured by the sun,
  A nothing and a shadow, but to be
Whiles that a few short years of time shall run,
  And vanish then forever—still, I say
Farewell! Farewell! It is but clay to clay.
Thou goest now, and I shall follow thee.

ROBERT B. WILSON.

ICH LIEBE DICH.

"ICH LIEBE DICH," was all he said,
And why I should have blushed so red
I can not say—I do not know;
The words could not have moved me so—
It must have been his look instead.

But why should I have hung my head,
And really almost felt afraid,
When what he meant I did not know?
  "Ich liebe dich."

"Three German words" they were, he said.
"Teach me the meaning? No, instead
The words themselves he'd teach, and so
The meaning soon enough I'd know."
And soon my faltering lips he led
To say the words himself had said—
  "Ich liebe dich."

JEAN WRIGHT.

A REVERIE.

The twilight falls in gloom;
All day the fitful sun and sparkling show'r
Have played at hide-and-seek amid the bloom—
    The varied tints of Spring's fresh bow'r.
Oh, sure each bud and blossom knows the spell,
Their subtle fragrance weaves about my brow;
Oh, sure a mystic tale their echoes tell—
    Love's soft, low-whisper'd vow.

    The deep'ning sky o'ercast,
The shadows slowly length'ning 'neath the trees,
The tender leaves swift in the vernal blast,
    To catch the music of the breeze;
The young lush grass a-peep above the earth,
The trailing vines that to the lattice cling,
Ah, these to fancies warm and true give birth,
    And o'er my senses fling.

    On landscape charms I glance;
The city's distant hum is lull'd to rest,
Athwart the sunset dark'ning clouds advance,
    And shut from sight the rosy west;
A dreamy orison enshrines my heart,
Deep shelter'd in the sacred haunts of home,
Where elfin sprites among the eeries dart,
    Irradiate in the gloam.

    Shine out, sweet love, unveil
Thy ecstasy erst wrought in accents wild;
Within my soul there breathes an anguish'd wail,
    Unsoothed by resignation mild.
I would not, if I might, give back the joy
That sweeps my pulses with enraptured thrill;
In transport pure the moments can not cloy—
    My craving lingers still.

Nor time may rend the tie;
The fealty that holds the captive will
In potent thrall, if sever'd, soon must die,
Poor human faith a-blight and chill.
O, birdlings, blossoms, leaflets, flow'rs,
Give forth chaste spirits to enchant the air;
Let silver'd mem'ries glad the lonely hours,
And crown my picture fair.

* * * * * * *

The night comes on apace;
The cricket's chirp, the woodland murmur's swell,
Bid nature's changeling melodies efface
The glamour of yon phantom spell.
The flashing morn adown the glist'ning aisles,
A dew-embower'd hill and grove and lea,
With ruthless light will scatter fairy wiles,
Nor leave my love to me.

EUGENIA DUNLAP POTTS.

SPRING AND SUMMER.

I HEARD a footstep on the hill;
The little brook began to trill.
I looked—a sweet and childish face,
Reflected like a blooming vase,
Was smiling from the water clear
With buttercups behind her ear.

A flock of swallows hove in sight;
On came Summer clad in white,
With sunshine falling from her hair
Upon her shoulders white and bare,
And, pressing through the tangled grass,
A daisy rose to watch her pass.

KATYDID.

LA GLU.

BRITTANY FOLK SONG.

ONCE upon a time there was a poor boy.
—Oulie oulai oulie oula—
Once upon a time there was a poor boy
    Who loved one
    Who loved him not.

She said to him, "Bring me to-day,"
—Oulie oulai oulie oula—
She said to him, "Bring me to-day
    The heart of thy mother
    For my dog."

He goes to his home and his mother kills.
—Oulie oulai oulie oula—
He goes to his home and his mother kills,
    Seizes the heart
    And runs away.

In running away down he falls.
—Oulie oulai oulie oula—
In running away down he falls,
    And the heart
    Rolls on the ground.

As it rolls it speaks to him.
—Oulie oulai oulie oula—
As it rolls it speaks to him—
    Listen thou
    To what it says.

As it rolls it weeping says,
—Oulie oulai oulie oula—
As it rolls it weeping says,
    "Art thou hurt
    My poor child?"

                          JEAN WRIGHT.

JENNIE JONES CUNNINGHAM.

LEFT ON THE BATTLE-FIELD.

WHAT, was it a dream? Am I all alone
  In the dreary night and the drizzling rain?
Hist!—Ah, it was only the river's moan;
  They have left me behind with the mangled slain.

Yes, now I remember it all too well!
  We met, from the battling ranks apart;
Together our weapons flashed and fell,
  And mine was sheathed in his quivering heart.

In the cypress gloom, where the deed was done,
  It was all too dark to see his face;
But I heard his death-groans, one by one,
  And he holds me still in a cold embrace.

He spoke but once, and I could not hear
  The words he said, for the cannon's roar;
But my heart grew cold with a deadly fear—
  O God! I had heard that voice before!

Had heard it before at our mother's knee,
  When we lisped the words of our evening prayer!
My brother! Would I had died for thee—
  This burden is more than my soul can bear!

I pressed my lips to his death-cold cheek,
  And begged him to show me, by word or sign,
That he knew and forgave me; he could not speak,
  But he nestled his poor cold face to mine.

The blood flowed fast from my wounded side,
  And then for a while I forgot my pain,
And over the lakelet we seemed to glide
  In our little boat, two boys again.

And then, in my dream, we stood alone
  On a forest path where the shadows fell;
And I heard again the tremulous tone,
  And the tender words of his last farewell.

But that parting was years, long years ago,
  He wandered away to a foreign land;
And our dear old mother will never know
  That he died to-night by his brother's hand.

* * * * * * * * *

The soldiers who hurried the dead away
  Disturbed not the clasp of that last embrace,
But laid them to sleep till the judgment day,
  Heart folded to heart, and face to face.

Bryant's Library of Poetry and Song.   SARAH T. BOLTON.

5:30 A. M.

OH, that proverbial early bird—
  The one that caught the worm—
I would that I had never heard
Of that proverbial early bird!
A pious fraud, a snare absurd,
  I boldly do affirm,
Was that proverbial early bird—
  The one that caught the worm.

ENVOI.

And Prince, the *worm*—
  He also rose betimes.
And yet, methinks his was a cruel fate.
  Would it not seem the moral of the tale
Were this—'t were best to lie full *late?*
JEAN WRIGHT.

SONG OF THE RAID.

On the Cumberland's bosom
  The moonbeams are bright,
And the path of the raiders
  Is plain by the light;
Across the broad riffle
  And up the steep bank,
The long winding column
  Moves rank after rank.

CHORUS.

Then Ho! for the Bluegrass—
  And welcome the chance—
No matter the danger
  That bids us advance;
The odds must be heavy
  To turn or deter
The lads who make war
  With the pistol and spur.

We haunt the wild border,
  We ever are near,
Giving hope to our friends
  And to enemies fear.
We hold idle armies
  Here, guarding this soil,
We snatch from swift battle
  Its glory and spoil.

Through the woodland's deep shade,
  By the meadow's green side,
Up hill and down valley
  We steadily ride;
But hushed now the laughter
  And silent the song,
As all night the squadrons
  Tramp swiftly along.

Th' advance guard is marching
   Away in the van,
Bold leader the captain,
   Tried soldier each man.
No challenge is passed
   When a foe they descry,
But the charge comes as fast
   As the hail from the sky.

By morn we see Glasgow,
   Columbia at noon,
Then march on again
   'Neath the smiles of the moon.
And at midnight on Lebanon
   Sudden swoop down
To flush the blue-jackets
   Who hold the good town.

Leave Bardstown to westward,
   Our right pushes in
The pickets to Danville
   With clatter and din;
Through Harrodsburg charging,
   Press hotly the chase,
Till Frankfort may witness
   The dust of the race.

Let Louisville listen,
   And Lexington wait,
We are lords of the heart
   Of the beautiful State.
The best steeds on Elkhorn
   We take as our right;
We must fight when we will,
   We must win when we fight.

We reach merry Georgetown—
   There's risk in delay—
But whatever happen
   We'll tarry one day;

Then down the white pike
    Cynthiana shall hear
The rifle's bold music,
    The rebel's wild cheer.

But now we draw bridle,
    Our purpose is done;
Our leader commands,
    And we turn with the sun;
But strong hearts are swelling,
    And eyes throb and burn,
For many go southward
    Who'll never return.

CHORUS.

Farewell to the Bluegrass,
    So sweet in my sight—
To its pastures so green
    And its waters so bright;
If it pass to the stranger,
    Be lost to the brave,
I'll ask of my birthland
    Enough for a grave.
                            B. W. DUKE.

THE SIGHT OF ANGELS.

THE angels come, the angels go,
    Through open doors of purer air;
Their moving presence oftentimes we know,
    It thrills us everywhere.

Sometimes we see them: lo, at night,
    Our eyes were shut but open'd seem:
The darkness breathes a breath of wondrous light—
    And then it was a dream!
                            JOHN JAMES PIATT.

THE WORKS OF NATURE.

A FRAGMENT.

I LOVE on Nature's lovely face to look;
Upon the landscape, stretching far and wide
Like a bright panorama to the view,
With its rich garniture of woods and fields,
And hills and vales and glens, and crystal streams
Gliding o'er golden sands.
      I love to gaze
On the high mountain with its rugged peaks
Piercing the skies, until at last it wreathes
Around its azure head a misty veil.
I love the thundering cataract to view,
Rolling in grandeur o'er the rocky steep,
While, like a diadem, upon its brow
The brilliant rainbow sits.
      I love to stand
On the broad lake's green margin, and to see,
Reflected in its sleeping waters clear,
O'erhanging cliffs and trees, and the blue vault
Of heaven in all its glory mirrored there.
* * * * * * *
And at the close of day, when sinks the sun
Behind the mountain-tops that bound the west,
Or slowly down into his ocean bed,
I love to watch the ever-changing clouds,
Now hung like crimson banners in the sky,
Now stretched, like gold-edged curtains, far and wide—
The bright and gorgeous drapery of Heaven.
And when, at night, the starry hosts appear
I fix my eyes upon those brilliant orbs
That move in silent grandeur o'er my head,
And think of Him whose glory they declare.
* * * * * * *
All Nature is an open book; and all
Who will may read therein—may read and learn

THE WORKS OF NATURE.

Their Maker; see His goodness and His power
In living characters displayed. And yet
How many look, like brutes irrational,
On this fair transcript of His attributes,
Nor love, nor power, nor goodness there behold,
Though plainly all appear!
* * * * * * *
Of all created beings, man alone
With reason is endowed, that he may read
This wide-spread volume.
     He alone is made
"With countenance erect," that he may look
"From nature up to nature's God."
       And yet
How oft does man, though fitted thus to hold
Communion with his Maker through His works,
Fix, like the brute, his dull and vacant gaze
On Heaven's great laboratory, and perceive
Nothing but what the brute itself may see,
And nothing feel but what that too may feel!

"*Rural Minstrelsy.*"   WILLIAM A. WASHINGTON.

DAVID AND GOLIATH.

A full and true account, in common metre, of this single combat, by an Irish Bard.

THE brightest boy ould Jesse had
  Was David—youngest son:
He was a bould and active lad,
  Well liked by ivery one.

Altho' he had to moind the sheep,
  To l'arn he was so sharp,
Whin other boys wor' fast asleep,
  He'd practice on the harp.

'T would make the birds of heaven hide
  Their heads to hear him sing;
He'd murther half the country side
  Wid pebbles and a sling.

And thin the sootherin' ways he knew
  To capture young and ould;
The female sex—Och, whillielu!
  'T was there wor' his best hould.

Whin David was some eighteen year
  Of age, or thereabout,
Betwane the haythen and Judaar
  A bloody war broke out.

His brothers 'listed for the war;
  Begorra! they wor' daisies—
His father tuk a conthract for
  To sell the army chaases.

"David," the ould man said one day,
  "You'd loike a little thramp;
Jist load some chaases on the dhray,
  And take 'em down to camp."

DAVID AND GOLIATH.

He dhrove to camp and sought straightway
  The commissary's tint;
He got a voucher for his pay,
  Thin to his brothers wint.

He found 'em lookin' mighty blue
  And in a dhreadful fright;
Retrate was what they wished to do,
  But divil a bit to fight.

A big, black bully, tin feet tall,
  Was bluffin' all the Jews,
And throops and staff and Gin'ral Saul
  Wor' quakin in their shoes.

Goliath was the craythur's name,
  A howlin' Philistine,
His sword was loike the lightnin's flame,
  His spear was loike a pine.

He wore upon his back and breast
  Tin thousand pounds of brass;
The shine of him, complately dhressed,
  Would smash a lookin'-glass.

And ivery day the baste would sthrut,
  Inflamed wid dhrink and pride,
And kept all Israel closely shut
  In lines well fortified.

"Come out," he'd bawl, "come out of there,
  Beyant your dirthy works;
Come, av ye dare, and fight me fair,
  Yez bloody Habrew Turks!"

But ivery faithful Israelite
  Said, "Lave the blaggard be:
Av coorse, no dacint Jew can fight
  Wid sich low thrash as he."

This sort of thing was well and good,
　　Till David jined the throop;
Whin he the matter understood,
　　Bedad! he raised a whoop:

"It is a burnin' sin and shame,"
　　He said, "upon me word,
To hear this haythen hound defame
　　The chosen of the Lord;

"And since no other mon has felt
　　A wish to tan his hide,
I'll fight him for the champion's belt,
　　And fifty pounds a side."

The corp'ril of the guard he tould
　　The off'sur of the day
What David said, and he made bould
　　To mintion it at tay.

The edge-du-kong was in that mess,
　　And heerd the whole discoorse:
So he—he couldn't do no less—
　　Tould Gin'ral Saul av coorse.

The Chafe of Staff tould the High Praste
　　To sind perempturous orthers
For David to report in haste
　　At Gin'ral Saul's headquarthers.

But whin the son of Jesse kim,
　　And Saul beheld the lad,
So young, so tindher-loike, and slim,
　　It made him tearin' mad.

"Oh, houly Moses! look at that,"
　　Said Saul—"the boy's consate;
How can it be that sich a brat
　　Can match that heavy weight?

"Wid that blood-suckin' giant thafe
 This baby can not sthrive;
The Philistine, it's my belafe,
 Would ate him up alive."

Thin David said, "Me Lord, it's thrue
 This seems a rash intint;
Yet while I weigh but nine stun' two,
 I'm full of divilmint.

"A lion and a bear kim down
 The mountain's rugged sides,
I slew the bastes, and wint to town
 And thraded off their hides.

"And since for roarin' brutes loike thim
 I've found I'm mon enough,
I'm quite convinced that I can thrim
 This blaggard pagan rough."

"Avick!" says Saul, "ye're full of pluck,
 And wag your little chin
Loike one who ra'ly thrusts his luck,
 And manes to thry and win.

"I'll give ye my best coat of mail—
 A new spring suit just made—
Tuck it a thrifle in the tail
 And pad the shoulder blade."

But David did n't understhand
 The use of sich a thing,
And only wanted in his hand
 His staff and thrusty sling.

Whin Goliath saw little David approachin', after having heerd proclamation that a gra'at champion was comin' out to fight him, musha, he laught fit to split his sides; and by rason of what passed betune them in the way of talk, I dhrap out of poethry for a bit, bekase, while poethry is mighty foine for a sintimental dialogue, it's no good at all for a ra'al strong, first class, breezy blaggardin' match.

"Oh, Jases!" said Goliath, wid the wather bilin' out of his eyes for laughin', "what sort av thing is that? May the divil admire me!" he says, "if I do n't believe it's a monkey escaped from au organ-grinder."

"Ye'll find me a moighty bad thing to monkey wid," says David, "ye big thafe, wid a pot on your head like a cupolo on a sthame fire ingine, and your dirthy black mouth loike the hole av a coal cellar."

"Ye little skinned pole-cat!" says Goliath, beginniu' to grow mad when he diskivered that David's rhethoric was suparior to his, "do ye think I'm a dog that ye've got a sthick to bate me wid?"

"Bedad," says David, "I would n't be afther doin' a dacent dog sich injustice; but it's dog's mate I'm goin' to make of ye."

"Hear that," says Goliath; "arrah, now, tache yure gran'mother to faad ducks!"

"Dhry up!" says David, "Bad scran to ye," he says; "ye have n't the sinse of a cat-fish. By the light that shines, yure bad ghrammar gives me a cramp in me stumnick." Och, David had a tongue in his head loike a jews-harp.

"Tear an' ouns!" says David. "I'll give the buzzards a picnic wid yer karkiss, and shure it'ull make 'em sick to ate ye."

"Ye're a liar!" says Goliath.

"Ye're another!" says David, "and an ophthalmic ould Cyclops to-boot."

Wid that Goliath lost his timper entirely. He pawed up the groun', and kim at David wid his eyes shut, a bellowin', and that bhrings me back to poethry:

Goliath poised his mighty spear,
'Twas fifty feet in length,
And unto David drawin' near,
He punched wid all his strength;

But David was surprisin' quick,
And sphry upon his pins;
So dodgin' nately, wid his sthick
He whacked Goliath's shins.

Wid pain the giant howled and grinned,
And dhrapped both shield and lance
To rub his leg the lick had skhinned,
Thin David saw his chance.

DAVID AND GOLIATH.

Takin' a brick from out his scrip,
  He put it in his sling,
And whirlin' it 'round head and hip,
  He let it dhrive full swing.

Right to the mark the darnick flies,
  As sthraight as to a hod;
It smote the wretch between the eyes,
  And stretched him on the sod.

Thin David, for to prove him dead,
  In sight of all beholders,
Chopped off his unbelavin' head
  From his blasphamious shoulders.

* * * * * * * *

Whin the Phenaysian sailors sought,
  Long since, ould Erin's strand,
A prince of David's blood they brought,
  Who settled in the land:

From him the Irish race had birth,
  And that's why we delight in,
Beyant all other tribes on earth,
  The harp's swate strains and fightin'.

That this surmeese is no wise thin
  Can aisily be shown,
For sthick and harp have iver been
  As Erin's imblims known.

So let her inemies beware
  How they indulge their hate,
Let England thrimble lest she share
  Goliath's dreadful fate.

                B. W. DUKE.

BENEATH THE VEIL.

Hooded nun with veiléd eyes,
Thou in whom the maiden dies
Unto Christ a sacrifice!

Thou who kneelest at the shrine,
Wedded to the love divine,
Making all its sorrows thine!

On thy brow the crown of sticks,
On thy lips the gall they mix,
On thy breast the crucifix.

Passion's agony and sweat,
Passion's hour when all forget;
Passion's cry on Olivet.

Masses sung and incense cold,
Vespers rung and pittance doled;
Beads in pain at midnight told;

Light of windows dim and quaint,
Sight of pale and paneled saint,
Throe of martyr torn and faint,

Are thy joys, O child of prayers,
Child of vigils, fasts and cares!
Ah, that none thy burden shares!

Were I weary, poor, distrest,
Thou, to give me shelter, rest,
Wouldst of all thyself divest.

Were I raving, fever-tost,
Homeless, friendless, spirit-lost,
Thou wouldst seek me, life the cost.

Were I dying 'mid the dead
On the field whence all had fled,
Thou wouldst lift my wounded head.

Ah, so tender for His sake,
Living but love's part to take,
Thou alone my heart dost break.

Worse am I than travel-worn,
Worse than needy, sick, forlorn,
Battle-spent or sorrow-torn.

Death were not so dolorous,
As to hear them ringing thus
For thy soul the Angelus.
JAMES LANE ALLEN.

MEMORIES OF GALILEE.

EACH cooing dove and sighing bough
  That makes the eve so blest to me,
Has something far diviner now—
  It bears me back to Galilee!

CHORUS.

O Galilee, sweet Galilee!
  Where Jesus loved so much to be;
O Galilee, blue Galilee!
  Come, sing thy song again to me!

Each flowery glen and mossy dell
  Where happy birds in song agree,
Thro' sunny noon the praises tell
  Of sights and sounds in Galilee!

And when I read the thrilling lore
  Of Him who walked upon the sea,
I long, oh! how I long once more
  To follow Him in Galilee!
ROBERT MORRIS.

MEETING RIVERS.

These verses were inspired by a scene at the meeting of the Ohio and Kentucky rivers.

I.

The sun on yonder line of hills
  Has placed a coronal of light,
And from its woven rays a sheen
Gilds their dark livery of green
  And makes its dullness bright.

He spreads his colors from the sky,
  Just where the rivers meet in one,
Until the mingled waters lie—
  The palette of the setting sun.

But never mortal artist mixed
  Such colors—wonderful and rare!
And never picture, new or old,
Shone in a frame of purer gold
  Than that which glitters there.

II.

The swift Kentucky's somber stream
  Rolls on in silence to the place
Where ends its "dark and bloody course,"
  Into the Ohio's wide embrace,
Ungladdened in its changeless gloom
By forethought of its brighter doom.

But on the glad Ohio's breast
  A thousand jewels blind the sight;
Gems that have gleamed since time has run,
Yet rise with every rising sun
  And perish with the night.

Sweet waters, twice named "beautiful!"
  On them the lingering sunbeams shed
Their slanting light till, near the land,
Shines clear and white the shell-strewn sand
  Upon their sloping bed;

And while the dark Kentucky strives to hide
Its treacherous depths beneath a muddy tide,
They open—plain to every careless glance—
Each bright recess beneath their broad expanse.

III.

Here, at the river's meeting-place,
  How fair the sights that greet the eye!
How pure the mirrored gold that gleams
Like Zion's limpid streets, and seems
  A pathway to the sky!

A tiny boat, all sail-clad, floats
  Straight down the paling path of light,
And as the white sails fade from view
The gilded pictures vanish too;
The sun collects each scattered hue
  And bids the world "good-night."

NANNIE MAYO FITZHUGH.

"ANSWERED."

I TOOK my sorrow where the swelling fields
  Lay circled by the low, caressing sky.
The soft enchantment that the morning yields
  Held all the murmurous air, and only I
Marred the rejoicing day, and drew apart.
  When joy came flooding till my pulse leaped high,
I told my gladness to the woods' deep heart,
  And all the forest answered with a sigh.
She heeds—sweet Nature—nay, she is not dumb!
  When from my prisoned soul the bars shall fall,
There waits an answer to my every cry,
Though yet her speech I may not know, in some
  Glad times my soul, bond-sundered, shall recall
In thousand-fold the sure and blest reply.

NANNIE MAYO FITZHUGH.

A NIGHT-TIME SONG.

Miss Casseday gave these words to the compiler as they came to her. She explained that a friend brought her three little pillows one day, and in her wakeful night hours she named these pillows Infinite Love, Infinite Power, and Infinite Goodness, placing the first-named under her head, the second under her back to hold her up, and finding much comfort from them all. The words of this poem came to her that night.

TEACH me to praise Thee, Father Dear,
For all Thy many mercies here,
As I recall these sent to-day
Help me for gratitude to pray.

The first and best of all is this—
That Jesus sends no pain amiss,
But with it all He sends His peace,
And makes my hopes and joys increase.

Lain on my couch for many years,
My days made up of hopes and fears,
I've learned at last my lesson sweet,
Lying in peace at Jesus' feet.

Often my eyes could scarcely see
This text spelt out so plain for me:
Infinite Wisdom knows the best,
Infinite Love will do the rest;

Infinite Goodness fills my cup,
Infinite Power holds me up,
Infinite Love helps me to see
That all things work for good to me.

When He withholds my sleep and rest
I know His purposes are best,
And precious night-time songs I sing
Beneath the shadow of His wing.

JENNIE CASSEDAY.

THE BURIED ORGAN.

FAR in a valley, green and lone,
  Lying within some legend old,
Sometimes is heard an Organ's tone,
  Tremulous, into the silence rolled;
In vanished years, the legend stands,
  To save it from the unhallowing prey
Of foemen's sacrilegious hands,
  The monks their Organ hid away.

None knows the spot wherein they laid
  That body of the heavenly soul
Of Music:—deep in forest shade,
  Forgot, the grave to which they stole
But oftentimes, in morning gold,
  Or through the twilight's hushing air,
Within that valley, green and old,
  The Organ's soul arises there.

Oh, soft and sweet, and weird and wild,
  It whispers to the holier air,
Gentle as lispings of a child,
  Mild as a mother's breathless prayer,
While silence trembles, deep and low;
  Then rapture bursts into the skies,
And chanting angels, winging slow
  On wings of music, seem to rise!

The herdsman sometimes, all alone,
  Is lost within that haunted air;
He hears the Buried Organ's tone—
  His hands are crossed, his breath is prayer!
And, while into his heart it steals,
  With hushing footsteps, downcast eyes,
Some deep cathedral's awe he feels—
  A church of air, and earth, and skies!

. . . Often when the sweet wand of Spring
　Has filled the woods with flowers unsown,
Or Autumn's dreamy breeze's wing
　Flutters through falling leaves, alone
I wander forth, and leave behind
　The city's dust, the sultry glare:
A shadowy dell, far off, I find—
　I know the Buried Organ there!

Within the city's noisy air
　I leave the creeds their Sabbath bells;
I cross my hands, my breath is prayer,
　Hearing that Organ's mystic swells.
The sweet birds sing, the soft winds blow,
　The flowers have whispers close, apart;
All wake within me, loud or low,
　The Buried Organ—in my heart!

JOHN JAMES PIATT.

NIGHT-THOUGHTS.

THEY come, in long procession rise before
　My wakeful sight, sweet thoughts, Belovèd, of thee
And of thy love, the dearest dream to me
That ever grew dear truth forevermore;
For, as to a child in his hush'd bed—the door
　Half-open where his mother's light may be
　A' comfort to his lonely sense when he,
Though waking, feels warm slumber reach the core
Of his fresh spirit—who drops his lids at last,
　Visiting Fairyland, while numberless
Lithe shadows pass and shapes created fast,
Charming him till he sleeps, and are his dream:
　So, while I breathe in tender wakefulness,
Sleep-bordering thoughts with blissful visions teem.

JOHN JAMES PIATT.

THE STRAWBERRY BOWL.

A private and confidential Epistle to Sam Gaines, Editor of the Hopkinsville *New Era*. Written for the Kentucky Press Association.

God might have made a better berry than the strawberry, but certainly he never did.—*Izaak Walton*.

MELROSE GARDEN, May, 1880.

YE SALUTATION.

BRING forth the bowl within whose round
No heart-consuming draught is found,
But berries glittering with the dew
Which south winds o'er the gardens strew,
Sweet souvenirs of Paradise,
With cheeks of flame and breath of spice,
Shedding for one bright hour their glow
O'er life's long Alpine waste of snow.

Breathes there a man with soul so dead,
Who never to himself hath said,
"O that I owned a strawberry bed?"
Whose heart hath ne'er within him burned,
As he beheld, in cream inurned,
Great sugared berries, coral red?
If such there be, go, mark him well;
Of berries never let him smell,
Where gathers the church festival
Or rings the merry marriage-bell;
Mark him—as thou wouldst mark a steer
Or swine—by cropping off his ear.

A WALK IN YE GARDEN.

Wake, winds of May, yon emerald waves,
Crested with flowers, like sea-foam white,
Where sparkle in their trefoil caves
Long coral reefs of berries bright;
Shaped like a gentle maiden's heart,
And bleeding, as from Cupid's dart,

The garden's earliest offering,
Crown-jewels on the brow of Spring;
The berry Izaak Walton loved,
And Downer's perfect taste approved;
Dispensing odors beatific,
Kentucky, Cumberland, Prolific,
Sharpless, and Monarch of the West,
And rare Charles Downing, last and best.
Thy leaves, sweet trefoil! symbols three
Of Faith and Hope and Love shall be;
Fair type of Christian hope to all,
The vine sleeps low 'neath snowy pall;
The resurrection blooms in May,
With flowers and fruits in bright array,
And soaring larks in countless throng
Singing their joyful Easter song,
And choir of mocking-birds on high,
Gray-plumed sopranos of the sky.

YE REVEL ON OLYMPUS.

Heap high the bowl! Ages ago,
Before the birth of Faust or Hoe,
Before *New Eras*, *Posts*, *and Suns*
Gave specials, paragraphs and puns,
When only Mercury bore the news
Around the skies, in winged shoes,
Such genial revels held the gods,
Juno and Jove, and other frauds;
In heaven's blue crystal urn each night
The stars, like berries, twinkled bright,
And the Great Dipper skimmed the cream
Where poured the Milky Way its stream;
Deserted is the Olympic hill;
Heaven, stars, girls, strawberries, bless us still.

YE INVOCATION.

Lord, we adore thy matchless bounty
And grace, which, after giving birth
To sun and moon and stars and earth,
Gave us a land of rarest worth,

THE STRAWBERRY BOWL. 263

And cast our lot in Christian County!
'Mid meek-eyed Jerseys, gifted mules,
Hopkinsville peaches, Public Schools,
Tobacco farms and gilt-edged bonds,
Wheat-fields and sheep and fishing-ponds,
Coveys of quail and double barrels,
Opossums, pheasants, doves and squirrels,
Damsels whose pamphanescent eyes,
If stars were quenched, would light the skies;
And for to-night, to make us merry,
Provided Izaak Walton's berry,
Ten inches round in lawful measure,
The garden's glory, pride and treasure—
Nor Brenner's brush nor Prentice's pen
Could tell their worth—and so, Amen!

YE PIC-NIC.

Fill high the bowl! In blissful vision
We wander over fields Elysian,
Through ever-lengthening colonnades
Of whispering elms and beechen shades;
Grave manhood's cares are cast away,
And all are boys again, to-day.
By one sure sign we know each other—
"The *strawberry mark!*—Our long lost brother!"
While all discourse on sylvan pipe
Of golden cream and berries ripe,
Or sound, on Memory's silver horn,
"I too was in Arcadia born!"
Sooth, 't is a goodly sight to see
The revellers' mutual ministry:
Stanton shall drive the Jersey cow,
Sam Gaines shall cause her milk to flow,
Logan shall hold her by the tail,
And Kelly bear the foaming pail;
Woodson shall crush the crystal ice,
Johnston hand spoons, all polished nice,
The *Courier-Journal* pass the berries,
With brisk champagne and golden sherries;

And he shall serve his country best
Who stores most berries 'neath his vest.
By shady glen and waterfall
Our early loves will we recall,
Maids whom no time can e'er eclipse,
With strawberry cheeks and sugared lips,
Phantoms which haunted boyhood's dream,
Life's fragrant, pure *creme de la creme—*
Delicious cream, which soured too soon,
And left us with an empty spoon!

YE PIONEER'S WILD STRAWBERRIES.

Father, thy locks are thin and gray,
Hast thou no legend for us, pray?
Sing of the wild strawberry's flame
When first Kentucky hunters came.

" 'Tis nigh on ninety years, I guess,
By the road called the 'Wilderness'—
Its story's told by Captain Speed,
A little book you all should read—
We pioneered to Old Kaintuck,
Woods swarmed with turkey, bear, and buck,
And by the 'Rock Spring' pitched our tents,
Them times wild strawberries was immense;
We did n't pick, we scooped 'em up
By bushels, with a bowl or cup;
And when our teams came home at night,
The critters' legs—they *wuz* a sight;
Seemed like they 'd swum in bloody seas,
The red juice splashed above their knees.
We rode one May-day 'cross the prairie,
Me and my wife and little Mary;
Come to a holler in the ground,
Where lots of strawberries grew around,
And herds of trampling buffalo
Made the red juice in rivers flow
And fill a pool some five foot deep—
Excuse me, pardners; I must weep—

THE STRAWBERRY BOWL.

Thanks! My throat *is* a leetle dry—
God knows I can not tell a lie! [Applause.]
Our hosses slipped and tumbled in,
We swum in juice up to the chin;
A half an hour we rose and sank,
At last we scrambled to the bank;
Me and my wife soon came around—"
(*Omnes.*) "But little Mary?"
"*She was drowned!*" [Groans.]
"Yes, drowned! My stricken heart, be calm!
Hers is the crown, the harp, the palm—
Thanks, yes, if you insist, a dram.
Blood flowed them days like strawberry juice
When Girty let his hell-hounds loose.
One day some Injin squaws allfired—"

There, old man, rest. You must be tired.
Share in our feast, Homeric sire;
Thanks to the Muse for such a lyre!

YE SILENT TOAST.

Fill high to-night the strawberry bowl
For friendship's feast and flow of soul,
Quickly, ere Psyche's brilliant flight
Shall vanish in the coming night.
Soon shall the parting word be spoken,
Soon friendship's golden bowl be broken;
Clasp hands and salutation send
To each true-hearted, absent friend;
Nor in our circle be forgot
The masters who before us wrought,
Titans of memorable days:
Penn, with his sheathless falchion's blaze,
Harney, the dauntless, true and strong,
And Prentice of the golden song,
Triad whose still ascending track
Flings its long rays of splendor back.

YE SMALL BOY'S DOWNFALL.

What spectres from the strawberry bowl
Flit through the galleries of the soul,
With shrill voice crying, "Grieve his heart;
Come like shadows; so depart!"
Strawberry cake, preserves, and jam!
I see thy mild eyes moisten, Sam,
Perchance at memory of the closet
Where once was stored the rare deposit,
High ranged upon the topmost shelf,
A skillful mother's richest pelf.
I see thee steal, at dead of night,
With cat-like footsteps, soft and light;
I see thee open slow the door,
Peep in, and cautiously explore;
I see young Sam the boxes pile,
Humming Longfellow's psalm the while:
" The heights to which the great have stept,
   Were not attained by sudden flight,
But they, while their companions slept,
   Were toiling upward in the night."
I hear a sudden scream—a crash—
I see a candle's fitful flash—
Tableau—A boy with downfallen breeches,
Loud sobs, salt tears, and stinging switches.

GOOD-NIGHT.

Heap high the bowl and pour the cream!
How bright the rosy berries gleam—
Red fruit and Jersey cream upon it,
The colors of my lady's bonnet.
In hues like these the western sun
Descends to rest when day is done;
And round his flaming couch are rolled
Bright curtained clouds of red and gold.
Not greedily the fruit devour;
Prolong the raptures of the hour;
Stain not with juice your linen fair,
And of the "strawberry nose" beware.

THE STRAWBERRY BOWL.

Think of the lovely—the sublime—
Niagara—California's clime;
The Mammoth Cave—Alaska's shore,
Where glaciers plunge and billows roar;
Balance each berry in your spoon,
Sink back in a delicious swoon,
And murmur in a Romeo's sigh:
"I have seen Naples—let me die!"

O, vital sparks of heavenly flame!
Whate'er your lineage, land, or name,
Pink buds which Mother Nature clips
From infant cherubs' finger tips,
Or earth-born babies' little toes,
Tinted like sea-shell or the rose,
Or notes from songs of home and love,
Which, floating to the skies above,
Are crystallized in heaven's pure air
And turn to crimson berries there—
Ambrosial fruit of heavenly birth,
By Ariel's fingers dropped on Earth—
Come o'er me and possess my soul,
Sweet spirit of the Strawberry Bowl!

For all the world's a strawberry bowl,
  Life the red fruit which fills the brim,
The daily papers spoon the whole,
  And women are the sugar and cream.

S. C. MERCER.

THE BEAUTIFUL.

I ASKED the artist, dreaming a dream,
  For the ideal of his soul,
As he sought to mirror the spirit's light
  That over his senses stole;
In the heavy sigh of his sad reply,
  I read how the task was vain,
To trace on the vacant canvas there
  The image of heart and brain.

I asked the poet one summer eve,
  Alone in the spell of his thought,
For the form that over his fancy stole,
  The shadow his spirit sought;
With a mournful voice he rose to tell
  How wildly and madly he strove
To link his rhyme to the silver chime
  Of the ringing stars above.

I asked his theme, in a musing mood,
  Of the proud philosopher,
His soul to the shrine of Nature wed,
  A votive worshiper.
He deigned to tell how the Beautiful
  Had lured him from his birth,
Leading his eye afar through the sky
  And over the wastes of earth.

I asked the good man, rising devout,
  One eve, from his silent prayer,
If ever a sense of the Beautiful
  Was his in devotion to share;
" 'T is the Spirit of God," was his answer meek,
  "Abroad in the earth and sky:
By day and by night its blazing light
  As a beacon to the eye."

I saw it then in the glow of a star,
  In the hue of the beautiful flower,
Its spell abroad in the glaring day,
  In the hush of the midnight hour;
Its image bright as a rainbow set
  In the murky cloud of sight,
At morn and eve sent down from heaven
  Its fountain of glory and light.
J. R. BARRICK.

NOVEMBER.

LONESOME like an' kinder dreary,
  Winds a sighin', soundin' weary,
Leaves a fallin' everywhere,
  Sadness some'ow in the air.
Birds so quiet—quit their singin'—
  'Pears like ever' day keeps bringin'
Longer hours for to fill,
  Heap o' time that's hard to kill.
Things seem mighty plain to say,
  "Life is passin' fast away."
Makes a fellow sorter blue,
  Sets him thinkin', wonderin' too,
'Bout this fleetin' thing called life,
  'Bout the death that ends the strife,
'Bout the friends that's come and went,
  'Bout the days already spent,
'Bout the absent, 'bout the dead,
  How they look, the words they said.
Winds a sighin', soundin' weary,
  Lonesome like an' kinder dreary.
LIZZIE WALKER.

VALEDICTORY.

Read at the closing meeting of the season of the Shakespeareau Club, at Flemingsburg, Kentucky, April, 1888.

TIME moves apace, and speeds the moment when
   With sad'ning words our parting comes at last;
   And years may pass ere we shall meet again
      As in the past.

Some eye of beauty may be dimmed in death;
   Some tuneful tongue forever hushed and still;
   Some mirthful heart, now stirred by playful breath,
      Lie mute and still.

Though one by one we fall, like autumn leaves
   From woodland boughs, tall oak, and creeping vine,
   As Death moves on to gather home his sheaves
      From Love's pure shrine,

Yet still to those who hold to memory dear
   The past, with all its lights and shadows gone,
   Some beams of joyous sunshine reappear
      To cheer us on.

From mem'ry's page, O let the hand of Time
   No line erase—no dark'ning shadows cast
   O'er childhood's grave, o'er manhood's glorious prime—
      The buried past!

Throw wide the book—close not the simple page,
   However marred by some ungrateful pen,
   As mem'ries sweet retrace the steps of age
      To youth again.

What though we gaze upon life's sweetest cup,
   And see, far down the lengthened space of years,
   Youth's bright and sunny hours come bubbling up
      Through smiles and tears;

VALEDICTORY.

What though, as yet we live each moment o'er,
  Long shadows creep adown the beaten track,
And spirit-voices fling from yonder shore
    Sad echoes back,

Does not the rainbow span the sunlit storm—
  The rosy morn move in the wake of night—
The stars their nightly office still perform
    Of love and light?

Does not the shade to happy sunshine yield,
  And to our weary steps its mantle spread,
And night, alike o'er meadow, heath, and field,
    Her dew-drops shed?

The green oasis 'mid the scorching plain
  With welcome greets the weary traveler's eye,
And cooling shades and gurgling streams again
    His thirst supply.

Then why despair? Why tune the burthened heart
  To songs of sadness, bitterness, and woe?
Since sweetest strains in choral accents start
    From long ago.

By faded lines with eager hands we trace
  The steps that mark the path of youth to age,
And meet with joy some long-forgotten face
    On mem'ry's page;

And so, in dreams, to life again recall
  The scenes we loved—bright childhood's sunny hours—
And gilded hopes—and blooming over all,
    Life's sweetest flowers.

For here and there, as down the path we stray
  And catch upon the breeze their sweet perfume,
Among the thorns that choke the narrow way
    Some flowers bloom.

The merry laugh—the groan of age—the breath
Of rosy spring—the chill of wintry blast—
The morn of life—the twilight eve of death,
    Come flitting past.

Though pleasures here may thrill us with delight,
And future hopes like shadows come and go,
Remember this: Each day must have its night
    For weal or woe.

And scanning thus our lives, this lesson then
We learn, whate'er we hope to do or dare,
Our lives are not alone what we have been,
    But what we are.

'Mid saddest grief, the very tears we shed
    Are but the dew-drops of the heart's pure love,
That strengthen hope, and lift the heart and head
    To thoughts above.

If hard the task, as o'er life's course we run,
    If by Thy hand we feel the chast'ning rod,
Then be it so—Thy will, not ours, be done
    On earth, O God.

Then let us each with energy anew
    Resume the toils allotted to our sphere,
Resolved our daily course of life pursue
    With happy cheer;

And profit by whatever here we've gained
    Of Friendship, Truth, Intelligence, and Love;
To Honor true, in Virtue's cause sustained
    By Heaven above.

That when at last, life's toils and cares are done,
    And all we are is veiled to mortal ken,
Our souls with well-earned Christian honors won,
    May meet again.

INGRAM CROCKETT.

And answer to the name of each, enrolled
Upon the book of life; to live and be
Where Truth and Light supernal shall unfold
    Eternity.

So then to Truth and Honor let us live;
To Faith and Hope forever firm and true;
As each fond heart in Friendship's ties receive
    A kind Adieu.
M. M. TEAGER.

CHRYSANTHEMUMS.

TRANQUIL and eager-eyed,
    The solitary pride
Of lonely garden-walks and leafless bowers,
Smiling where buried lie the summer flowers.

    Ye were not once so fair,
    Your smiles were not so rare,
Before Jack Frost, with bitter, blighting breath,
Had kissed your fragile sisters to their death.

    The leafless maples spread
    Their white arms overhead,
And, hopping in and out, the friendly sparrow
Chirps out his praise to you, to *them* his sorrow.

    Thus on life's common way
    Of toil and tempest they
Shine brightest in the end, who dauntless stand,
Bidding defiance to Fate's ruthless hand.
MATTIE N. BROWN.

A CHRISTMAS PANSY.

I CHIDED thee but now, sweet flower, that thou hast dared to bloom,
To shed a gleam of radiance o'er summer-beauty's tomb,
To come amid the darkness, the rain, and wintry sleet,
A sign, the joyous impress of the Christmas Angel's feet.

There is an ancient legend, these violets have their birth
Where'er the feet of angels have touched the darkened earth;
If so, my garden flower-bed is henceforth holy ground,
For there these angel foot-prints at Christmas have been found.

Thou pretty little trembler, caught 'neath our alien skies,
Thou'st wandered from the gardens of the golden Paradise,
And it is thy sweet mission to bring to one of earth
The hallowed recollections of the gentle Savior's birth.

The wintry winds are coldly rude to smite thy velvet cheek,
To freeze the pearly tear-drop in thine eye so softly meek;
But more rude are they to thee, fair summer's orphan flower,
Than was this life to Jesus from his earliest mortal hour.

'Tis said some sisters of thy race sprang from the holy sod,
Where Jesus in his agony was bowed before his God,
And as in loving sympathy, expectant, near they stood,
Their tender leaves were sprinkled with the fearful sweat of blood.

Empurpled by these priceless drops, the meek-eyed angel-flower
Has worn its robe of mourning since that midnight's awful hour,
And always is it cherished now the dearer for the stain,
Which brings to mind His agony, His undeserved pain.

Heart's Ease! the name of all thy names the dearest to my
    heart,
What tender recollections thy presence doth impart!
Type of the everlasting Love, which 'mid the wintriest
    gloom
Shows to the soul a cheering glimpse of life beyond the
    tomb.
                            FLORENCE ANDERSON CLARK.

DEATH—A LIVING KING.

A DAY is done;
The sun adown the west
    Will light another day begun,
While this doth sleep and rest.

A love is done;
The heart with its bequest
    Will cheer another love begun,
While this doth sleep and rest.

A life is done;
The soul so oft oppressed
    Will crown another life begun,
While this doth sleep and rest.

Then whyfore sad?
Each day, each love, each strife,
    Though hid from view, still maketh glad
Some other form of life.
                            ANNA J. HAMILTON.

IN LOOKING ON THE HAPPY AUTUMN FIELDS.

AH, happy fields, at rest from fruitfulness!
   No careless storm of the ungentle Spring
   Uptore your venturing roots, nor pierced the sting
Of spiteful frost your early promises.
The skies were blue above you. With caress
   Of gentlest beams the sun lured you to bring
   Your blushing blossoms forth, and from the wing
Of night were shaken dews their thirst to bless.
For shadows had ye but the bounteous clouds
That, passing, spanned you with the arch of hope;
   No canker-worms made of your leaves their shrouds,
   Nor envious hand sowed tares on every slope.
   And now the jocund harvesters have blest you,
   Ye happy fields, that from your labors rest you.

Kind Heaven! so order the uncertain days
   Of my brief mortal season, so defend
   From frost and drought and tempest, so befriend
With sun and dew, and bows of promise raise,
So temper to me all the cold world's ways
   That not in vain my toiling strength I spend,
   But come in ripeness to the perfect end,
And be at rest in life's autumnal haze!
Nought were it then upon the heart to take
The ice of death and in it lie entombed,
   As when on you the snows of winter break,
Ye mourn not for the spring-time when ye bloomed.
   Ah! let me know the harvesters have blest me,
   Ere I from all my labor come to rest me!

JAMES LANE ALLEN.

BUILDING CASTLES.

I SIT me where the fire-light's glare
    Before my vision dances,
And castles fair build high in air,
    Adorned with idle fancies.
My wife so true and children two
    Sit by my side unheeding—
Content are they, with naught to say,
    Some pleasant stories reading.

And fairer days shed brighter rays
    Athwart my dreamy vision;
Sweet prospects rife crown all my life,
    Through golden fields Elysian.
In wreaths and curls the smoke it whirls
    In shapely forms around me;
From my pipe of clay I puff away,
    Redoubled joys surround me—

Amid the daze of smoke and blaze,
    My heavy eyelids closing,
As Morpheus plays in luring ways,
    And sets me all a-dozing;
To my surprise I ope my eyes,
    For some one I hear calling—
And rousing me, what do I see,
    But all my castles falling.

                ALFRED W. HARRIS.

DREAMY SEPTEMBER.

THE work of the year seemeth ended,
   And Nature is taking a rest,
As she sleeps through this dreamy September,
   With hands folded loose on her breast.

The great busy loom of the spring-time
   In indolent silence doth stay;
No threads of a leaf to be woven
   Are wound on its shuttle to-day;

No buds to be chiseled or polished,
   Or carved into eloquent grace—
And the tools are so quietly hanging,
   No sign of their presence we trace.

Scarce a breath stirs the infinite stillness
   Of the languorous, luminous air—
E'en the fall of a shadow might startle
   The silence so golden and rare.

'T is delicious, oh, dreamy September,
   To fall in with thy sweet, restful mood
And attune all my soul to the quiet
   With which every day is imbued.

To sit with my hands idly folded,
   Forgetting to dust or to sweep,
To drive every care from my bosom,
   And rock all my sorrows to sleep;

To cherish the idlest of fancies,
   And think through a portal of rose,
With naught to disturb the Elysian
   I find in this perfect repose.

                    BELLE WILSON STAPP.

A DASH THROUGH THE LINES.

A ROYAL night for the row before us,
  The moon goes down in a bank of cloud,
One star to westward trembles o'er us,
  Wrapped like a corpse in its pallid shroud.

The lamp burns dim in the fisher's dwelling
  Filled with the Southern refugees;
Hist! to the cannon's thunder swelling
  Far away on the tired breeze.

I can hear the creek's black waters lapping
  The sandy beach and the wooded shores,
And the dying wind like a night-bird flapping
  Its dusky wings o'er the idle oars.

Five miles off is the wide, wide river—
  Five miles off the Potomac flood;
I can scarcely tell why I pause and shiver,
  Dragging the boat up out of the mud.

'T is a risky thing we're about, old fellow,
  Deserters afloat on the river wide,
Where the gunboats peer, with their eyes so yellow,
  Like panthers loose on the sullen tide.

'T is the last, last time I shall venture over,
  Risking my neck for the gold so bright—
Just one long whiff of the Maryland clover,
  One last dash through the lines to-night.

Lift up the lantern and hold it steady;
  Call out the women, the children, too;
The moon is down and the boat is ready,
  But the blockade running is yet to do.

All aboard! Push off now quickly,
  We must hug the shore till the river shines.
Look, where those lights burn pale and sickly,
  Over there are the Union lines.

I can see the river straight before us;
    Muffle the oars, nor cry, nor speak,
Let us hurry on, through the darkness o'er us,
    Into the river and out of the creek.

Woman, hush! there are foes behind us,
    The wolves are seeking their prey abroad:
Quiet the children or death will find us—
    For you the water, for me the cord.

Hist! 'tis only the black waves creeping
    Under the stern of our trusty boat.
The Yankee gunners must all be sleeping
    To leave us here on the tide afloat.

God be thanked, we are half way over!
    Near at hand are the welcome shores.
I can smell the blooms of the Maryland clover;
    Row for the land, now bend to the oars.

Haste, make haste, ere the gray dawn whitens
    Over the east, for I dreamt last night
I walked through a land that no beam e'er lightens,
    With a troop of spectres gaunt and white.

I must reach the shore but to look once only
    On a face upraised to the skies above;
'Mid the green woods there, in her cottage lonely,
    Waiting to greet me, is she I love.

She—there's a light—hush, hush, no screaming;
    Keep quite still in your places here;
'Tis the lamp from a prowling gunboat gleaming
    Over the waters far and near.

Make for the land—strike out—they've seen us.
    Zip! 'twas a cannon's deadly hiss,
But there's many a watery gap between us—
    They may fire again—so they fire and miss.

They're bearing down on us sure and steady,
   Zip, zip, zip—how the water boils!
Crouch, so the next shot finds us ready—
   A few strong pulls and we 'scape their toils.

We'll hurry in where the bank curves under
   That fringe of trees whose long boughs enlace;
Then, while their cannon boom and thunder,
   We'll seek the woods for our hiding-place.

A few more strokes and we leave the river;
   The land lies there where the long waves swell;
God! how the balls ricochet and shiver
   Till the air is strong with the powder's smell.

One stroke more—oh, my God! 't is over!
   That last shot told; ah, they aimed aright!
Good-bye to the Maryland fields of clover,
   And—tell her—I can not—come—to-night.

ELVIRA SYDNOR MILLER.

THE INGLESIDE.

IT's rare to see the morning bleeze,
   Like a bonfire frae the sea;
It's fair to see the burnie kiss
   The lip o' the flowery lee;
An' fine it is on green hillside,
   When hums the hinny bee;
But rarer, fairer, finer fair
   Is the ingleside to me.

Glens may be gilt wi' gowans rare,
   The birds may fill the tree,
An' haughs hae a' the scented ware
   That simmer's growth can gie;
But the cantie hearth where cronies meet,
   An' the darling o' our e'e,
That makes to us a warld complete,
   O, the ingleside's for me.

HEW AINSLIE.

THE GOLDEN WEDDING.

ONCE more the golden harp is strung,
    Attuned to joy and welcome cheer;
The voice of Love, the tuneful tongue
    To Friendship sweet—to mem'ry dear,
The light and blithesome heart of youth—
    Sweet dreams and hopes of long ago—
The pledge of Friendship, Love, and Truth,
    With all its measured numbers flow.

Now gently touch that harp once more—
    Call forth the sweet, melodious strain;
Faint echoes from the distant shore,
    Restored to Love and life again.
As vespers on the light winds play,
    Each joyous note, each gentle trill,
Like angel voices far away,
    Comes floating down through mem'ry still.

Here, fifty years ago to-night,
    Those notes did hope and joy awake,
And Heaven two hearts in one unite
    Till Heaven the silken cord should break;
And here again, at Love's pure shrine,
    Those hearts, still faithful, constant, true,
About each brow fresh laurels twine,
    And o'er life's path fresh flowers strew.

And as the joyous echoes start
    From far-off whispers, soft and low,
We see again here rolled apart
    The faded scroll of long ago;
And here, upon the sacred page,
    As each fond hope renewed appears,
The bloom of youth, the frosts of age
    Attest the lengthened flight of years.

THE GOLDEN WEDDING.

Old age, far down the slopes of time—
　Mid age upon the heights above—
Stern youth, in manhood's early prime—
　Sweet prattling innocence and love;
Long-cherished friends of other days—
　Strong hearts, untouched by grief or fear—
Gay, joyous mirth, sweet songs of praise,
　With beauty's bloom are mingled here.

How sweet, when mem'ry steals along
　Where life's cool murmuring waters flow,
To hear once more the rapturous song
　That thrilled us fifty years ago;
To call, in beauteous visions, up
　Again each well-remembered face
Of those who pledged to us the cup
　Of joy through life's eventful race.

To live those hallowed moments o'er
　When first our plighted faith was given,
And sealed with solemn vows before
　The bright eternal courts of Heaven.
To look beyond where first began
　Life's toils, its sorrows, griefs, and fears,
And measure but a single span
　To bridge the tide of fifty years.

But sweeter is it far to dwell,
　With furrowed cheek and care-worn brow,
Upon each word, as lisping fell
　From trembling lips the nuptial vow;
To breathe those sacred words again,
　And know still, ere life's sun is set,
The hearts we pledged each other then
　Are faithful to each other yet.

　　　　　　　　　　　M. M. TEAGER.

THE SONG OF STEAM.

HARNESS me down with your iron bands,
  Be sure of your curb and rein,
For I scorn the power of your puny hands
  As the tempest scorns a chain.
How I laughed, as I lay concealed from sight
  For many a countless hour,
At the childish boast of human might,
  And the pride of human power.

When I saw an army upon the land,
  A navy upon the seas,
Creeping along, a snail-like band,
  Or waiting the wayward breeze;
When I marked the peasant faintly reel
  With the toil which he daily bore,
As he feebly turned the tardy wheel
  Or tugged away at the oar;

When I measured the panting courser's speed,
  The flight of the carrier dove,
As they bore the law of a king decreed,
  Or the lines of impatient love,
I could not but think how the world would feel
  As these were outstripp'd afar,
When I should be bound to the rushing keel
  Or chained to the flying car.

Ha! ha! ha! they found me at last;
  They invited me forth at length;
And I rushed to my throne with a thunder-blast,
  And laughed in my iron strength.
O then ye saw a wondrous change,
  On the earth and the ocean wide,
Where now my fiery armies range,
  Nor wait for wind nor tide.

THE SONG OF STEAM.

Hurrah! Hurrah! the waters o'er,
  The mountain's steep decline,
Time—space—have yielded to my power;
  The world! the world is mine!
The rivers the sun hath earliest blest,
  Or those where his beams decline,
The giant streams of the queenly West,
  Or the Orient floods divine.

The ocean pales where'er I sweep—
  I hear my strength rejoice;
And the monsters of the briny deep
  Cower, trembling, at my voice.
I carry the wealth and the lord of earth,
  The thoughts of his god-like mind;
The mind lags after my going forth,
  The lightning is left behind.

In the darksome depths of the fathomless mine
  My tireless arm doth play,
Where the rocks never saw the sun decline,
  Or the dawn of the glorious day;
I bring earth's glittering jewels up
  From the hidden caves below,
And I make the fountain's granite cup
  With a crystal gush o'erflow.

I blow the bellows, I forge the steel
  In all the shops of trade;
I hammer the ore and turn the wheel
  Where my arms of strength are made;
I manage the furnace, the mill, the mint;
  I carry, I spin, I weave;
And all of my doings I put into print
  On every Saturday eve.

I 've no muscle to weary, no breast to decay,
  No bones to be "laid on the shelf,"
And soon I intend you may "go and play,"
  While I manage this world myself.

But harness me down with your iron bands,
  Be sure of your curb and rein,
For I scorn the power of your puny hands
  As the tempest scorns a chain.

GEORGE W. CUTTER.

A BUNCH OF MAGNOLIAS.

He gathered a bunch of poems
  From a garden in the sky,
And they were flower poems
  That came from oh, so high!

He gave one to a lady,
  Because her slender hand
Seemed made to hold a poem
  That came from blossom-land.

And one went to a prison,
  And a sweet message took—
One far away is dreaming,
  Its smile pressed in a book.

One, filled with angel whispers,
  He to my boudoir gave,
And one weeps in his memory,
  Its face hid on—a grave.

KATYDID.

RAPTURES.

PROCUL ESTE PROFANA.

WHILE youth in blooming Spring invites
To warm embraces, sweet delights,
   I'll yield to nature's voice,
I'll clasp my dear Narcissa, press'd
Close to my love-enraptured breast
   In mutual melting joys.

From flowery vales and verdant trees
The genial gales and balmy breeze
   O'er worlds enchanted move,
And nature all around conspires
To kindle all the soft desires
   Into a flame of love.

And can that fascinating frame
A cold, unfeeling heart contain
   Which passions never move;
A heart unform'd the joys to know
Which from the thrills and transports flow
   Of life-entrancing love.

No, the dear image of that day,
When in her circling arms I lay
   In ecstasy divine,
May something more than hope impart,
It tells my fondly fluttering heart
   She will be ever mine.

Each fond endearment of every kiss
Is present joy—and promised bliss—
   From my all-yielding bride,
While fancy's fairy power employs
The dear remembrance of past joys,
   As pledge for joy untried.

                              WILLIAM LITTELL.
"Festoons of Fancy."

EVENING THOUGHTS.

Most beautiful is the dark midnight sky:
Above ten thousand worlds in grandeur roll,
Hymning their Author's praise in anthems sweet
And high. The pulses of our being throb
In solemn awe; we tremble, and our life
Seems but a thought of the Eternal Mind
That formed this glorious scene of wonder, light,
And majesty.
          Beneath and all around
What silence and what beauty! On each flower
There hangs a drop of silver dew serene
And bright and trembling, while a zephyr cool
Soothes it to slumber with her gentle wing.

And now a soft, low music thrill floats out
Upon the air, so dim, so faint, we still
Our breathing, lest we lose the echoing
Of its strange sweetness. O'er the lake's bright waves
The airy zephyr lingers long to kiss
The stars that tremble there, like bright, glad thoughts,
Which struggle from the imprisoned soul to leap
Up to the fount of all true beauty, love,
And holiness.
          How softly rests the moon's
Calm smile on yonder sweet and grassy slope,
Where 'neath the cypress dear Leora sleeps:
Her life was like the rose-bud but half blown,
Within whose fragrant breast the poison worm
Lies hid; or like a harp, whose strings were tuned
To notes of joy, but which a careless hand
Too rudely broke. She faded gently, like
The bright close of a peaceful summer day,
And 'mid the flowers we laid the fair young head
Which once was fairer than themselves.
                                    Ah, life
Is a most fearful thing. Our being may

But seem a gentle star-beam flashing o'er
Time's rushing waters, but its light will guide
With fearful truth the frail and tossing bark
Of many wanderers o'er life's mystic sea.
Bright be our guidance then, and tho' our song
May be but faint and low, it yet may wake
Within some heart a happy dream, and bid
Sweet flowers of hope to softly bloom again
With dewy freshness in some saddened breast.

JENNIE T. MCHENRY.

SONG.

I.

A GENTLE wind, unvoiced,
    Along its viewless way,
By chance smote on a Lily bell
    Wherein a Dew-drop lay;
The drop in perfumed fragments fell,
    And whispering in my ears,
The Spring wind sigh'd and sweetly said,
    "I've kissed a Beauty's tears."

II.

That wind was as my thought,
    Which wandered here and there,
Loving, but restless not to find
    A love-shrine anywhere,
Till smiting on thy love-dewed heart
    The spell of silence broke,
And through the chambers of my soul
    Exquisite music woke.

J. V. COSBY.

THE BOATMAN'S HORN.

O, BOATMAN! wind that horn again,
  For never did the listening air
  Upon its lambent bosom bear
So wild, so soft, so sweet a strain!
  What though thy notes are sad and few,
  By every simple boatman blown,
    Yet is each pulse to nature true,
    And melody in every tone.
  How oft in boyhood's joyous day,
  Unmindful of the lapsing hours,
  I've loitered on my homeward way
  By wild Ohio's bank of flowers;
    While some lone boatman from the deck
    Poured his soft numbers to that tide,
  As if to charm from storm and wreck
  The boat where all his fortunes ride.

Delighted, Nature drank the sound,
Enchanted, Echo bore it 'round,
In whispers soft and softer still,
From hill to plain and plain to hill,
Till e'en the thoughtless frolic boy,
Elate with hope and wild with joy,
Who gamboled by the river's side
And sported with the fretting tide,
Feels something new pervade his breast,
Change his light steps, repress his jest.
Bends o'er the flood his eager ear,
To catch the sounds far off, yet dear—
Drinks the sweet draught, but knows not why
The tear of rapture fills his eye.
And can he now, to manhood grown,
Tell why those notes, simple and lone,
As on the ravished ear they fell,
Bind every sense in magic spell?
There is a tide of feeling given

To all on earth—its fountain heaven—
Beginning with the dewy flower
Just ope'd in Flora's vernal bower,
Rising creation's orders through,
With louder murmur, brighter hue.
That tide is sympathy. Its ebb and flow
Give life its hues, its joy and woe.
Music, the master spirit that can move
Its waves to war or lull them into love,
Can cheer the sinking sailor 'mid the wave,
And bid the warrior on, nor fear the grave,
Inspire the fainting pilgrim on his road
And elevate his soul to claim his God.
Then boatman wind that horn again;
Though much of sorrow mark its strain,
Yet are its notes to sorrow dear;
What though they wake fond memory's tear,
Tears are sad memory's sacred feast,
And rapture oft her chosen guest.

WM. O. BUTLER.

TWILIGHT IN KENTUCKY.

THE day was weary and upon the West
    Had leaned.
Night held one star aloft,
And slow and soft
    The twilight screened
The sun for Nature's rest.

How gently came repose—a whisper bold
    Of song
From a near woodland bird
Was all we heard,
    Save where a throng
Of lambs cried for the fold.

Across the field the weary farmer sped
  Knee deep
In rye; behind him lay
Fresh furrows—Day
  Smiles though asleep
And points him to his bed.
                              KATYDID.

A SONG.

WE stood beside the window—
  It was the very same
Where years ago together
  We wrote each other's name.
I listened for the dear words
  I used to hear from thee—
I listened, but there came not
  One loving word for me.

I looked into the blue depths
  Of those beloved eyes;
I longed to see them glisten
  With thoughts of former ties.
I looked, but oh! they spoke not
  The tenderness of old;
I thought my very heart-strings
  Would break, they were so cold.

My hand, I laid it gently—
  How gently!—on to thine;
I thought its pulse beat quicker;
  I thought it answered mine.
But no, there was no pressure;
  My dream of bliss was o'er;
I knew the spell was broken—
  That I was loved no more.
                            FORTUNATUS COSBY.

THE BLUEBIRD.

Though Winter's power fades away,
　The tyrant does not yield;
But still he holds a waning sway
　O'er hill and grove and field.

But while he still is lingering,
　Some lovely days appear—
Bright heralds from the train of Spring,
　To tell that she is near.

It is as if a day of heaven
　Had fallen from on high,
And God's own smiles for sunlight given
　Were beaming through the sky.

The bluebird now with joyous note
　His song of welcome sings;
Joy swells melodious in his throat;
　Joy quivers in his wings.

No cunning show of art severe,
　But soft and low his lay—
A sunbeam shining to the ear—
　Spring's softest, brightest ray.

Those magic tones call from the past
　The sunny hours of youth;
And shining hopes come thronging fast
　From worlds of love and truth.

The harmony is seen and heard,
　For notes and rays combine,
And joys and hopes and sun and bird
　All seem to sing and shine.
　　　　　　　　Noble Butler.

TO WHITTIER,

ON HIS SEVENTY-SIXTH BIRTHDAY.

How lightly falls the snow of age
    Upon the whitening locks of one
Who, be he poet, priest, or sage,
    Can say, at life's declining sun:
"Master, from that thou gavest me,
A hundred-fold I bring to thee."

That heart retains its freshness still,
    Though time-worn be its house of clay,
That like some calm and shaded rill
    Keeps ever singing on its way,
While all around it storm and strife
Rage fiercely on the shore of life.

Thus, Poet, on thine honored head
    The snow of age doth gently fall,
And thou mayst seek thy restful bed
    When Death's resistless voice shall call,
Wrapped close in tender dreams, as one
Assured the day's work was well done.

How like an evergreen thy heart,
    Retaining all its verdure still,
Though long ago did spring depart
    And leave thee to the winter's chill;
Yet, resting on its foliage green,
Is summer's lingering beauty seen.

Ah! soft and sweet thy melodies
    Shall sound through many a troubled heart;
Though tuneless then, the silent keys
    On which thy hand hath played its part,
Chords from thy music-soul shall be
Thus wafted to eternity.

Beloved Poet, though my song
  With rhythmic flow charm not thine ear,
From all the world's applauding throng
  Thou ne'er hadst tribute more sincere.
Accept these words, that would express
To thee a heart's deep tenderness.

MRS. W. P. McDOWELL.

TWO SONGS.

"I'LL make my song so grand and high—
  So high," he said, "that those who hear
Will stand and gaze into the sky,
  As on a soaring bird they fear
    That earthward turns,
And where some planet shines alone
  My song shall sit, and those who see
Will say the star has higher grown,
  And all, perchance, because of me
    It brighter burns."

"And I would stay close to the grass—
  So near that a sweet child could kiss
My song," she said, "where those who pass
  Would brush its bloom, and I could miss
    One fragrance less.
I'd have my song so sweet, its wing
  So fragile yet so perfect wrought,
That both would seem some spirit thing
  Of comfort, down from Heaven brought
    For men to bless."

KATYDID.

GENTLENESS: A SONNET.*

FAR in mid-ocean rose a rugged cliff.
Seas lashed its feet in fury; storm and wind
Roared round its wrinkled head, hoarse, cold, unkind.
Flocks of wild sea-birds flying over, stiff
And stark fell headlong down, their life resigned.
Dark vapors rolled about its hoary height
In murky density. There suns glowered pale;
Nor moon nor stars came in the shadowed night
To vex its solitude. In the far flight
Of time men came, and with an iron hail
Of cannon 'gainst this crag did thundering ring.
The rock disdainful stood. At last a flower,
The asphodel, waif on a zephyr's wing,
Touched it in love. It trembled to love's power.

WILLIAM J. DAVIS.

* Ptolemy Hephestion, in his geography of the world, tells of a rock in the ocean, famous in his day, which, shaped like a huge inverted cone and resting on a narrow foundation, resisted the violence of winds and waves, and all human efforts to destroy its equilibrium, but was shaken to its center when its surface was touched by the little flower called asphodel.

MARCUS BLAKEY ALLMOND.

BIOGRAPHICAL SKETCHES.

BIOGRAPHICAL SKETCHES

OF AUTHORS REPRESENTED IN THIS VOLUME.

PROFESSOR MARCUS BLAKEY ALLMOND, A. M.

Born in Stanardsville, Virginia, 1851. Married Miss Virginia Carey Meade, of that State, who is the real heroine of his poem "Estelle." President Noah Porter, of Yale College, wrote him a very complimentary letter upon this, his longest poem, in which letter he says: "It is sweet in its spirit, lovely in its picture, and admirably felicitous in its diction. What could I say more? and I should not say less, if I say any thing." Professor Allmond held the chair of Ancient Languages in the Male High School of Louisville, Kentucky, for several years, and is now President of the University School in that city. He was magazine medalist at the University of Virginia, of which institution he is a graduate. * * *

HEW AINSLIE

Was born in Scotland in 1792. When Sir Walter Scott, James Hogg, and others were making Scotland a " hunting field " after her " ancient minstrelsie," he was a clerk in the Register House, Edinburgh. In 1822 Mr. Ainslie emigrated to America and settled in the then "far West," making his home in Louisville. In 1855 he published a volume of poems in his mother tongue, entitled, " Scottish Songs, Ballads, and Poems." He died in Louisville. * *

JAMES LANE ALLEN.

The friends who know Mr. Allen best say that his full strength is yet untried, that the best in him is yet untold, and that with health and time he will give it permanent artistic shape. He has already won the first place among American short-story writers. An English critic compares him to Washington Irving, another to Nathaniel Hawthorne. He has written less poetry than prose, and always takes a modest view of his own work. By birth, rearing, and education Mr. Allen is a Kentuckian. He was born near Lexington, Kentucky, on a bluegrass farm not far from the spot where the generations of his family had lived since the first emigration from Virginia. Mr. Allen began his career as a writer several years ago in Harper's Monthly and The Century, with a series of articles descriptive of life, character, and social iustitutions in Kentucky. He has continued to be a favorite with those magazines, and has an article in one or both nearly every month. His beautiful story of "The Flute and The Violin" is illustrated and sold in book form, and one could not conceive of a more exquisite story.

SARAH H. HENTON.

JOSEPH ALLGOOD

Is connected with The Bradley and Gilbert Company, of Louisville, and is very modest as to his ability as a writer, yet his poems are seen in all the leading newspapers, and he certainly has many friends who admire his unaffected style. * *

JAMES R. BARRICK

Was born in Barren County, Kentucky, in 1829. Attended Urania College at Glasgow. Began to write poetry at an early age, and was a frequent contributor to the "Poet's Corner" of the Louisville Journal. There has never been a volume of his poems published, but his family have a splendid collection ready for the press. During the Civil War he went South and edited several different papers. At the time of his death, which occurred April 30, 1869, he was editor of the Atlanta Constitution.

SARAH T. BOLTON

Is now seventy-two years old; a resident of Indianapolis, Indiana. She was born in Newport, Kentucky, but became an adopted child of our sister State in early girlhood, and was married at the age of sixteen to Nathaniel Bolton, then editor of a paper at Madison. After marriage financial reverses came, and her singing was hushed for a while. She met these troubles bravely, and when the clouds passed away, as a cloud passes from before the sun, and the brightness shines forth into every corner, so did her sweet songs burst forth and fill all the land with their radiance. During her sojourn abroad, when her husband was Consul to Geneva, Switzerland, she caught the sweet influence of the beauties of the country and wove them in her songs. "Lake Leman," "Mont Blanc," and others instance this. W. D. Gallagher, our venerable Kentucky poet, in writing of Mrs. Bolton, said: "She sings because song is the language of her heart, and she *must* sing or her heart must ache with its suppressed emotions." The channel of the Ohio River is not so broad—Mrs. Bolton has built a bridge —of song. * * *

MISS ALLINE BROTHER

Is the only daughter of Dr. William Brother, of Fort Spring, Woodford County, Kentucky. Born in the heart of the bluegrass country, she combines much fresh young beauty with rare intellectual gifts. Is a writer of both prose and poetry. * *

MARY E. BETTS.

Mary E. Wilson-Betts was born at Maysville, Kentucky, 1830, and was married to Morgan L. Betts in 1854. She died the same year.

MATTIE N. BROWN.

Born in 1844, and reared among the romantic hills of Spencer County, Kentucky. Her poetic talent developed early, and she left a volume of poems which receive much praise. Married Salem Brown, of Louisville, and died in that city, March 4, 1887.   * *

STANTON PIERCE BRYAN

Was born in Spencer County, Kentucky, July 22, 1827. Is an active practitioner of medicine in Oldham County, having taken a full course of study in Dublin, Ireland. Married Adelaide Thomas in 1853, and raised five daughters, one of whom recently died a missionary in China. In the midst of his duties as a physician Dr. Bryan finds it a recreation to indulge his passion for writing poetry, and finds an entrance to the leading papers and magazines.   * *

WILLIAM O. BUTLER.

Born in Jessamine County, Kentucky, 1793. Was a lawyer by profession, but enlisted in the war of 1812. At the battle of Raisin he was one of the few who escaped massacre after being wounded. Was Major-General in the war with Mexico, and led the charge at Monterey. In early life wrote some excellent verse.   * *

NOBLE BUTLER

Was born in Pennsylvania, but became a citizen of Kentucky in early life, and was identified with the schools of Louisville—teaching as a profession and writing text-books—prominent among which his Grammar took high rank, being adopted in all the schools. He wrote much for the press, but little poetry.   * *

MISS JENNIE CASSEDAY

Is a resident of Louisville, and her name is a household word. She is extensively known for her charities. Has recently built "Rest Cottage" at Pewee Valley, a summer home where working girls from the city may spend a vacation of rest. Miss Casseday is President of the Flower Mission for the Universe, and her sweet influence reaches to every land; yet she has been an invalid thirty years. She composes some beautiful verses and calls them "Night-time Songs." She says they come to her as an inspiration in the lone, wakeful night-hours. To know her is a sweet inspiration for good.   * *

MADISON CAWEIN.

Born in Louisville, March 23, 1865. Was graduated from the High School in 1886. Has published successively "Blooms of the Berry," "Triumph of Music," "Accolon of Gaul," "Lyrics and Idyls," and "Days and Dreams." His latest volume is entitled " Moods and Memories." Although a young man he has won the appreciation of such critics as Edmund Clarence Stedman, W. D. Howells, Frank Dempster Sherman, and James Lane Allen. James Whitcomb Riley dedicated his last book of poems to Mr. Cawein, and says of him: "He is a *soul* as well as a singer."

The following extract is from the New York World, whose literary editor pays Mr. Cawein a handsome tribute:

"Mr. Cawein is a Kentuckian. To a foreigner unacquainted with our geography and social latitudes that statement may mean nothing more than the indication of a section with a curious name. To many Americans it signifies no more than a place where quick-tempered men and pretty women abound, and where the thoroughbreds prance in pastures of bluegrass. The New Englander, even the Northern poet, may think of Kentucky as one of the fertile divisions of the Union, which may in time produce a cultured Daniel Boone. The Southerner alone knows what Kentucky is, and he knows it is, as Joaquin Miller would say, 'God's own country.' So, of course, from Kentucky we might expect a poet to come. American poetry must puzzle the less informed of our foreign readers, especially the Germans, and every educated German now reads our poetry. Poetry, more decidedly than prose, is identified by its 'atmosphere.' How confusing must our different atmospheres be to strangers. And to complicate matters, here is a Southern poet with the Greece of Keats in his fancy, the Italy of Rossetti in his expression, and occasionally the imagination of Coleridge."

RUFUS J. CHILDRESS,

A poet of the people, was born on a small farm near Paducah, Kentucky, in the year 1852. His fondness for literature manifested itself at a very early age, and most of his spare time was spent poring over books or setting his vagrant fancies to song. While a mere youth he published a small volume of verses, the modest success of which inspired him with a desire to seek a broader field for his talents. Later on, therefore, we find him at Louisville, where his contributions to the local papers speedily attracted the attention of all lovers of pure thought and delicate imaginings. Though a dweller in the mart, toiling unceasingly from morning till night, Mr. Childress has never ceased to be an Arcadian; his songs breathe of the woods, the green countryside, blue skies, and murmuring waters, and through the smoke and dust, the turmoil and striving of Babylon, the dream of these fair things shines always starlike before him. Mr. Childress has been a welcome contributor to the Courier-Journal, Belford's Magazine, the Round Table, the New South, and other well-known magazines and journals. A brief biography, and some of his poems also, appeared in the Library of Western Song, published at Chicago. I am pleased to state that he is now engaged in compiling a second volume of verse, which will probably appear in the near future. Having been honored with his friendship for many years, I can say nothing but what is good of him. He is a devoted husband, an affectionate father, a faithful friend, and upright citizen. Would there were more like him.

ELVIRA SYDNOR MILLER.

FLORENCE ANDERSON CLARK

Was reared in the beautiful bluegrass region of Kentucky, where nature in its fairest aspects fostered the dreamy tendencies of a poetic temperament. In 1869 she was married to Captain James B. Clark, of Jackson, Mississippi, who was for six years editor of The Kentucky People, at Harrodsburg, Kentucky. For this paper much of Mrs. Clark's literary work was done. In 1875 they removed to Austin, Texas, where her husband is Librarian of the State University.

FORTUNATUS COSBY, JR.

Was born near the city of Louisville, May 2, 1802. He studied at Transylvania University, but was graduated from Yale College. Afterward studied law and was admitted to the bar, but his talents were of a too versatile nature to allow him to remain loyal to that engrossing profession, and we find him a clerk in the Treasury Department at Washington, and subsequently, for several years, United States Consul at Geneva, Switzerland. Between 1840 and 1850 he was a frequent contributor of both prose and verse to newspapers at Louisville, and was intimately associated with the brilliant George D. Prentice, and died but six months after him, June, 1871.

MRS. JENNIE JONES CUNNINGHAM

Is a native of Tennessee, but has lived in Louisville, Kentucky, for sixteen years. Her poems have been readily accepted by leading papers. She is well known as a writer, but lives a very quiet and rather oriental life. She is the wife of J. A. Cunningham, who is the author of several books on scientific and theologic research.

MRS. W. LESLIE COLLINS

Lives at Frankfort. She published a small volume of poems in 1888, entitled, " Sea Waifs and Other Poems."

REV. JOUETT VERNON COSBY.

A native of Staunton, Virginia, but for many years a citizen of Bardstown, Kentucky. A theologian of note. Wrote many fugitive poems, but never published a volume.

INGRAM CROCKETT.

Born at Henderson, Kentucky, 1856. His father, John W. Crockett, was famous throughout the State for his powers of oratory. His mother was a Miss Ingram, daughter of one of the early settlers of Henderson. Mr. Crockett has been more successful than most young writers. His poetry is eagerly sought, and he has been welcomed by the leading periodicals. In all his writing there is a quiet, gentle dignity and loftiness of purpose which illustrate his "manliness of soul." Mr. Crockett was married in Henderson, and is connected with the Planters State Bank at that place. * *

GEORGE WASHINGTON CUTTER

Was born in Massachusetts about 1809, and died in Washington City in 1865, but he was many years a resident of Kentucky and fully identified with her people. It was while commanding a company of Kentuckians in the war with Mexico that he wrote his beautiful poem, "Buena Vista." He practiced law for several years at Covington. His poem, "The Song of Steam," is widely known.

GEORGE M. DAVIE.

George Montgomery Davie was born in Christian County, Kentucky. Graduating at Princeton University, New Jersey, in 1868, his life has since been that of a studious and laborious lawyer. He married, in 1878, Margaret Howard, daughter of General William Preston. His home is in Louisville. The exactions of professional life have forbidden him to seriously indulge his taste for literary work; his verses have been "occasional" ones, some of which have been published in different periodicals.

MAJOR WILLIAM J. DAVIS

Was born in South Carolina, March 23, 1839. After finishing his education, which was both classical and military, and in both branches of which he excelled, he entered the Confederate service at the beginning of the war and continued to its close. After the war he studied law and practiced for some time, but finally became engaged in educational and scientific pursuits. In 1877 he became Secretary of the Board of Trustees of the Public Schools of Louisville, and still holds that place. He is an accomplished scholar, scientist, and writer.

Yours truly — S. P. Bryan.

BIOGRAPHICAL SKETCHES. 305

MRS. MAY SMITH DOWNS.

Born in Missouri, but reared in Kentucky. A daughter of Joseph W. Smith, of Glasgow. She was married in 1889 to Professor J. M. N. Downs, the present Superintendent of Public Schools at Somerset.

GENERAL BASIL W. DUKE

Was born in Scott County, Kentucky, on May 28, 1837; was educated at Georgetown and at Center College, and commenced the practice of law in 1856 at St. Louis. His taste and talent for military life led to his becoming a captain in the State Guard; and in 1861 he gave his services to the Confederacy at Bowling Green, Kentucky. His career as a cavalry leader, in a line of service created by himself and General Morgan, was as brilliant as it was novel in warfare. The close of the war found him a Brigadier-General, with an independent command. Returning to civil life with the fall of the Confederacy, he resumed the practice of the law at Louisville; served in the Kentucky Legislature, and as Commonwealth's Attorney for Louisville, and is now one of the counsel of the Louisville and Nashville Railroad Company. He was married in the year 1861 to a sister of General John H. Morgan.

During the war General Duke was the author of a "System of Cavalry Tactics," and, since the war, of a "History of Morgan's Command;" and for several years one of the editors, in his odd hours, of The Southern Bivouac. His brilliant and versatile talents, his singularly striking and high character, and his social powers and position have given him an enviable place and distinction in Kentucky. G. M. D.

REUBEN THOMAS DURRETT.

Born in Henry County, Kentucky, January 22, 1824. After two years at Georgetown (Kentucky) College he went to Brown University, Providence, Rhode Island, where he graduated in 1849. The same year he entered the Law Department of the University of Louisville and graduated with the degree of LL. B. in 1850. After thirty years of successful practice at the Louisville bar he was able to retire on the competency he had earned.

In his earlier years Mr. Durrett yielded to an imagination which demanded the expression of thoughts in verse, and had he not acquired distinction in other lines he might have been widely known as a poet. In poetry he was exceedingly versatile, and passed from the humorous to the grave with marked facility. His serious humor, however, predominated, and his best productions may be considered in this vein. His "Night Scene at Drennon's Springs," in 1850; his "Thoughts over the Grave of Rev. Thomas Smith," 1852; and his "Old Year and New in the Coliseum at Rome," in 1856, each of which

20

was published when written, are fine specimens of classic thought expressed in blank verse, and entitle him to high rank among Western poets.

It is as a prose writer, however, that Mr. Durrett will be most favorably and most enduringly known. After retiring from the bar in 1880, he devoted much of his leisure to historic studies, for which he always had an inclination. His numerous historic articles, published in the Courier-Journal since 1880, have been widely read and much admired for their original research and the new colors with which they invested important events and subjects.

In 1884 a few of his associates of similar tastes joined Mr. Durrett in establishing an association in Louisville for co-operative effort in the collecting and preserving and publishing of historic matter relating to Kentucky. This association was named the "Filson Club," in honor of John Filson, the first historian of Kentucky, and Mr. Durrett, who was made its president, prepared and read the first paper before it. This paper was the "Life and Times of John Filson," which was published as number one of the series of Club publications. It is a quarto of 132 pages, so full of original matter and so beautifully written that it at once gave the Club a prominent stand among kindred associations.

In his literary studies Mr. Durrett has always bought the books he needed, and in thus purchasing from year to year he has accumulated a large and valuable library. The volumes and pamphlets and papers and manuscripts upon his shelves number more than fifty thousand, and he is adding to them every day. His collection embraces the best works in almost every branch of human knowledge, but is particularly rich in history, and especially in American history. He is so familiar with his books that he can promptly lay his hands on any one of the fifty thousand volumes without the aid of a catalogue; but, better than this, he is as familiar with the contents of his books as he is with their location upon the shelves.

In 1852 Mr. Durrett was married to Miss Elizabeth H. Bates, the only daughter of Caleb and Elizabeth (*nee* Humphreys) Bates, of Cincinnati, Ohio.

Mr. Durrett, now in his sixty-eighth year, is a well preserved man of health and vigor, who bids fair to be among those who, at the age of seventy-six, will cross over from the nineteenth to the twentieth century. He belongs to the school of old Virginia gentlemen, now so rare among us, and his hospitable home is ever open to those who wish to see him. His collection of books and antiquities has made him a kind of show in Louisville, whither strangers as well as acquaintances resort with an assurance of seeing something worth seeing and learning something worth learning. He is never more delighted than when in his great library with one or more persons in search of information from rare books and manuscripts. In this way most literary persons at home and many from abroad have been placed under obligations to him, and his constant regret is that he has not been able to do more good to others with his books. WM. H. PERRIN.

SYDNER DYER

Was a resident of Louisville for many years, where he entered the ministry of the Baptist Church. In 1845 he published his first volume of poems, and a second one in 1855. He afterward became a citizen of Indiana. * * *

ALEXANDER EVANS.

Born in Middletown, Kentucky, November 9, 1814. Engaged in commercial pursuits until 1847, when he was appointed Lieutenant, by President Polk, in the 16th U. S. Infantry. In 1848 the regiment disbanded, and he was again in commercial life until 1861, when he went South and was Major in Breckinridge's Division. Since the close of the Civil War Major Evans has engaged in business pursuits in Louisville until his age forced him into retirement. His poems appeared in the Louisville papers as early as 1837, and from that time at frequent intervals. Even at his advanced age Major Evans writes beautiful verse, filled with all the bright imagery of youth. He has published several books. * *

MISS NANNIE MAYO FITZHUGH

Lives at Lexington, and is known as one of the most gifted writers of the Bluegrass State. Her poetry is quite familiar to readers of The Century, Harper, New Orleans Times, and New York Sun, and many other leading periodicals publish her exquisite sonnets. Her descriptive powers probably reach their highest limit in the beautiful poem entitled "Meeting Rivers." "T'other Miss Mandy," published by Harper, has given her a national reputation. *

MANLIUS THOMPSON FLIPPIN.

Born in Monroe County, Kentucky. He still lives at the county-seat, Tompkinsville, and is Judge of the County Court. Has recently published a volume of poems. *

THOMAS B. FORD.

Born in Owen County, Kentucky, but has lived in Frankfort many years. President of the Southern Literary Association and a prime factor in the new literary movement of the South. His life has been devoted principally to public interests. His efforts in a literary way have been very successful. A drama, an opera, and several novels, besides his poetry, show his versatility of talent. * *

LAURA CATHERINE FORD,

Now the wife of Dr. Hugh Smith, who was chief surgeon of the famous "Orphan Brigade," lives in Owenton, Kentucky, in the same county in which she was born. Is a sister of Colonel Thomas Ford. She writes more prose than poetry. * *

WILLIAM W. FOSDICK

Was educated at Transylvania University, Lexington, Kentucky, and after graduating there went to Louisville to pursue the study of law. After completing his studies with Judge Prior he began the practice of law in Covington, where he was a partner of James Southgate. * *

STEPHEN COLLINS FOSTER

Was born in Pittsburgh, Pennsylvania, in 1826. Died in 1864. He lived many years in Kentucky, and gave to us the "Old Kentucky Home." It appears in Bryant's Library of Poetry, and every Kentuckian can testify to its touching sentiment who has ever listened to it sung in a strange land. * * * *

WILLIAM DAVIS GALLAGHER.

Born in Philadelphia, August 21, 1808. After the death of his father, when he was but eight years old, his mother moved to Cincinnati. His first literary work was for an agricultural paper called The Tiller. He was editorially connected with many different newspapers for about three-score years. With the Gazette, of Cincinnati, from 1839 to 1850, and the Courier, of Louisville, from 1853 to 1854.

The characteristic of Mr. Gallagher's writings is purity of style and purity of matter. A thorough search through the broad range of his writings in the newspapers and periodicals for the last six and sixty years may be made without finding one vulgar sentence or one immoral sentiment. The cultured gentleman and the unswerving moralist go with his pen wherever it is used.

During the Civil War he was connected with the governmental service in the Customs and the Pension Departments at Louisville.

As a poet Mr. Gallagher has been widely and favorably known. He has published several books of poetry. "Miama Woods, A Golden Wedding, and other Poems" was issued in 1881. It is a good volume on which to rest his fame. There are in it descriptions of nature, songs of patriotism, and lyrics of the affections, and legends and odes that will live as long as our country exists and the English language is spoken. He now resides in his humble cottage at Pewee Valley, at the venerable age of eighty-four, full of the priceless riches of literary fame, but poor in this world's goods.   R. T. DURRETT.

BIOGRAPHICAL SKETCHES. 309

MISS ANNA J. HAMILTON.

Born in Louisville, April 20, 1860. Was graduated from the High School in 1878. Occupies the Commercial chair in the Normal School in that city. A late number of the Magazine of Poetry contains an interesting sketch of Miss Hamilton and her poetry. She is at present editing the Kentucky edition of "The Women of the Century," to be published soon by Charles Wells Moulton, of Buffalo, New York.

JOHN M. HARNEY.

Practiced medicine at Bardstown, Kentucky, and married a daughter of Judge Rowan there in 1814. His wife died in a few years, and he traveled abroad. Receiving a naval appointment to Buenas Ayres he made that his home for several years, but finally returned to Bardstown, and died on the 15th of January, 1825. He wrote "Crystalina, a Fairy Tale," in six cantos, in 1816, which received much praise from Eastern magazines. It was completed before he reached his twenty-third year. Many other shorter poems met with wide circulation in the leading periodicals of that day. His poem "Echo and the Lover" occupies a place in Bryant's Library of Poetry and Song.   * * *

WILL WALLACE HARNEY.

Born at Bloomington, Indiana, June 21, 1831, but was brought to Kentucky by his parents in 1833. Educated at home under Professor Noble Butler. The name Harney is Celtic and signifies strong in mind—headstrong. His father, John H. Harney, was for twenty-five years editor of the Louisville Democrat.

Mr. Harney was the first principal of the Louisville High School. Held chair of Belles Letters in the Normal Department of Transylvania University.

Was married in 1868 to Miss Mary St. Mayer Randolph, and moved to Florida in 1869. His wife died in 1870, after which he spent much of his time exploring the Everglades, which he did as far south as Florida Keys.

His letters descriptive of the climate and the phosphate beds of Florida, published in the Northern periodicals, attracted much attention to that State. His poetry is published in Harper's and The Century, and is widely copied in books of selections, both English and American, and much used by elocutionists for qualities adapted to vocal expression.   * *

ALFRED W. HARRIS.

Born in Louisville, January 27, 1842. Has held several Government positions. Married to Miss Maggie Heimers in 1870. Member of the Filson Club.

JOEL T. HART.

Born in Clark County, Kentucky in 1810. He has made for himself an everlasting record in his life-work, "The Triumph of Chastity," which he was twenty years in completing. It was modeled from the same clay used for Powers' "Greek Slave," and is now the property of the ladies of Lexington, Kentucky. Hart's poems were written while he was in Italy, where he spent the best years of his life, and where he died. His remains were brought home and interred at Frankfort.

COLONEL WILL S. HAYS

Was born in Louisville, Kentucky, July 19, 1837. He first entered the field of journalism thirty-seven years ago on the Louisville Democrat as river editor. He remained with that paper until it went out of existence during the close of the late war, and then spent two or three years of his life on the river as captain and clerk on various boats, the last one being the famous Jacob Strader. He finally drifted back into newspaper life, and was for a long time amanuensis to the late George D. Prentice. When Prentice died Colonel Hays went over to the Courier-Journal after they were consolidated, and, with the exception of about one year, he has been with that great paper as its marine editor ever since.

There are few men now living who have done more for the marine interests of the great Southwest than Will S. Hays. His reputation as a song-writer is world-wide. He has written and composed more popular ballads than any man living, and bears his worldly fame and envied name with becoming modesty.

EDWIN SYLVESTER HOPKINS

Was born in Covington, of Kentucky parentage, but traces his origin to the Hopkins family of New England. The removal of his parents to Greencastle, Indiana, at that time the most prominent seat of learning in the State, placed him in an atmosphere of culture and refinement that largely influenced his subsequent career.

With a strong affection for the woods and fields where his holidays were spent, his thoughts naturally sought poetic expression, and among his first contributions to literature was a series of twelve poems illustrating the various moods of nature during the year, and published in the Indianapolis Journal and in the Courier-Journal.

After graduation he was elected to a professorship in Franklin College, Indiana, and was married to a lady in Danville, Kentucky, a graduate of Caldwell Institute, and a contributor to several leading magazines. After several years spent in teaching he gave up the profession, and removing to the bluegrass region of his native State became a Bourbon County farmer and stock raiser, which calling he still finds

BIOGRAPHICAL SKETCHES. 311

congenial, allowing sufficient leisure for an occasional contribution to The Judge, Peterson's, The Free Press, Indianapolis Journal, and Courier-Journal, and many other publications.

JOHN HOSKINS.

Born in Cornwall, England, February 25, 1827. Came to Kentucky in 1845. Has lived in Louisville since 1850. His poems are noticeable for their rhythmic flow, and are easily adapted to music. He writes music as well, and his publications find ready sale.

COLONEL J. STODDARD JOHNSTON

Was born in New Orleans, February 10, 1833, but has for long years been a Kentuckian, and comes of a family who were among the pioneers of the State. He was graduated from Yale College in 1853, and from the Law Department of the University of Louisville in 1854. He was in the Confederate army from 1862 to the close of the war, and held important positions on the staffs of Generals Bragg, Breckinridge, and Buckner. Since the war Colonel Johnson has been a leading politician, and held the office of Secretary of State under Governors Leslie and McCreary. He was for many years editor of the Frankfort Yeoman. He is an able writer and noted for a wide range of knowledge and scholarly attainments.

ROSA VERTNER JEFFREY.

Rosa Vertner Jeffrey is one of the most gifted poets of the South. She is a native of Natchez, Mississippi, but in early life removed to Lexington, Kentucky, with her maternal aunt and adopted mother, Mrs. Vertner, by whose name she was known. Her mother (who died when Rosa was only a few months old) was the daughter of an Episcopal clergyman, Rev. James Abercrombie, at one time rector of old St. Peter's, Philadelphia. Her father, J. T. Griffith, was the well-known author of "Indian Stones," and other writings published both in this country and England.

At an early age Rosa Vertner was married to Claude M. Johnson, of Lexington, Kentucky. Her present husband was born in Edinburgh, and belongs to a distinguished Scotch family.

Mrs. Jeffrey resides in Lexington, where she dispenses in a quiet way an elegant hospitality. Her crown of snowy hair enhances the classic features of a still lovely face. She possesses a very versatile genius; her poetry is of the most genuine kind, natural, lucid, and spontaneous; her style is refined and without affectation. With the subtlety of her intensely human sympathy for humanity she woos and wins. She is a poet born, not made. When her first volume was published by Messrs. Ticknor & Fields, in 1859, it was received both in the North and South without an adverse criticism. I mention this because the trend of thought has been to accord so much less culture in literary pursuits to the South than it really deserves. Mrs. Jeffrey's poems were highly eulogized by the best critics of the day, Theodore O'Hara, George D. Prentice, Paul Shipman, of the Courier-Journal, and many others.

The following poem, inscribed to her by George D. Prentice, is inserted by request in this sketch:

TO ROSA.

Not in the Grecian isles,
    Not where the bright flowers of Illyssus shine,
E'er moved a breathing form whose beauty's wiles
    Could match with thine.

Not where the golden glow
    Of Italy's clear sky is pure and clear,
Not where the beauteous waves of Leman flow,
    Hast thou thy peer.

Not where the sunlight falls
    On bright Circassia through the perfumed air,
Nor in Stamboul's oriental halls,
    Dwells one so fair.

No fabled form of old,
    Not hers who rose from out the foaming sea,
Though deemed more fair than aught of earthly mould,
    Transcended thee.

In thy dark eyes a spell
    Of beauty lingers, but their glance of fire,
When thy proud spirit is aroused, might quell
    The lion's ire.

Thou movest floatingly
    As the light cloud that to the zephyr yields,
But with a step proud as a queen's might be
    O'er conquered fields.

And thou hast that strange gift,
    The gift of genius, high and proud and strong,
At whose behest thoughts beautiful and swift
    Around thee throng.

They come to thee from far,
    From air, and earth, and ocean's boundless deeps;
They rush in glory from each shining star
    On heaven's blue steeps.

They leap from earth's far bound—
    Forth from the red volcano's depths they start—
From bow and cloud they float, and gather round
    Thy burning heart.

> Then at thy high command
> They stand all marshaled in thy peerless lay,
> As some great warrior marshals his proud band
> In bright array.
>
> Thy hand has power to trace
> Words as enduring as yon planet's flame,
> Words that forever 'mid our changing race
> Will keep thy name.
>
> Linked with bright song alone,
> That name o'er time's wild heaving waves will sweep,
> As o'er the water sweeps the bugle tone
> At midnight deep.
>
> Thy magic strains will make
> A portion of earth's living music heard
> Forever, like the cadences of lake
> And breeze and bird.
>
> The world of nature glows
> In thy bright page more lovely to the eye,
> As when o'er hills and plain, the sunset throws
> Its golden dye.
>
> And thou art very dear
> To many hearts, thou bright and gifted one,
> Aye, men adore thee, as the Persian seer
> Adored the sun.

The "Legend of the Opal," written at the age of fifteen, is inimitable. "Baby Power," "Nina, or the Last Night at Pompeii," "The Frozen Ship," and "The First Eclipse" are choice productions, but too long for publication in this sketch.

M. M. HODGES.

ANDREW W. KELLEY.

In 1872 Kelley left Schenectady, New York, where he had been employed as a reporter on a small afternoon newspaper, and went to Tennessee. Here he employed his time with writing poems and sketches, mainly for the New York Mercury, until the autumn of 1873, when he went to Franklin, Kentucky, and took a position as associate editor of The Patriot. He did not remain long on the paper, indeed, no one remained long on The Patriot, and I might say with equal truth that nothing stuck to that paper, absolutely nothing, except a mortgage about the size of an ordinary blanket, and a libel suit brought by a citizen of Bear Wallow, Allen County, whose book of sylvan verse had been "roasted" to such a degree as warranted an action at law.

It was Kelley's intention, year after year, to go East, but he sat in his room and dreamed and dreamed; and time, regardless of dreams or poetic fancies, moved steadily along, and finally stopped one day. And then the green sward in the cemetery was disturbed, and the dreamer was lowered into the "dreamless bed."

A gentle child of genius, smiling or deeply brooding, laughing or in sorrow, he was the soother of distress and the encourager of faltering footsteps. In verse, he had a most merry faculty of humor, and a most tender faculty of pathos. In a line he would draw a character tittering with the jollity of its own conceit; a word-flash, a change, and the mellow light of fond sympathy falls like a yellow drapery of richest silk, and with a warm beauty dignifies drollery and gives to a whimsical chuckle a tone of appealing pathos.

The country has surely produced greater poets than "Parmenas Mix," but I doubt if we shall ever know a truer lover of Nature's divine impulses. He lightened the heart and made it tender, surely a noble mission; he talked to the lowly, he flashed the diamond of his genius into many a dark recess. He preached the gospel of good will; he sang a beautiful song.   OPIE READ.

MRS. ANNIE CHAMBERS-KETCHUM

Was born near Georgetown, Kentucky, and is noted for her poetic talent. Her "Semper Fidelis," published in Harper's Magazine several years ago, is said to be one of the most finished productions of American literature.

OLIVER LUCAS.

Born in Orange County, Indiana, June 1827. At the age of sixteen he adopted the business of practical printing. At New Albany he and Hon. A. M. Bradley published the New Albany Democrat. Later he moved to Louisville, where he became connected with the Louisville Democrat. In 1856 he was the legislative correspondent of the Louisville Journal at Frankfort, and also reported for the Frankfort Yeoman. In May, 1863, he was elected clerk of the Board of Aldermen of the city of Louisville, and has been elected twenty-eight times successively. It was almost accidental that he became a writer of verse, his productions being principally of a local character, and published over the *nom de plume* of "The Poet of the Asfaltus."   LAF. JOSEPH.

MRS. MARY THORNTON McABOY

Has a fadeless reputation as a writer of very sweet songs. She was born in Bourbon County, Kentucky, and contributed her poetry to many of the leading papers in the State, and yet she claimed for it no especial literary merit.

NELLY MARSHALL McAFEE.

Louisville, Kentucky, was the birthplace and is the home of Nelly Marshall McAfee. She is the scion of a noble race, who have few peers and no superior. Her ancestral line, without a break in its ramifications, runs back to 1172, when William le Mareschal came over to England with the Army of the Northern Conquerer. "Nelly Marshall" was the boast and pride of her State, and she has lost none of her prestige since her marriage with Captain John J. McAfee, which event occurred some years ago.

Mrs. McAfee is not only a writer of verse but of fiction, which has fixed her position in the South and the Southwest as a literary leader in her State. She is a brilliant lecturer, a superb elocutionist, and, remarkable to state, she is called an "orator" rather than a public speaker. She handles her pen only when she feels the inspiration move her to industry. Her name ranks high in the histories of her State, and in the biographies and eucyclopedias of the country. She sings with no uncertain sound. And she deserves everything kind that could be said of her. Gifted with grace, beauty and genius, these endowments are supplemented by culture, refinement and accomplishments. She is a magnificent pianist, and paints with great grace and delicacy.   H. T. H.

THOMAS F. McBEATH.

Born in Wayne county, Kentucky, 1852; completed his education at Urania College, Glasgow, Kentucky, in 1882, and was chosen Valedictorian of his class of twenty members. His poem, "Biopsis," has been pronounced one of the finest poems that has been contributed to the literature of the South. He is now President of the Normal College at Daleville, Mississippi.   * *

MRS. KATE GOLDSBOROUGH McDOWELL

Was born in Louisville, and still lives there. A daughter of J. H. Wright, and wife of William Preston McDowell. She has written a great deal but never published a volume. The poet Whittier wrote her a very graceful and complimentary letter of thanks for the lines she addressed him on his seventy-sixth birthday.   * *

JENNIE T. McHENRY,

Of Hartford, Kentucky, wrote over the *nom de plume* of "Rosine." Her poems were collected and published in a small volume in 1867.

MRS. CLARA LOVELL McILVAIN.

Born in Cincinnati, Ohio, November 26, 1836. Was educated at Nazareth, Kentucky, and became a convert to the Catholic religion. Soon after leaving school she was married to J. Banks McIlvain, of Louisville, Kentucky. In her collection of poems, "Echoes of the Past," edited by her daughter, Charlotte McIlvaine Moore, will be found the story of her life, breathed in such sweet measures as to win for her the love of all. She died in Louisville, August 26, 1881.

MRS. KATE SLAUGHTER McKINNEY (KATYDID)

Was born at London, Laurel County, Kentucky. When she was seven years old her parents moved to Kirksville, Madison County. She was graduated in 1876 at Daughter's College, and some years ago was married to Mr. J. I. McKinney, now Superintendent of the Louisville and Nashville Railroad at Montgomery, Alabama. She has issued one volume, "Katydid's Poems," made up, for the most part, of the lightest of gentle zephyrs; but they are laden with the perfume of mountain flowers in the spring-time and with the soothing odors of pines and birches. Their great merit is in their perfect naturalness and simplicity. She finds beauty in homely things, and makes them grow into our affections.
CHAS. J. O'MALLEY.

S. C. MERCER.

Mr. S. C. Mercer is a resident of Hopkinsville, Kentucky, where he occupies himself as a farmer. He has been connected with the press in various capacities in Kentucky, and from 1862 to 1869 edited a paper in Nashville, Tennessee. He was born in Washington County, Pennsylvania, but his life has been identified with Kentucky. He is widely known as an excellent and original writer of prose and verse, and a very accomplished literary man.

MISS ELVIRA SYDNOR MILLER,

Whose taking fairy tales and beautiful poetry have won for her the widest reputation of any woman writer in Kentucky, was a Virginian by birth and only adopted Louisville as a home. Her great-grandfather was John O. Donnell, Quartermaster General of the Revolution. Her mother's ancestors were Italian; this probably accounts for the poetic vein which permeates her whole soul. She is a great lover of children, horses, and flowers, and her mother says is a "sad Bohemian." She is brilliant and fascinating, and always leaves a pleasant memory with those who meet her. Besides her "Songs of the Heart," and other volumes, she has ready for the press a story, "The Home of the Dead Belle," which deals with Louisville's social history. * *

ALICE HAWTHORNE MUDD.

Descended from the Maryland headlights of literature—Nathaniel Hawthorne and Washington Irving. She was born in Louisville, Kentucky, educated at Roseland Academy, Bardstown, Kentucky. In 1876 she was on the editor's staff collecting historic facts for the "Encyclopedia of Kentucky." The next year she was on the staff of the Sunday Argus and Trade Gazette, and wrote over the *nom de plume* of "Patsy Dean" and "George Francis Piltcher." The same year she brought out her first book of poems, "Hawthorne Leaves." * *

BIOGRAPHICAL SKETCHES.

ROBERT MORRIS.

Born near Boston, Massachusetts, 1816. He first became a citizen of Kentucky in 1852, locating at Fulton. Was prominently identified with all the interests of Freemasonry, and contributed largely to its literature. His songs, "The Level and the Square" and "Gallilee," are very popular. The latter is found in all modern Sunday-school song-books. He died at LaGrange, Kentucky, July 31, 1888.

IDA GOLDSMITH MORRIS.

Born in Louisville, Kentucky, October, 1870. Was graduated from the High School in 1888, being elected poet of the class. She was married January 12, 1891, to Mr. Herman Morris, a lawyer of Glasgow, Kentucky. * *

ELIZABETH LEE MURPHEY.

Happy the soul that comes upon its literary mission and finds a public ready to receive it. More happy still that people who entertain these angels unawares. The influence of the cultured man or woman upon the community in which he lives is priceless beyond value in all that goes to make up a great and free people. These thoughts easily adjust themselves to the personal history of Elizabeth Lee Murphey *nee* Hays, one of the most gifted and useful of Kentucky women. In her home she is the center of a most charming circle, and an earnest, devoted wife and mother. In addition to these duties she has for the past two years been engaged in literary work, and at present is one of the editors of The Round Table, published at Dallas, Texas. She wields a pure influence in the literary world, and her career is watched with much interest by her friends and admirers. She has written many beautiful poems, which have been widely copied and read, and in them all there breathes the warm, rich spirit of heroism and devotion. Her style is at once gentle and strong, lofty and winning. She stands at the center of the literary life of a big, bustling, Western city, and does much to give tone and direction to its movements.

A. W. MELL.

VIRGINIA F. NOBLE

Was born in Louisville, but from childhood has resided in Paducah. Her father, Colonel John C. Noble, has for many years been widely known among the literary people of Kentucky, and his researches have covered many fields of thought, and upon his talented daughter has fallen his mantle of greatness. Miss Noble's writings partake largely of the analytic in character. Not, however, after the fashion of most analytical writers are her productions dispassionate. Womanly feeling and sentiment are breathed in every line of her poetry and prose. For several years her work has been gladly accepted by Eastern magazines, to which she is a regular contributor. She is the founder of the "Castalian" literary club of Paducah, and is a firm believer in the future literary pre-eminence of Southern talent. ADA BRAZLETON.

THEODORE O'HARA.

It is purposed here to sketch briefly the life of a Southern soldier who builded for himself an enduring fame as a poet upon four lines. These lines, together with other stanzas of the poem in which they occur, may be seen in the national cemeteries of the United States, cast in iron and placed along the silent ways which wander among the dead, to commemorate the sleeping brave of North and South alike; and these four immortal lines, which have sufficed to secure their author's name a place in the sacred annals, are inscribed also over the gateway of the National Cemetery at Washington. Though the man who wrote them fought upon the opposing side, even to the end, these lines seem no whit less fitting here than when we find them placed above the wearers of the gray who rest in the cemetery at New Orleans. Thus does the spirit of poesy triumph over material issues, appealing to something within us before which mere differences of political opinion, strong and abiding as they seem to be, sink out of sight and are lost forever. To forget the questions upon which they have been divided to their hurt, let men cherish those truths upon which they are one.

Theodore O'Hara, soldier, poet, and journalist, was born in Danville, Kentucky, February 11, 1820. He was the son of Kane O'Hara, an Irish gentleman who, after having left his own land on account of political oppression, became distinguished in Kentucky as an educator of great learning and ability. The family finally settled in the vicinity of Frankfort, Kentucky. After being prepared under the teaching of his father, Theodore was sent to St. Joseph's College at Bardstown, Kentucky, where he graduated with high honors. After this he practiced law for a time, but in 1845 he held a position in the Treasury Department at Washington, and the next year was appointed captain in the old United States Army.

He served through the Mexican War, and was brevetted major on the field for gallantry and meritorious conduct. He then practiced law in Washington for a time, but when Lopez attempted the liberation of Cuba, O'Hara joined the expedition, and led a regiment at Cardenas, in which battle he was severely wounded. Subsequently he was concerned in Walker's adventurous expedition to Central America. He afterward conducted several newspapers in the South with great ability and brilliancy, among them the Mobile Register.

At the beginning of the War of the Rebellion he joined the service at once, and was put in command of the fort at the entrance of Mobile Bay, which he bravely defended until ordered to retire. After this he served on Albert Sydney Johnston's staff, and was beside that officer when he fell at Shiloh. Later on he was chief-of-staff to General John C. Breckinridge, and was in the famous charge at Stone River. He served as chief-of-staff until the end of the war. After the war he engaged in some commercial transactions in Columbus, Georgia, but finally retired to a plantation on the Alabama side of the Chattahoochee River, where he died of fever on the 7th of June, 1867. In 1873 the legislature of Kentucky provided for the bringing back of his body to his native State, and in 1874 he was buried with military honors in the State Cemetery at Frankfort. This is a brief record of O'Hara's life.

O'Hara wrote only two poems which have been preserved to history—one entitled "The Bivouac of the Dead," and one "A Dirge for the Brave Old Pioneer." These are identical in the manner of their construction, and they are both elegiac and commemorative poems. He seems to have written only when special demand was made upon him, and then only in this one vein. It is upon this first-mentioned poem, "The Bivouac of the Dead," that O'Hara's claim for immortality must rest. It was written to commemorate the death of his comrades who fell in Mexico, and was read by him upon the occasion of their burial in the plot of ground set apart by the State for their reception in the cemetery at Frankfort. O'Hara now sleeps within the same ground, and may be said to have sung his own memorial, standing upon his unmade grave. The opening stanza of this poem, especially the second quatrain of it, remains unsurpassed in its own field.

From Sketch in The Century. ROBERT BURNS WILSON.

CHARLES J. O'MALLEY

Was born in Union County, Kentucky, in 1857. His mother was of Spanish descent. His father was Irish, nearly related to the poet-priest, Father Ryan. In 1882 he was married to Miss Sallie M. Hill, of Calhoun, Missouri. Like many other young writers Mr. O'Malley first became known through The Current. He wrote, besides poetry, a number of light scientific papers: "Summer in Kentucky," "By Marsh and Pool," "Our Native Evergreens." He also wrote "The Botany, Ornithology, and Geology of Union County." A series of articles on the "Poets and Poetry of Southwest Kentucky," written by him for the Henderson Journal, attracted much attention. He knows Kentucky like a book, having been over every county but one in the State. In his writings he not only stimulates his fellow-workers, but cultivates a taste in them for things above the gross and commonplace, and smoothes and refines the life about him. His poems are to be found in The Century, Youths' Companion, and other leading periodicals. "The Building of the Moon" is one of the most thoroughly original things in the English language. ARCH POOL.

MRS. SALLIE MARGARET HILL O'MALLEY.

Born in Indiana, educated in Missouri. Was married to Charles J. O'Malley, and became a resident of Kentucky in 1882. Her poetry is much in sympathy with the every-day things of life.

DANIEL E. O'SULLIVAN

Was born in Bowling Green, Kentucky, September, 1858. Is at present editor and owner of the Sunday Critic, Louisville, Kentucky. Barely in his thirties, Mr. O'Sullivan has crowded much work into his life. For two years he was managing editor of the Courier-Journal; then on the staff of the New York World, and later managing editor of the Louisville Commercial. Was married in 1886 to Miss Bertha Bijur, of Louisville. Mr. O'Sullivan's poetry was written before he became such a busy journalist. In either capacity he is a success.

* *

EUGENIA PARHAM

Is a daughter of the late Dr. W. H. Parham, of McCracken County, Kentucky. At the early age of sixteen she adopted the profession of teacher, and has held successively positions in Blandville College, Paducah public schools, West Kentucky College, and for two years past has held the chair of English Literature and Moral Philosophy in the old Judson Institute at Marion, Alabama. She has more than a local reputation as an essayist, but her literary work has all been done amid the busy cares of a teacher. Her poems are published in the Courier-Journal and other leading papers.

JO. A. PARKER

Is editor of The Index, published at LaGrange, Kentucky, and is also secretary of the Southern Literary Association. Though he has scarcely attained his majority he has made a reputation for intelligence quite above the ordinary.

* * *

JOHN JAMES PIATT

Has been for ten years United States Consul at Queenstown, Ireland; but he is a poet that time and the ocean can not separate from the hearts of his countrymen. Although not a Kentuckian by birth he married Sallie Morgan Bryan, of Kentucky, and his daughter Marian was born in Kentucky, and by virtue of his long and intimate association with George D. Prentice and several years' residence in Louisville, Mr. Piatt is certainly entitled to recognition by Kentuckians, and his poems are gladly accorded a place in this collection.

Among his earlier volumes was "Poems by Two Friends," a joint production by W. D. Howells and himself. His next volumes were "Western Windows" and "Land Marks." A few years ago he edited

CLINT RUBY.

a very remarkable compilation under the title of "The Union of Literature and Art." "Idylls and Lyrics of the Ohio Valley" is another of his popular volumes.

In 1889 was published in London "A Book of Gold—A Quarter Century of Sonnets"—twenty-five most exquisite sonnets. The Spectator says, "Mr. Piatt's best things are undoubtedly those which smell of the Western soil." The Morning Post: "Mr. Piatt's poems have a distinct transatlantic ring which lends them an additional attraction."

* *

\ SARAH M. B. PIATT.

Sarah Morgan Bryan was born in Fayette County, Kentucky, in 1836, and is a granddaughter of one of the pioneers. She was graduated from the Henry Female College at Newcastle, Kentucky. In early girlhood a strong poetic temperament was developed, and she soon gained substantial recognition as a poet. She was married in 1861 to John James Piatt, and soon after published her volume, "Nests at Washington." In 1871 "A Woman's Poems" was published. During the ten years spent abroad Mrs. Piatt has published several smaller volumes of verse, and the English and Irish press notices are very complimentary. The St. James Gazette says: "We find Mrs. Piatt's Muse is the Muse of the American Girl, and we confess, for our own part, the more completely she is the Muse of the American Girl the better we like her." "A Voyage to the Fortunate Isles," "A Wall Between," "An Irish Garland," and "In Primrose Time" are the titles of different volumes. "The Witch in the Glass," etc. is her volume of 1890.

* *

MRS. EUGENIA DUNLAP POTTS

Was born near Lancaster, Kentucky. Was graduated at Franklin Female Institute in Lancaster, and finished a course in music and French at Philadelphia. In 1874 she published the "Song of Lancaster," a metrical history after the versification of Longfellow's Hiawatha. The great poet's letter of commendation is among the author's treasures. Mrs. Potts is at present editor of The Illustrated Kentuckian, published at Lexington.

GEORGE DENNISON PRENTICE.

There is in front of the Courier-Journal building in Louisville, above the entrance, a life-size statue of Mr. Prentice in Carrara marble representing him sitting in his chair in a familiar pose. "This," says John James Piatt, "is a fitting local monument of the honored editor, statesman, and patriot, but I believe there is something in his volume of poems, which, although it may not be a moving, an active force in this busy world, will survive the marble effigy in the memory of men."

George D. Prentice was born in Connecticut in 1802, and came to

Kentucky in 1830 for the purpose of writing a biography of Henry Clay to be used in the campaign in New England, but fortune favored Kentuckians when a tide in his affairs brought Mr. Prentice permanently into our State and made him a citizen of it—made him our *very own*.

All along from youth to old age Mr. Prentice exhibited his love of poetry, and while his principal longer poems were written early in life many of his later ones are of equal strength and beauty, and through all of his serious poems the current of feeling is in sympathy with nature's great works. "Mammoth Cave" is admired by many above his "Closing Year," which is ranked with Bryant's "Thanatopsis," as one of the finest pieces of blank verse in the English language. "The River in Mammoth Cave" is peculiarly impressive, as mournful in tone as the strange, weird river it celebrates, and having once visited this river one reads the poem with profound awe.

In the South, where literature is slow of recognition, such a disposition as Mr. Prentice showed, amid the busy cares of a journalist's life, to encourage poetic talent and hold out a helping hand, is something not to be forgotten in the history of our country and American literature, and in the hearts of all Kentuckians he lives enshrined. He died January 22, 1870. * *

DR. FRANK H. RHEA.

Born at Madisonville, Kentucky, in 1855, but now lives at Waverly, Union County, where he practices his profession. His poetry is thoroughly original. One striking characteristic of it is the employment of words of Latin rather than of Anglo-Saxon extraction, and this is but one of many ways in which his writings are entirely different from those of any other Kentucky poet. * *

HARRISON ROBERTSON

Is managing editor of the Courier-Journal. He is a poet, but like many others he allows the cares of a journalist's life to crowd out the Muse, and says he will probably never write another poem. His poems were published in Harper's and The Century. * *

MRS. ADELAIDE D. ROLLSTON

Was born near Paducah, Kentucky, and has lived since her early womanhood and marriage in that city. At a very early age she began to contribute both verse and prose to Eastern journals, and she has since confined herself principally to the delineation of character, feeling that it is her true field of labor, and she finds a ready acceptance of her work. Her poetry is characterized by simplicity of structure and faultless rhythm.

BIOGRAPHICAL SKETCHES. 323

CLINT RUBY

Was born in Henderson, Kentucky, twelve years ago, and is widely known as the Boy Elocutionist. At an early age he gave evidence of poetic talent, and was possessed of a remarkably retentive memory, repeating page after page of verse after once hearing it. He has devoted his time to public readings, and meets with the greatest encouragement. His literary talent is inherited from his parents. His mother, Mrs. Alice L. O. Ruby, being a contributor to various magazines. He now lives at Madisonville, Hopkins County, Kentucky.

* *

THOMAS H. SHREVE

Is remembered as a citizen of Louisville, Kentucky—a man whose versatility of talent was remarkable. He had proven himself capable as a merchant, but his ambition was for literary work, and he soon established a reputation as one of the best young writers of the time, preparing papers of rare excellence in various departments of literature. His artistic talent also developed, and he left many excellent paintings to illustrate it. His poetry has been widely copied and admired. W. D. Gallagher says of it: "He was as joyous in his verse as the lark soaring in the early morn and singing at heaven's gate." Mr. Shreve was employed on the editorial staff of the Louisville Journal at the time of his death, which occurred on the morning of December 23, 1853.

* *

MRS. MATTIE PEARSON SMITH,

Though now an adopted daughter of the State of Minnesota, Kentucky may fairly lay claim to at least an interest in the genius of this gifted authoress, as many of her earlier years were passed at Covington in this State, where her education was chiefly obtained, and where also for a number of years she taught school. Mrs. Smith has written much beautiful verse, and has contributed liberally to the press and periodicals, and all her published work would make several large volumes. She lives at present at Le Sueur, Minnesota, at which place her husband, Edson R. Smith, is a prominent banker and mill-owner.

* *

CAPTAIN THOMAS SPEED

Is a practicing lawyer in Louisville. He was born at Bardstown, Kentucky. His ancestors came from Virginia in the pioneer days. He was educated at Center College, and served in the Civil War as Adjutant of the 12th Kentucky Veteran Volunteer Infantry. He has written a number of prose pieces, but is not much accustomed to court the Muses. He is the author of "The Wilderness Road." The skill with which he appeals to national feeling shows that he has the heart of a poet.

HENRY COOLIDGE SEMPLE.

Born in Louisville, May 11, 1871. Was graduated from the High School in that city, and is at present teaching in Funk Seminary at LaGrange, Kentucky. At the early age of thirteen years he began to scribble verse, and though he has written but few pieces of merit, these are characterized by that genuine overflow of poetic spirit that answers no man's bidding.

MAJOR THOMAS SPEED.

Born in Virginia in 1768. His father removed to Kentucky in 1782, and he lived for a while at Danville, but from 1793 till his death at Bardstown. He was major in the war of 1812, and member of Congress in 1817. Died 1842. He was the grandfather of Captain Thomas Speed, and wrote the poem "Autumn Leaves" in 1806.

FREDERIC M. SPOTSWOOD

Lives at Lexington, Kentucky, where he edits The National Guard, a sheet devoted to the interests of the State Military. He has written a number of songs that have sold well, and his vein is chiefly the Anacreontic. The "Queen of Night," his longest poem, was born of the beauty revealed by a moonlight view of " The Meadows," one of the handsomest homes in the Bluegrass country.   * *

MRS. BELLE WILSON STAPP

Is a writer of ability. Before her marriage she wrote a great deal and received large compensation for prose work, but ill health has for many years interrupted her literary work. We see a poem from her pen occasionally in the Courier-Journal. All of the Kentucky papers give her a cordial welcome. She resides at Buckeye, Garrard County.
* *
HENRY T. STANTON

Was born on the 30th of June, 1834. His father, Hon. Richard H. Stanton, of Maysville, Kentucky, was for a number of years a member of Congress from that District, and subsequently Judge of the Circuit Court. His son, who was his first born, had the benefit of a thorough education, and early evinced a taste for literary pursuits and a genius for poetry. He was, at different times, editor of the Maysville Bulletin and Frankfort Yeoman, in which papers most of his poetical contributions, since published in two volumes, originally appeared. He served during the war in the Confederate army as Adjutant-General upon the staffs of General Williams, General Morgan, and General Breckinridge. In early life he married Miss Martha Lindsey, of Mt. Sterling, Kentucky, and their union has been blessed with nine children, six daughters and three sons. Since 1870 he has resided in Frankfort, his present occupation being that of an insurance agent. From time to time he continues to write verses of a high order, and gives readings from his poems to popular audiences. Personally he is of pleasing address, vivacious in conversation, happy in his family relations, and esteemed by a circle of friends co-extensive with the State. J. S. J.

MISS JEANNETTE SWING.

She is the niece of Rev. David Swing, of Chicago, so well known in literary circles. Was born at Cincinnati, Ohio, but removed during her childhood to Dayton, Kentucky, where she was graduated from the High School in 1886. At an early age she gave evidence of literary talent, and at the age of eighteen her first story appeared in a large Cincinnati daily. Since then she has contributed both prose and poetry to many of the papers, and has been unusually successful.

MICHAEL MOORES TEAGER

Was born in Bath County, Kentucky, May 1, 1833. His father, Jacob Teager, was of German extraction, but a native of Mason County, Kentucky. His mother, Louisa (Moores) Teager, was born in Bath County, Kentucky, and daughter of Michael Moores, who came to Kentucky soon after the Revolutionary War, in which he participated. He was admitted to the bar in 1860, and entered upon the practice of law at Flemingsburg, Kentucky, where he now resides. In 1862 he enlisted in the Confederate service with the 2d Battalion, Kentucky Mounted Rifles, and served during the war, after which, on the 11th May, 1871, he was married to Miss Irene Emma Stealy, of Jeffersonville, Indiana.

SARAH CAMPBELL HARRIS-THORNTON.

Born in Mason County, Kentucky, 1825. Her poem, "Beyond the Grave," was written at the age of fifteen, and appeared in the Lexington Intelligencer. Some time after marriage moved to Texas, where she died in 1880.

CATHERINE A. WARFIELD.

Catherine Ann Ware was born in the State of Mississippi, but educated in Philadelphia. She was married to Elisha Warfield, of Lexington, Kentucky, in 1833, and after several years' travel abroad, and a protracted residence in Texas, they finally settled in Lexington, where Mrs. Warfield became one of the chief ornaments to the refined and intellectual circle of that section of Kentucky society. In 1846 a volume of poems, entitled "Poems by two Sisters of the West," from the pen of Mrs. Warfield, and her sister, Mrs. Eleanor Percy Lee, was published and quite favorably received, but Mrs. Warfield's best poems were contributed singly to the Louisville Journal. * *

LIZZIE WALKER,

Of Hartford, easily takes rank among the most beautiful and versatile of the younger writers whose songs are adding so much to the literature of the South. Her mother was Elvira English, of Hardin County, Kentucky, and her father is the eminent Judge E. Dudley Walker. Miss Walker seems to have been born for the literary career. Her talents shone forth brightly from early girlhood. She has cultivated several varieties of verse. The reflective element enters into her writings more than might be expected in one so young and joyous. This quality appears in the poem entitled "The Old Year." She uses dialect freely in the expression of her sympathies and loves for the external world. It is not often so exquisite a piece of nature-painting is found as that given in Miss Walker's poem, "November."

JOHN CLARK RIDPATH.

THOMAS WALSH

Was born near Connersville, Indiana, December 14, 1859. In his fifteenth year he began his academic course at St. Meinrad's College, Spencer County, Indiana. He studied here for four years and then entered St. Xavier's College, Cincinnati, Ohio, completing his classical course of study a year later. Shortly afterward he located at Louisville, Kentucky. He was engaged for a year or two in the publication of The Celtic Review, a weekly journal devoted to the interests of the Irish people. Abandoning this pursuit he entered the legal profession, in which he has since continued, having by his ability and energy built up a large and lucrative practice. He is an exceedingly eloquent and popular speaker, is noted for the fervency, wit, and pathos of his efforts at the bar and before the people. He has written occasional poems for the Courier-Journal and the Times, of Louisville.

ASHER G. CARUTH.

WILLIAM A. WASHINGTON

Was a direct descendant of George Washington, and a man of fine character. Many years of his life were spent in Logan County, where he wrote and published his poems. One volume, entitled "Rural Minstrelsy," was published in 1860. He died in Owensboro, having almost rounded out his century. He was never married, but lived with his two sisters, who were also unmarried, and who died a short time before him. ♦ ♦

LIZZIE WILSON.

Born in Louisville, Kentucky, December 30, 1835. Died there March 19, 1858. In 1860 a volume entitled "Poems by Lizzie," was published, dedicated to George D. Prentice.

BIOGRAPHICAL SKETCHES.

HENRY WATTERSON,

Son of Hon. Harvey Watterson, lately deceased. He was born in Washington City, February 16, 1840. Became editor of the Louisville Journal in 1868, and has been editor-in-chief of the Courier-Journal since it first appeared. He served in Congress in 1876. Mr. Watterson is one of the most powerful leaders of the Democratic party. His poetry was written in early life.

AMELIA B. WELBY

Was born February 3, 1819, at St. Michaels, in Maryland. In 1834 her parents removed with her to Louisville, Kentucky, where her poetic genius first became known to the public, and where she died on the 3d of May, 1852. Her first published work was a poem, in 1837, in the Louisville Journal. In 1845 she issued the first collected edition of her poems, which met with such ready and extensive sale that the publishers of the country contended for the privilege of issuing a second edition, which the Appletons did in 1846, and they have since found it necessary to issue some twenty additional editions. She was married to George Welby, Esq., an excellent gentleman, of Louisville, Kentucky, in June, 1838.

FORCEYTHE WILSON

Was a native of New York, but for many years a resident of Kentucky. A brother of the Hon. Augustus Wilson of Louisville. He contributed many beautiful poems to the Courier-Journal while George D. Prentice was editor, and afterward published a volume of poems, entitled "The Old Sargeant, and other Poems." John James Piatt said of him: "One of those rare poets whose poetry is first in their life, and perhaps grows poorer in their last verses." * *

ROBERT BURNS WILSON

Was born near Washington, Pennsylvania, but his childhood was passed in West Virginia. He received his education partly at Wheeling, and afterward at Pittsburgh. Having lost his mother at the early age of ten years, and being of a sensitive nature, his grief for her has had a sad effect upon his life. In his poem dedicated to her he says, "All that's best in me and in my art is thine." In 1886 Mr. Wilson went to Louisville, Kentucky, where he gained an enviable reputation as an artist by a crayon portrait of Henry Watterson. Two years later he adopted Frankfort as his home, and there continues his art-work. His first poem, "A Wild Violet in November," made his reputation as a poet, and when his first volume, "Life and Love," was issued, there was a great demand for it.

No idle rhymer of trifling verse, but a strong-voiced singer who has walked with Nature and drawn his inspiration from her, his observant eye mirrors the beauties of the world, and with pen and brush he portrays them with the grace and truth of an artist.   * *

HENRY CLEVELAND WOOD

Is a native Kentuckian, descended on his mother's side from the Cleveland and Whitney families of New England. His paternal ancestors settled permanently in Kentucky before Daniel Boone built his first cabin here.

Mr. Wood's first literary venture was a sketch written at the age of twelve years and contributed to Appleton's Journal, for which he received compensation. This success, doubtless, gave him more exquisite joy than any he has since achieved. In 1874 he began contributing to the English magazines, and from that time has frequently appeared in The Quiver, Good Words, and other periodicals. In this country he has contributed to The Aldine, The Cosmopolitan, The Current, Belford's, Our Continent, Youth's Companion, Literary Life, Demorest, Peterson, Once a Week, Harper's Weekly, and many other of the leading publications.

Mr. Wood has very great artistic and musical talent. He draws freely, paints, and executes various designs in wood carving, his own home being handsomely decorated by himself. He is yet unmarried, and devoted to his venerable grandmother and mother who live with him at Harrodsburg.   * *

MISS JEAN WRIGHT.

The father of Miss Jean Wright is General J. M. Wright, a graduate of West Point, a brilliant young officer in the Civil War, member of the Kentucky Legislature, Adjutant-General of Kentucky, and now Marshal of the United States Supreme Court. Her mother is the daughter of Dr. Ewing, and a niece of General William O. Butler, one of Kentucky's early soldier-poets. A native of Louisville, Miss Wright has inherited talent and literary taste. Her first offering is a delicious little volume of poems published in 1892, and charmingly illustrated by her young cousin, Emma Keats Speed.

EUGENIA DUNLAP POTTS.

To MRS. FANNIE PORTER DICKEY.

THE MOODS OF YOU.

The moods of you in colors blent
  Would make a rainbow, vivid, fair,
Such as to clouds whose glory lent
  Makes gorgeous roses in the air,
Which float off, darkening as they go;
  Yet you—with face of sun and mist—
Are with them in their ebb and flow,
  With ruby gleam and amethyst,
To mystic depths and trackless fields
  Of shadow, thickening as each crowds
Where old Aquarius stands and wields
  His rain-flail on the flashing clouds.

Though vast the region they traverse,
  These blessed messengers of rain,
I watch them, whether they disperse
  Or link themselves in endless chain—
The throbbing air about them filled
  With glint of sun and slanting ray,
Whereby a red-gold seems instilled
  Into them, turning cold and gray—
Down from the zenith's glowing haze
  Sparse wandering or condensed in storm,
These flying clouds in every phase
  But hold you in some lovely form.

And, though the thunder smiles and pains,
    Where they wax eerie, low and dim,
They breathe you through their watery veins
    Into the very soul of them;
And cast into your eyes the gray,
    Transfer their sun-glints to your hair;
Your cheeks they sprinkle with the spray
    Of red-gold bronzing your face fair;
And thus they make your being whole,
    And you with all their moods endow,
And leave their glory in your soul,
    Their softer shadows on your brow.

Yet more than this in moods of you,
    And lovelier, meets discerning eyes;
For one perceives the luscious blue
    Which fills the hollow morning skies.
And fragrance of the grassy lawn,
    And freshness of the mountain brook,
Into your breezy nature drawn,
    Reveal themselves to all who look;
Indeed, one used to fairy dreams
    Sees in your face the budding sheaf,
The lucent glint of sylvan gleams,
    And purity of bloom and leaf.

The Genii and arts that please
    In simple culture serve you good,
For your companions, which are trees,
    Conspire by symbols understood—
Each trembling, swaying where it stands,
    To airy twig of topmost limb,
And, reaching down with leafy hands,
    So glad to touch your garment's hem!—

And join with you in gnarly feud
  To help you catch on canvas screen,
Within some beechen solitude,
  The glint of gold amongst the green.

Ye poets, souls that dream and dream,
  This Naiad, loving song and sky,
Newborn of native grove and stream,
  In guise of woman heavenly high—
Let us decree for love and lore,
  This friend who heaps our laurels up,
That she shall drink forevermore
  The wine of joy from golden cup,
And down the ages ring clear-toned
  The praise each sweet shell now prolongs,
And crown her where she sits enthroned
  Upon the tops of our best songs.

RUFUS J. CHILDRESS.

www.ingramcontent.com/pod-product-compliance
Lightning Source LLC
Chambersburg PA
CBHW032012220426
43664CB00006B/216